ONTARIO'S AMAZING MUSEUMS

ONTARIO'S AMAZING MUSEUMS

A GUIDE TO ONTARIO'S MOST INTERESTING
AND UNUSUAL MUSEUMS, ARCHIVES,
EDUCATION CENTRES, AND COLLECTIONS

Julia Pine

ECW PRESS

CANADIAN CATALOGUING IN PUBLICATION DATA

Pine, Julia
Ontario's amazing museums

ISBN 1-55022-208-2

1. Museums – Ontario – Guidebooks. I. Title

AM21.06P5 1994 069 .09713 C94-930589-8

Design and imaging by ECW Type & Art, Oakville, Ontario.
Printed by Kromar Printing, Winnipeg, Manitoba.

Distributed by General Distribution Services,
30 Lesmill Road, Toronto, Ontario M3B 2T6,
(416) 445-3333, (800) 387-0172 (Canada), FAX (416) 445-5967.

Published by ECW PRESS,
2120 Queen Street East, Suite 200, Toronto, Ontario, Canada M4E 1E2.

ACKNOWLEDGEMENTS

Many thanks to the following people for their help, encouragement, and time: André Gravelle, Elizabeth and Lee Gold, Max Dublin, Keith Miller, Mrs. Sonja Bata and all the staff at the Bata Shoe Museum, especially Ada "the Eye" Hopkins, Robert Barron, Trish Brown, Mary Ellen Simko, Ken Rentner, Dr. Martin Ruck, everyone at ECW PRESS, Tony and Jeannie Westell, Carol Shaina and Freddie Litwack, Manny Albino, Janet Strong, Farenc Szabo, Major Stewart Bull, Dr. Laura Ford, Peter Scott, Anna Jarvis, The Ontario Museum Association, The Canadian Museums Association, The Ontario Historical Society, C.H.P. Heritage Centre, Olive Koyama, Clement Virgo, everyone at all the museums, archives, and sites listed, Michael Pine, and especially to my mother, the amazing Monica Pine.

INTRODUCTION

The idea for *Ontario's Amazing Museums* came about when I began to discover more and more interesting museums and collections throughout Ontario — a museum of contraception, a shoe museum, the Football Hall of Fame, and so on. Surely, I thought, everyone in Ontario should know about these places, and since no commercial guide existed, I took it upon myself to root through tourist information centres and hotel lobbies, follow hunches, approach strangers, contact historical societies, harass my friends and family, and scour the province. The results were fantastic, and I discovered something about Ontario that few people know: it is a goldmine of unique, weird, educational, cheesy, fascinating, historical, and often world-class museums and collections.

I have stretched the definition of the word "museum" to mean "a collection of neat stuff," and as long as a place is set up to educate, inspire, or entertain people through the display and use of objects, I have included it. However, *Ontario's Amazing Museums* is by no means comprehensive. Art galleries, most community museums, and many historic sites, like mills and houses, have been excluded, as their inclusion would have been a monumental task. Comprehensive listings of recognized museums can be accessed through the Ontario Historical Society and the Canadian Museums Association, and *Slate* magazine, available in art-friendly locations, gives regular gallery updates. There were also several places about which I heard, but could not locate, such as the Trapper's Museum, which seems to have gotten lost in the woods, and the Haileybury Fire Museum, which was as elusive as a waft of smoke. Also, museums are in a constant state of flux and it is hard to keep up with them all. Locations, hours, staff, and exhibitions all change; new places open and established ones close.

My hope is that *Ontario's Amazing Museums* will help create awareness of and interest in Ontario's wonderful range of museums, archives, education centres, and collections: they are important keys to our past, present, and future. Hopefully too, in years to come Canada will allot more funding, organization, and recognition to its museum community, and Canadians will develop a greater appreciation for this amazing resource — these places need funding and visitors to survive. And to all the collectors, curators, archivists, volunteers, directors, exhibit designers, conservators, tour guides, and museum movers and shakers — may your halls sing and your cash registers ring!

Julia Pine

HOW TO USE THIS GUIDE

Site listings are in alphabetical order, although descriptive words, like "Museum of" or "Centre for," have occasionally been overlooked to make reference easier. For example, the "Museum of Mental Health Services" will be found under "Mental Health Services." A Location Index lists sites by the closest city or town, and the Subject Index will be of use to people looking for institutions with a particular focus.

The address, location, hours, admission fee, and other particulars, where applicable, are at the top of each listing. These were, to my knowledge, accurate at the time this guide went to press, but *always call to check before you go anywhere,* as changes occur frequently, especially during holidays. All holidays mentioned are Canadian, and many, like Easter, fall on different dates each year. Don't forget that Canadian Thanksgiving is different from U.S. Thanksgiving. Listings are intended to give an overview and a few highlights of each site. Quoted material, unless indicated otherwise, comes from institution brochures or information kits.

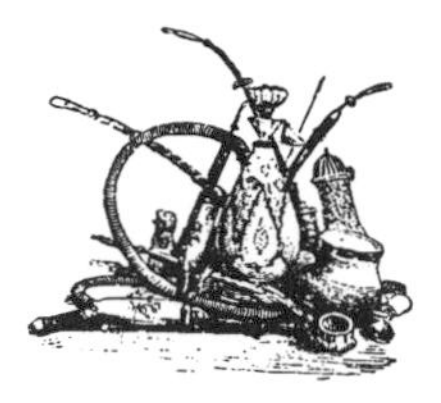

Addiction Research Foundation Museum

- 33 Russell Street, Toronto, Ontario, M5S 2S1
- (416) 595-6144
- Open Monday – Friday, 9:00 – 5:00
- Free admission

"Strange and Curious Drugs" was the original title of a now nameless hallway exhibit at Toronto's Addiction Research Foundation, exploring themes in the history of substance use and abuse. The display interprets many different aspects of drugs, including their physical and cultural origins and social attitudes towards them. Alcohol, caffeine, cocaine, opium, morphine, folk medicine, and "Grannies' cures," such as "tying a spider onto a thimble and suspending it from the neck of an ailing person" are explained through photos and text, in conjunction with artifacts ranging from printed ephemera and opium pipes to North American '70s style plastic water bongs. Key figures in reform and temperance movements are discussed, and trivia, such as Sherlock Holmes' "seven percent solution," i.e., his addiction to cocaine, are presented. The historical use of substances like codeine and cocaine in common products like cola drinks and cough syrup is also explained. Although the display is quite small and focuses on Canadian content, the collection proper consists of about one thousand artifacts and archival materials from around the world.

AECL Research, Chalk River Laboratories

- Chalk River, Ontario, KOJ 1JO
  LOCATION: 8 kilometres north of Highway 17
- (613) 584-3311, ext. 4429
- Visitor's Centre open weekdays, July – August, 8:30 – 4:00; by appointment rest of year
- Free tours and admission

AECL (Atomic Energy of Canada Laboratories) Chalk River Laboratories is the home of Canada's first nuclear program and of the first nuclear reactor in the world outside of the U.S. This early reactor, known as ZEEP, for Zero Energy Experimental Pile, has now been declared a National Historic Site. Two-hour guided bus tours throughout the summer from June to September offer a ride around the site and a visit to one or more operational facilities which, besides ZEEP, include five research reactors, a tandem accelerator superconducting cyclotron, the world's most powerful high-energy industrial accelerator, and a 4,000-hectare outdoor lab used for environmental research. Also on site is the Visitor's Centre, set up to create awareness and promote understanding of nuclear energy and its role in Canada. The Centre offers a variety of displays, films and models related to the Canadian nuclear industry, and visitors can even try out a pair of mechanical arms. Valid I.D. must be presented to take a tour, and children must be over the age of 12, but any age can access the Visitor's Centre. Picnic facilities face the Ottawa River.

Agawa Bay Exhibit Centre

- c/o Lake Superior Provincial Park, P.O. Box 267, Wawa, Ontario, POS IKO
  LOCATION: Agawa Bay Campground, Highway 17
- (705) 856-2284
- Open end of July and August, 4 hours a day; interpreter on pictograph site daily during this period
- Free admission

Agawa Bay campground is located in Lake Superior Provincial Park, some 1,550 square kilometres of Ontario terrain, between Sault Ste. Marie, Wawa and the Agawa River with beautiful lakes, rivers, pebbled beaches, forest, Canadian Shield rock and wildlife, canoe routes and hiking trails. The park itself has a lively, typically Canadian history. The Canadian Shield bedrock that lays the foundation of the Bay and surrounding area was moulded by earthquakes, ice, and volcanoes over a span of about two million years. Next came the ancestors of the Ojibwa people who left many legacies, including pictographs on the surfaces of Agawa Rock, which can still be seen today. Later came fur traders, and later still, artists, including the Group of Seven, who immortalized the area in their paintings. The Exhibit Centre provides text, photographs, rocks, maps, and information on area history, camping, hiking, geology, flora and fauna. Interpretive activities are held regularly in season, including discussion of the pictographs.

Agricultural Museum

- CEF-2000, Building 86, Central Experimental Farm, Ottawa, Ontario, K1R 0C6
  LOCATION: Prince of Wales Drive, Ottawa
- (613) 995-9554, toll-free 1-800-538-9110
- Open daily, 9:30 – 5:00
- Admission fee

The Agricultural Museum is located in an enormous dairy barn *circa* the 1920s, on the grounds of Ottawa's Central Experimental Farm. A joint project of Agriculture Canada and the National Museum of Science and Technology, the museum focuses on agricultural equipment and methods in Canada. Threshers, scythes, containers, scaled-down recreations of barns, and old advertisements offer a human perspective of farming, while machinery that was once state-of-the-art conveys what a science agriculture is, and how far it has come technically. The collection is well displayed and interpretation is provided through exhibit labels and bilingual commentary at earphone stations — all that is missing is the dirt. The museum has a great gift shop, and, being located in the heart of the Experimental Farm, is just minutes away from several delightful outdoor attractions.

Museum Ship Alexander Henry

- c/o Marine Museum of the Great Lakes, 55 Ontario Street, Kingston, Ontario, K7L 2Y2
  LOCATION: docked next to the Marine Museum of the Great Lakes
- (613) 542-2261
- Bed and Breakfast from $38.00 to $65.00 per cabin per night, available mid-May to Labour Day; tours until Thanksgiving

Owned and operated by the Marine Museum of the Great Lakes, the Museum Ship *Alexander Henry* not only lets you float on the waters of time, but you actually sleep on them! The *Alexander Henry* has been converted into a 64-metre Bed and Breakfast aboard ship. The beds are really berths, in cabins, all of which are on the outside of the ship, which means portholes with a view. All have washing facilities and some have private washrooms. The cabins are described as "modest but comfortable" and are kept in "shipshape and Bristol fashion," but if you decide to take the plunge it won't be for the space, but for the experience, and for a good cause, as proceeds go back into the ship and the Marine Museum. Breakfast is Continental and held in the small but grand oak-walled officers' mess. The *Alexander Henry* is docked next to the Marine Museum and is only a stone's throw from Kingston's downtown core. Tours of the ship are offered throughout the summer months.

Algonquin Park Logging Museum

* P.O. Box 219, Whitney, Ontario, K0J 2M0
  LOCATION: Kilometre 54.5, Algonquin Park
* (613) 637-2828
* Open weekends, late May – late June, 10:00 – 6:00; daily, late June – early October, 10:00 – 6:00
* Free admission with valid park permit

Visitors may go into the Algonquin Park Pioneer Logging Exhibit with absolutely no knowledge or interest in logging, but if they are attentive, they are guaranteed to come out with a firm understanding of the profession and a tremendous amount of respect for the men who have braved its extreme dangers and discomforts. Although not completely finished, the current exhibit has been superbly researched and planned, and consists of 20 stations placed on a 1.3 kilometres walking trail. The trek begins with the distribution of guide books and a modern building housing a shop, information services, and a theatre showing a short introductory video. The first station is a recreated loggers' lodgings of the 1800s, which comes alive in all its squalor, claustrophobia, and occasional good times. The next several stations hold examples of logs and equipment in various stages of manufacture and technology where visitors can learn about transportation, communication, forest regrowth, blacksmithing, and can touch and feel logs, vehicles and equipment essential to the logger's trade. Of particular interest is the rebuilt steam-powered "Alligator" invented in 1889, and tidbits of social history included in the guide book, such as the custom of nailing a logger's boots to his grave marker if he drowned while breaking up a log jam.

ALGONQUIN PARK VISITOR CENTRE

- P.O. Box 219, Whitney, Ontario, KOJ 2MO
  LOCATION: Kilometre 43, Highway 60, Algonquin Park
- (613) 637-2828
- Open daily, late May – late June, 10:00 – 6:00; late June – early September, 9:00 – 9:00; early September – early October, 10:00 – 6:00; early October – end of October, 10:00 – 5:00; early November – late May, 11:00 – 5:00, weekends only
- Free admission with valid park permit

Algonquin Park, established a century ago, is the oldest and one of the largest provincial parks in Ontario. Holding true to its founding purpose as a "public park and forest reservation, fish and game preserve," the park covers over 4,600,000 hectares, and plays host to half a million people every year. The new Visitor Centre was set up to educate this multitude about Algonquin Park and features a multi-media exhibit combining stuffed and mounted animals, enlarged, colourized photographs, audio-visual displays, artifacts, and recreations. The presentation of facts, figures, displays of the park's water and wildlife, flora and fauna, natural and social history, railway heritage, indigenous occupation, and immortalization by famous artists all give the visitor a greater understanding and respect of Algonquin Park's many facets. The Centre also contains a theatre, restaurant, shop, and a spectacular lookout, making it a great place to spend a cold or rained-out camping day.

Allan Gardens

- c/o Department of Parks and Recreation, 21st floor, East Tower, City Hall, Toronto, Ontario, M5H 2N2
  LOCATION: south side of Carlton Street, between Jarvis and Sherbourne
- (416) 392-7288
- Open daily, Monday – Friday, 9:00 – 4:00; weekends, 10:00 – 5:00
- Free admission

Allan Gardens is known as "an oasis in downtown Toronto," and certainly, with its beautiful greenhouses and conservatory, filled with between 5,000 and 7,000 tropical and sub-tropical plants at any given time, what else could you call it? The Gardens' long and eventful history began in 1860 when the grounds were opened by the Prince of Wales. A fine wood, iron, and glass pavilion was built in 1879 and used for gala balls, concerts, and flower shows. This burned down in 1902, and was later replaced by the glass-domed Palm House, a lovely classical structure in the tradition of the great Victorian glass houses. This building still stands, although other greenhouses have been added. Stepping into Allan Gardens today is like entering a tropical paradise: towering palms and hanging vines fill the domed glass nucleus out of which fan rooms full of exotic plants, flowers, and cacti and laced with streams and ponds full of fish. The Gardens are delightful in the summer, but are perhaps most magical in winter, especially at Christmas when they feature the Victorian Christmas flower show.

The Arboretum, University of Guelph

* c/o Guelph, Ontario, N1G 2W1
  LOCATION: east side of University of Guelph campus
* (519) 824-4120 ext. 2113
* Open daily, dawn to dusk; Arboretum Centre open weekdays, 8:30 – 4:30; J.C. Taylor Nature Centre open weekends, 9:00 – 4:00
* Free admission, except for group programs

The Arboretum at the University of Guelph is a 165-hectare botanical and biological park that functions as an educational and scientific facility, as well as being a delightful place to visit. Its many charms include interpretive nature trails, plant collections, and a Nature Centre. Close to 3,000 kinds of trees and shrubs can be seen including maples, sumacs, smoke-trees, pines, spruces, dogwoods, chestnuts, and dwarf conifers. Fragrant lilac and rose collections can also be enjoyed in season, as well as the Gosling Wildlife gardens, a gravel pit rehabilitation, gene banks, seed orchards, and a memorial forest. The Arboretum hosts nature interpretation programs, special projects such as the Children's Restoration Forest Project, dinner theatre among the trees, and educational programs and events year-round. The Arboretum Centre, designed by architect Raymond Moriyama, includes an outdoor patio, boardroom, and auditorium, and can be rented for special events.

Archival Teaching and Research Museum

* P.O. Box 2532, Terminal A, London, Ontario, N6A 4H1
  LOCATION: London Psychiatric Hospital, 850 Highbury Avenue, London
* (519) 455-5110
* Open Monday – Friday, 8:15 – 4:30, by appointment only
* Free admission

The London Insane Asylum opened in 1870, two miles from London, in response to a public outcry for proper housing for "deprived citizens." Over the years the Asylum grew quite self sufficient, carrying out several trades on the premises and boasting its own chapel and bakery. Many pioneering efforts in psychiatry began at the London Insane Asylum, and today the institution, now known as the London Psychiatric Hospital, has a strong educational focus. In the late '60s, after the original Asylum buildings had been replaced, hospital administration felt that the history of the old Asylum should be preserved, with the result being the Archival Teaching and Research Museum. The old Superintendent's office was rebuilt in the basement area of the S-wing, as were bedrooms, treatment facilities, an historic washroom, and a continuous water bath room. Display areas have also been set up to exhibit artifacts chronicling the progress of psychiatric treatment, and a research library is housed in the Superintendent's office. The Archival Teaching and Research Museum is used in the education of both graduate and undergraduate students, but is open to the public by appointment.

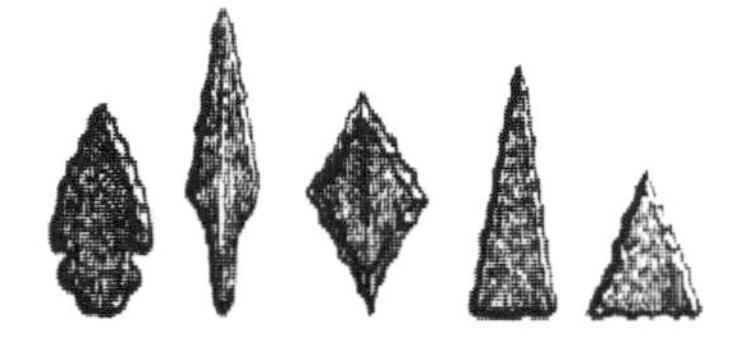

Arkona Lions' Museum and Information Centre

- R.R. 3, Exeter, Ontario, NOM 1S5
  LOCATION: Rock Glen Conservation Area, 2 kilometres northeast of Arkona
- April – October (519) 828-3071,
  November – March (519) 235-2610
- May, June, September, and October, noon – 5:00 on weekends and by appointment; July and August, daily, noon – 5:00
- Free with admission to conservation area

The Arkona Lions' Museum was started by a man named Ted Baxter, a local expert on Native North American material culture and fossils from the Devonian Era. Over the years, from his own expeditions and through donations, Baxter amassed a considerable collection of artifacts. His original museum was housed in another location until the current building was erected in 1985, thanks to the Arkona Lions' Club and the Ausable Bayfield Conservation Authority. Fossils, rocks, minerals, semi-precious stones, petrified wood, and early Native North American items including drills, skinning stones, scrapers, and arrowheads are the type of artifacts visitors can examine. The Centre also features information on the surrounding conservation area and Carolinian (hardwood) forests in Canada.

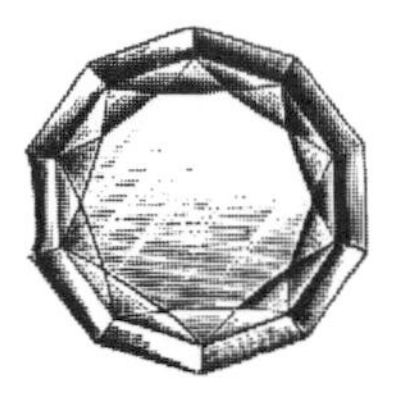

Ashley's Crystal Museum

* 50 Bloor Street West, Toronto, Ontario, M4W 3L8
* (416) 964-2900
* Open Monday – Wednesday, 10:00 – 6:00; Thursday and Friday, 10:00 – 7:00; Saturday, 9:30 – 5:30; closed some Fridays
* Free admission

Nestled upstairs in Ashley China Limited's fine china and tableware shop is a small, luxurious display of about a dozen fine pieces of etched Czechoslovakian crystal sculpture. These are from the private collection of a local businessman who obviously knows and loves crystal, although the museum is quite mysterious, providing no information about the collection or the pieces displayed, including artist, date, or title of the work. The only things that distinguish the museum from the rest of the shop are low lighting, missing price tags, and the sign that says "Museum." However, the unidentified pieces are lovely, and an interesting video on the history and technology of glass and crystal, with a focus on Canadian production, runs continuously. For some people, the best part of the visit will be walking through Ashley China where there is plenty of table finery to see. The store even has a few of its own "museum" pieces displayed in the stairwells.

ATHENS HISTORICAL MURALS

* c/o Athens Municipal Office, 1 Main Street West, Athens, Ontario, KOE IBO
  LOCATION: Athens, Ontario
* (613) 924-2044
* Open all year, no charge

Although Welland may have more giant murals, Athens was the first town in Ontario to try using paintings, size extra large, as a tourist attraction. The project began in 1986 when several top Canadian artists were commissioned to paint murals on buildings and other large, flat surfaces to celebrate the small, quaint rural town's heritage. So far about a dozen murals have gone up, painted by artists such as Lorrie Maruscak, Dan Sawatsky, and Pierre Hardy, depicting events like gatherings at the local (now gone) train station, townspeople gathered around a stove, or picnicking by the water, and a summer band concert *circa* 1925. The town also holds special events throughout the year such as the April Maple Syrup Festival and the July Steam Fair and Craft Show.

Backus Heritage Conservation Area

* R.R. 1, Port Rowan, Ontario, NOE 1MO
  LOCATION: off Regional Road 42, access from Highway 24 or Highway 59
* (519) 586-2201
* Open daily, May 1 – October 31, 10:00 – 5:00; call for off-season hours
* Admission fee

Backus Heritage Conservation Area, named after John Backhouse, a local mill owner of the late 1800s, consists of about 485 hectares of land featuring the largest remaining area of Carolinian, or hardwood, forest in Canada, nature trails, a conservation area, campgrounds, and a Conservation Education Centre. Also on the site is Backus Heritage Village, the heart of which is the original gristmill built by John Backhouse, which remained in operation for 160 years, and is now boasted by the village as the "longest operating grist mill in Upper Canada." Over a dozen restored and reconstructed buildings are staffed seasonally by interpreters and include a craft shop, general store, sawmill, threshing barn, windmill, blacksmith shop, cider press, church, schoolhouse, cemetery, and an agricultural museum containing machinery and tools *circa* 1900. Tours, interpretive programs, and special events regarding both the conservation and heritage aspects of the area are featured throughout the year.

Baldwin Room

- Metro Toronto Reference Library, 789 Yonge Street, Toronto, Ontario, M4W 2G8
- (416) 393-7154
- Open Monday – Thursday, 9:00 – 9:00; (9:00 – 8:00 July and August); Friday, 9:00 – 6:00; Saturday, 9:00 – 5:00; Sunday, 1:30 – 5:00, Thanksgiving – April 30
- Free admission

The Baldwin Room in the Metro Toronto Reference Library is named after the nineteenth-century reformer and statesman Robert Baldwin. It contains a large collection of primary source material relating to Canadian history and consists of five major research collections: books, pamphlets and periodicals; manuscripts; broadsides and printed ephemera; newspapers and pictures. Gems of the collection include a 1512 edition of Eusebius's *Chronicon*, which holds the first known references in print to Native North Americans; an extensive set of the Jesuit *Relations*; journals of an employee of the NorthWest Company who was involved in the fur trade between 1802 and 1839; popular printed media such as posters, handbills, restaurant menus, and train tickets, and a collection of Canadian historic visual materials in the form of paintings, drawings, photographs, and postcards. Reproduction services are offered and standard archival procedures apply.

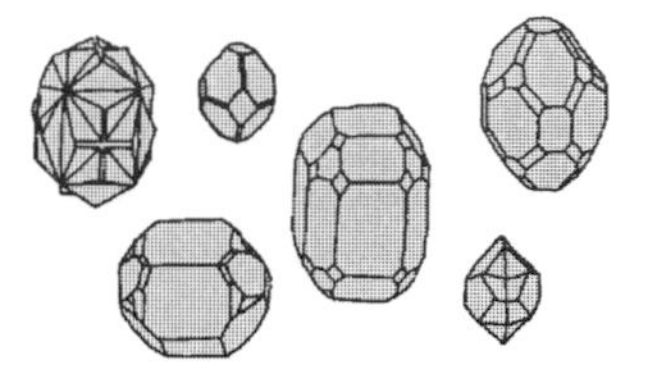

Bancroft Mineral Museum

* c/o Bancroft and District Chamber of Commerce, Box 539, Bancroft, Ontario, KOL 1CO
  LOCATION: Station Street in the Old Station
* (613) 332-1513
* Open daily all summer, 9:00 – 4:00; Monday – Saturday in spring and fall; Monday – Friday in winter
* Free admission, donations appreciated

The Bancroft Mineral Museum was first opened in 1985 as the joint effort of the District Chamber of Commerce and the Bancroft Gem and Mineral Club, many members of which have contributed to the collection. The museum is housed in one room of the Chamber of Commerce building and features modest displays of local, Ontario, United States, and international minerals as well as gems and lapidary materials. A mine model, ore car, ore bucket, and several photographs are also exhibited, along with a mining display. Bancroft calls itself the "Mineral Capital of Canada" and holds the Annual Rockhound Gemboree, a four-day rock festival every August, where minerals, gems, and lapidary materials and jewellery are bought and traded. Guided field excursions are also offered during the Gemboree.

Banting Museum and Education Centre

* 442 Adelaide Street North, London, Ontario, N6B 3H8
* (519) 673-1752
* Open Tuesday to Saturday, 12:00 – 4:30; public holidays, May – October, 12:00 – 4:30
* Admission fee, tours by appointment

Sir Frederick G. Banting, the man who discovered insulin and developed its use for the control of diabetes, is an important figure in Canadian and international medical history. Commemorating his achievements, the Banting Museum and Education Centre is located in the house were Doctor Banting lived and held his medical practice in the 1920s. Various exhibits explain the history of diabetes up until the discovery of insulin and explore the work of Dr. Banting, including his efforts in World War I, and his winning of the Nobel Prize. A restored doctor's office and a diorama of a battlefield from a World War I casualty area give insight into the life of a Canadian doctor earlier in this century. A statue of Banting stands on the grounds next to the museum, and a Flame of Hope burns continually in nearby Sir Frederick G. Banting Square, dedicated to diabetics of the world. The Queen Mother lit the flame on a visit to the museum in 1989, and it is intended to burn until an actual cure for diabetes is found.

BATA SHOE MUSEUM

- c/o 59 Wynford Drive, Don Mills, Ontario, M3C 1K3
  LOCATION: 131 Bloor Street West, Toronto (after spring, 1995, at the corner of Bloor Street West and St. George Street)
- (416) 924-7463
- Open Tuesday – Sunday, 11:00 – 6:00; call for new hours after spring, 1995; will be closed September 1994 – April 1995
- Admission fee, tours by appointment

The Bata Shoe Museum is one of a handful of shoe museums throughout the world, and the only one in North America. Its extensive and comprehensive collection of over 9,000 shoes, boots, and related artifacts begins with a plaster cast of the first known hominid footprint, donated by archaeologist Mary Leakey, and spans nearly all periods and cultures where people have covered their feet. Egyptian funerary sandals from 2,500 B.C., Pablo Picasso's zebra-striped walking shoes, Queen Victoria's slippers, and Elvis Presley's bulging blue-and-white vinyl shoes keep visitors on their toes, while footwear for weird and wonderful purposes like crushing chestnuts and carrying out ritual executions will send them head over heels. The museum also boasts the world's finest collection of Native North American footwear, a wide range of historical shoe fashions and an impressive collection from the circumpolar region. In spring 1995 the entire Bata Shoe Museum Collection will march into a new three-storey facility in downtown Toronto, designed by architect Raymond Moriyama. Tours, lectures, educational programs, and special events are offered all year.

Beaver Valley Military Museum

* P.O. Box 40, Clarksburg, Ontario, NOH 1J0
  LOCATION: Marsh Street, Clarksburg
* (519) 599-3031
* Open daily, third week of June – Labour Day, 10:00 – 12:00 and 1:00 – 4:00; weekends, Victoria Day – November 11, 1:00 – 5:00; by appointment off season
* Admission fee

The Beaver Valley Military Museum holds a sizeable collection of military artifacts from the Canadian Armed Forces and abroad, dating from 1880. The focus is on local Grey County, which produced flying ace Billy Bishop and the Grey and Simcoe Foresters, and covers the South African War, World Wars I and II, and the Korean War. Photographs, uniforms, weapons, and equipment on view include replicas of the 31st Grey Regiment uniforms, a complete Red Cross nurse's uniform from World War I, a pair of copper and wood trench boots, mortar bombs, and radio sets. Among the museum's objectives are "to perpetuate the memory and deeds of all who served or who have died in active service in Her Majesty's Forces" and "to maintain the traditions of patriotism, loyalty and a sense of duty to Canada for which they stood."

BELL HOMESTEAD

* 94 Tutela Heights Road, Brantford, Ontario, N3T 1A1
* (519) 756-6220
* Open all year 10:00 – 6:00; open holiday Mondays, closed following Tuesday
* Admission fee

Make a personal call to the home of the Bell family, the place where the inventor of the telephone once lived and worked. The Bells emigrated to Canada from Scotland in 1870, hoping to improve the poor health of their son Alexander Graham. Here the young man recovered, became a teacher of speech, moved to Boston in 1871 and opened a school for teachers of the deaf. On March 10, 1876, after several years of experimenting with the idea of a telephone, Bell uttered the famous first teletransmitted words, "Mr. Watson, come here, I want you!" on his Gallows Frame Telephone, the world's first telephone. Although this call was made in the United States, Bell declared his Brantford, Ontario, home the place where the telephone was actually invented. Certainly it was the site for the world's first long-distance telephone call, which was received in a boot store in Paris, Ontario, on August 10, 1876. The Bells' lovely home is preserved with many original furnishings owned and used by the family, including a stuffed duckbill platypus brought by relatives from Australia in 1874.

Beth Tzedec Reuben and Helene Dennis Museum

* 1700 Bathurst Street, Toronto, Ontario, M5P 3K3
* (416) 781-3511
* Open Monday, Wednesday and Thursday 11:00 – 5:00, Sunday 11:00 – 2:00; closed Sundays in summer, or by appointment
* Free admission, fee for some special events

The Beth Tzedec Reuben and Helene Dennis Museum is located in Beth Tzedec Synagogue, which has some very interesting features beyond the museum walls, including the Max and Beatrice Wolfe Library and original lithographs, signed by Marc Chagall, of the Jerusalem Windows in the Hadassah Hebrew Medical Centre in the Judaean Hills overlooking Jerusalem. The museum itself contains many rare and beautiful artifacts and includes the outstanding Cecil Roth Collection of Judaica. Visitors can see Hanukkah lamps from many different countries, and a collection of Sabbath lamps, one of which is thought to be the oldest in existence. Bowls, seals, medals, coins, Torah ornaments, platters, dishes, textiles, and documents can all be admired and examined. One of the collection's many highlights is a rare scroll of the Book of Esther from the historic Chinese Jewish community in Kaifeng Fu, China. The manuscript is illuminated, mostly in gold, with butterflies, lotus blossoms, and dragonflies. Tours of the museum and chapels, lectures, and exhibits are offered in the Synagogue throughout the year.

Bethune Memorial House

- 235 John Street North, Gravenhurst, Ontario, PIP IG4
- (705) 687-4261
- May – October, daily 10:00 – 5:00; winter, weekdays 10:00 – 5:00
- Free admission

Bethune Memorial House is the birthplace of Canadian hero Norman Bethune, renowned for his medical achievements and self-sacrifice. This extraordinary man gained international recognition for innovative surgical techniques and instruments. He developed the first mobile blood transfusion service on the battlefields of the Spanish Civil War and is most revered for his work in China, prior to his death in 1939, as a field surgeon and medical educator. In China Norman Bethune is remembered as a martyr and several monuments and museums there pay tribute to his efforts. The Bethune Memorial House is a lovely two-storey Victorian Presbyterian manse that has been meticulously restored to reflect life *circa* 1890 among the Bethune family, and includes several household items once belonging to the Bethunes. The Visitors' Centre features audio-visual materials and a display of gifts from the People's Republic of China. Tours by appointment.

The Big Apple and Brian McFarlane's Hockey Museum

* c/o Sunshine Orchards, Colborne, Ontario, KOK 1S0
  LOCATION: Highway 401, Exit 497
* (905) 355-2574 or (905) 355-3155,
  Hockey Museum (905) 355-5533
* Open daily, May – October, 8:00 a.m. – 9:00 p.m.;
  November – April, 8:00 p.m. – 7:00 p.m.
* Admission fee to some attractions

Anyone who has driven on Highway 401 past Colborne, Ontario, will be familiar with "The Big Apple." In fact, it is actually the world's *biggest* apple, or apple-shaped building, at 10.7 metres high, 11.6 metres wide, and weighing in at 38,100 kilograms. Inside Big Red are educational exhibits about the local apple industry and there is a lookout at the top. The grounds include a variety of things to see and do, like a shop with a veritable orchard of apple-themed items, a bakery featuring more apple tarts, pies, and turnovers than most people have ever seen, and an observation window so the bakers can be viewed in action. Nearby are Animal Land where children can pet geese, goats, and llamas, the Garden of Eden nature walk, a mini golf course, and picnic facilities. Also on site is Brian McFarlane's Hockey Museum, the official home of Peter Puck, which includes a collection of hockey photos and videos, and the Peter Puck Theatre.

Big Nickel Mine / Path of Discovery

- c/o Science North, 100 Ramsey Lake Road, Sudbury, Ontario, P3E 5S9
  LOCATION: Lorne Street at Big Nickel Mine Road, Sudbury
- (705) 522-3701
- Open daily, late June – Labour Day, 9:00 – 6:00; May 1 – late June and day after Labour Day – Thanksgiving, 9:00 – 5:00 Path of Discovery: daily, late June – Labour Day
- Admission and tour fee

Operated by Sudbury's Science North Science Centre, the Big Nickel Mine includes a half-hour guided tour to the underworld of a nickel mine. Visitors will see a miner's workplace, 20 metres underground, learn about mining techniques, emergency quarters and explosives, and see a recreated blasting display. While down under visitors can mail a letter from Canada's only subsurface mailbox, and see lettuce and tree seedlings growing underground. Outside the Big Nickel Mine is, naturally, a big nickel, actually the world's biggest coin at 9 metres high and 61 cm thick. Visits can be followed by the "Path of Discovery," a two-and-one-half-hour bus tour that takes visitors to significant sites in Sudbury's mining history and present-day operations. The tour starts at the Big Nickel and visits the Frood open pit mine, the Copper Cliff Smelter, a copper refinery, and the site where nickel was first discovered in the area. Visitors are encouraged to wear long sleeves and pants, and footwear that covers the feet completely.

Billy Bishop Heritage Museum

* P.O. Box 535, Owen Sound, Ontario, N4K 5R1
  LOCATION: 948 3rd Avenue West, Owen Sound, Ontario, N4K 4P6
* (519) 371-0031
* Open weekends, Victoria Day – Thanksgiving, 1:00 – 4:00; daily, July 1 – Labour Day, 1:00 – 4:00
* Admission by donation

Despite being expelled from military college in 1914, Billy Bishop went on to become Canada's number one flying ace in World War I, with 72 official victories – he even scrapped with the Red Baron, and later offered his military services in World War II and wrote a book called *Winged Peace*. Bishop was hired to do the first aerial show over the CNE in 1920, in which his airborne exuberance caused panic among "Ex" onlookers. Billy Bishop has remained a national hero, and his memory is still carried in the Maple Leaf roundel, used by the Royal Canadian Air Force, which is a modified version of a logo Bishop designed. A museum dedicated to the flying ace and his achievements is located in the house built by Bishop's father, where Billy was born and grew up. The house, furnished to period, has three fireplaces, dark-stained oak floors and woodwork, and displays many items used by Billy Bishop and his family.

Biology-Earth Sciences Museum

* Rooms 370 and 371, Biology One Building, University of Waterloo, Waterloo, Ontario, N2L 3G1
* (519) 885-1211 ext. 2469
* Open weekdays, 9:00 – 5:00; evenings and weekends by request; Geological Garden open daily
* Free admission

The Biology-Earth Sciences Museum has been run by the Biology-Earth Sciences department of the University of Waterloo since 1968. Here visitors can learn all about the Planet Earth, from its beginnings, billions of years ago, to the present. On display are rocks, gems, minerals, and fossils from Ontario and the world over. Mounted birds, including a passenger pigeon, animal bones, and remains of extinct mammals such as the mastodon and sabre-toothed tiger can be viewed as well as skeletons and replicas of dinosaurs and dinosaur eggs. Crystals can be examined through microscopes and the forces behind volcanoes are explained. Dioramas of Burgess Shale, Yoho National Park, and the Hungry Hollow formation are on display, as well as a feature on groundwater with computerized and hands-on facilities. Outside is a geological "rock garden" featuring a 27,215 kilogram collection of carefully labelled rocks from all over Ontario.

Black Creek Pioneer Village

* 1000 Murray Ross Parkway, North York, Ontario, M3J 2P3
  LOCATION: Jane Street and Steeles Avenue West
* (416) 736-1733
* Open March – April/October – November, Wednesday – Friday and weekends and holidays, 10:00 – 4:30; May – August, daily, 10:00 – 5:00; September, Wednesday – Sunday, 10:00 – 5:00; December, 10:00 – 4:30 daily
* Admission fee

Come and experience "life in the past lane" at this charming recreated 1860s rural Victorian community. Black Creek Pioneer Village features over 35 homes and workshops, country roads and boardwalks, and public and farm buildings all brought to life with costumed interpreters working and living as they would over 100 years ago. A printing office, weaver's shop, mill, drygoods emporium, the "Half Way House" inn, and shops and work spaces for black- and gun-smithing and clock-, barrel- and broom-making are all brought to life with period furniture, tools, toys, textiles, and equipment. Tours and educational programs cover a wide range of subjects, and special events, workshops, and displays are held year-round, from fiddle contests to summer theatre. Refreshments are available and the modern Visitors Centre houses a great gift shop; also, Village-made crafts and goods can be purchased in homes and workshops on site. Black Creek Pioneer Village is the only living history village in Metro Toronto.

Bowmanville Museum

* P.O. Box 188, Bowmanville, Ontario, L1C 3K9
  LOCATION: 37 Silver Street, Bowmanville
* (905) 623-2734
* Open April – June/September – December, Tuesday – Saturday, 9:30 – 4:30, Sundays, 1:30 – 4:30, holiday Mondays, 1:30 – 4:30; July and August, Monday – Saturday, 9:30 – 4:30
* Admission fee

The Bowmanville Museum was the result of a whopping donation in 1960 of $50,000 by local resident Sara Jane Williams to the Town of Bowmanville, on the condition that the town establish a museum. Opened in 1961, the Bowmanville Museum is located in what started out in 1846 as a Regency Style cottage, transformed to Provincial Italianate in the 1860s. Nine period rooms contain Victorian furnishings, textiles, costumes, artifacts and displays on local history, and rotating exhibits. The museum also houses what is possibly the largest doll collection in Canada, featuring over 4,000 dolls from across Europe and North America dating from the late 1800s. Wax, bisque, porcelain, straw, wood, and plastic lovelies line the walls, and connoisseurs will particularly admire an Eaton's Beauty, a complete set of Dionne Quints dolls, and Royal dolls made in honour of the coronation of George VI. Special events are held, and there is a gift shop on the premises.

Bowmanville Zoo

* 340 King Street East, Bowmanville, Ontario, L1C 3K5
  LOCATION: off Highway 401, exit 432, then 1.6 kilometres north on Liberty Street and 1 kilometre east to 340 King Street East
* (905) 623-5655
* Open May, daily, 10:00 – 5:00; June, weekdays, 10:00 – 5:00, weekends, 10:00 – 6:00; July and August, daily, 10:00 – 6:00; September, weekdays, 10:00 – 4:00, weekends, 10:00 – 5:00; October, weekends only, 10:00 – 4:00
* Admission fee

The Bowmanville Zoo, established in 1919, is the oldest operating zoo in the country. Dedicated to the preservation of endangered species, the zoo features hundreds of animals from all over the world, many of whom are rare and endangered. Peacocks, fallow deer, lions, tigers, elephants, zebras, hippos, camels, wild boar, pygmy goats, Burmese pythons, swans, ostriches, emus and droves of other wild and wonderful beasts inhabit the 18-hectare site. There is an Animal Kingdom Show where creatures display their performing abilities, as well as elephant rides, friendly animal encounters throughout the day, lion feedings at 5:00 p.m., and a petting zoo. Carnival rides, picnic facilities, a gift shop, restaurant, and free parking are available. The Bowmanville Zoo also features a variety of educational programs geared to different age and interest groups, including outreach programs that bring animals right into the classroom.

Brantford and Area Sports Hall of Recognition

* Wayne Gretzky Sports Centre, 254 North Park Street, Brantford, Ontario, N3R 4L1
* (519) 756-9900 ext. 223
* Open Monday – Friday, 10:00 – 8:30; Thursdays, 10:30 – 8:30; Saturday and Sunday, 11:00 – 6:00 Summer hours may vary
* Free admission

In response to numerous requests to see Wayne Gretzky memorabilia at the Wayne Gretzky Sports Centre, the Brantford and Area Sports Hall of Recognition was set up in 1991 to pay tribute to Gretzky and other outstanding sports celebrities from Brantford and the surrounding area. Hockey, football, lacrosse, swimming, boxing, wrestling, skiing, horse-racing, bowling, golf, figure skating, badminton, track and field, baseball, and the marathon are all represented through Canadian sports greats from skier Todd Brooker to runner Tom Longboat. Trophies, uniforms, boxing gloves, medals, ribbons and more are displayed, including the Great One's Hart Trophy, and Enos Williams' hand-made lacrosse stick. An audio-visual presentation called *The Makings of a Champion* is also available for viewing.

Bunker Military Museum

- Cobalt ONR Station, P.O. Box 43, Cobalt, Ontario, P0J 1C0
- (705) 679-5220
- Open daily, June 1 – September 1, 9:00 – 5:00
- Admission fee, tours by appointment

Located in a 1910 Ontario Northland Railway Station overlooking Cobalt Lake is the Bunker Military Museum, appropriately described as "a diamond in the rough." The museum holds an abundance of military artifacts and memorabilia from Canada and around the world, consisting of the private collection of owner/curator Jim Jones and significant donations. Trophies, medals, souvenirs, photos, postcards, rations, shaving kits, flags, posters, and an extensive military library are available for admiration and perusal. Uniforms are displayed on hand-crafted wooden mannequins, among them a paratrooper and open parachute hanging from the ceiling. Highlights include many women's military uniforms and items from Desert Storm. Set up as a tribute to military history, the Bunker's motto is "Not to glorify war . . . but to rekindle fond memories!"

BYTOWN MUSEUM

* P.O. Box 523, Station B, Ottawa, Ontario, K1P 5P6
  LOCATION: Rideau Canal off Wellington Street at the Ottawa Locks
* (613) 234-4570
* Open April 1 – 30 and Thanksgiving to November 30, weekdays, 10:00 – 4:00; May to Thanksgiving, Monday – Saturday, 10:00 – 4:00; Sunday 2:00 – 5:00, closed Tuesday
* Admission fee

The Bytown Museum is housed in the oldest stone building in Ottawa, the former commissariat used by Colonel By and the Royal Engineers during the construction of the Rideau Canal. Built in the early 19th century, it still stands in one of the most historically rich areas of Ottawa, next to the Rideau Canal locks, between Parliament Hill and the Chateau Laurier. Personal and military artifacts owed by Colonel By, the founder of "Bytown," now Ottawa, are featured, along with items from Bytown, Ottawa, and the Ottawa Valley from 1826 to the present. Kitchen and household furnishings and implements, toys, furniture, costumes, and a large picture collection are also on display. Special exhibits, such as a recent feature focusing on ten local long-running businesses, are staged regularly. The Bytown Museum has a research library, archives, and a gift shop and tours can be arranged by appointment. Also, accessible through the double doors facing the Canal, is an exhibit set up by the Canadian Parks Service on the builders of the Rideau Canal.

Campbell House

- 160 Queen Street West, Toronto, Ontario, M5H 3H3
- (416) 597-0227
- Open Monday – Friday, 9:30 – 4:30 all year;
  late May – New Year's, weekends, 12:00 – 4:30
- Admission fee

Campbell House, the only surviving building of its scale from the original town of York, is the restored home of Sir William Campbell, former Chief of Justice of Upper Canada. The fine mansion, a rare example of Canadian Georgian architecture, was built in 1822 and looks rather out of place on Toronto's trendy Queen Street, but it hasn't always been located there. The building originally sat on nearby Adelaide Street, but in March 1972, in a move that lasted 6 1/2 hours, Campbell House was jacked three metres off the ground and dollied to its current location. To clear the way, 1.3 kilometres of trolley wire, electricity poles, traffic lights, signs, and 82 street lights had to be removed, and 65 manhole covers had to be filled to hold the weight of the 272,000 kilogram edifice. The move was a success and now Campbell House functions as a restored period house, furnished to reflect the lifestyle of a prosperous man of taste and his family. Features include a portrait of Sir William and Lady Campbell, and a model of the Town of York *circa* 1825, with over 40 buildings. Costumed interpreters greet visitors at the door for tours of the lovely home.

Canada's Sports Hall of Fame

* Exhibition Place (centre of grounds), Toronto, Ontario, M6K 3C3
* (416) 260-6789
* Open daily, 10:00 – 4:30
* Free admission

Canada's Sports Hall of Fame was established in 1955, and consists of three storeys of displays of photographs, trophies, uniforms, and sports-wear worn by Canada's best builders and athletes to date. Visitors will learn about the development of Canadian sports in the Heritage Gallery and the Hall of Fame Gallery highlighting Honoured Members. Athletes like Marilyn Bell, Alex Baumann, Nancy Greene, and Terry Fox and those outstanding in sports from rowing to swimming and skiing to horse racing are all commemorated. Interactive displays on great moments in Canadian sport history and quizzes are available for use. The Sports Hall of Fame also inducts Honoured Members yearly, when choices are made by a nationwide selection committee. Group tours by appointment.

CANADIAN AUTOMOTIVE MUSEUM

- 99 Simcoe Street South, Oshawa, Ontario, L1H 4G7
  LOCATION: 1.5 kilometres north of Highway 401, exit 417
- (905) 576-1222
- Open daily, Tuesday – Friday, 9:00 – 5:00; Saturday, Sunday, and holidays, 10:00 – 6:00
- Admission fee

Oshawa is considered the birthplace of the Canadian auto industry, and with over one third of the city's residents still employed in auto-related jobs, it makes a good parking spot for the Canadian Automotive Museum. The museum interprets auto development in Canada and its impact on Canadian life and is set up in an authentic car dealership of the 1920s. Over 70 automobiles are displayed, many with dioramas and lively anecdotes, both inside and outside the building. Of note are a Fisher Electric from 1898, a Redpath Messenger from 1903, a 1912 Rolls Royce limo, owned originally by Lady Eaton, a Talbot Roadster from the thirties, a good old Plymouth "K" car from '81, and a West German Amphicar of 1965, which could travel on both land and water, although it never caught on commercially. Also on exhibit are bicycles, motorcycles, gas pumps, washing machines, musical instruments and other historical items. There is a gift shop on the premises and parking is free.

Canadian Broadcasting Corporation Museum

* 250 Front Street West, Toronto, Ontario, M5W 1E6
* (416) 205-3311
* Open Monday – Friday, 9:00 – 5:00
* Free admission

The Canadian Broadcasting Corporation has been keeping Canadians in touch with each other and the world for decades through television and radio, and has become an integral part of Canadian history and identity. The CBC Museum is a collection of corporation equipment and ephemera that has been accumulating since the late 1960s. Once obsolete, larger CBC items are sent to the Museum of Science and Technology in Ottawa but smaller artifacts, like microphones, receivers, TVs, radios, cameras, and tape machines (some of which used paper tape) from the CBC's early days up to the satellite era can be seen in the museum which is off the Barbara Frum Atrium in the Toronto CBC building. Gems of the collection are an award from Sylvania, given to the CBC for being the first company in North America to get footage of Queen Elizabeth's coronation in 1953, an impressive selection of microphones from the early 1930s, and Knowlton Nash's typewriter. Tours of CBC Toronto include a visit to the museum, an 8-minute video on the history of the CBC, and visits to important parts of the building such as the storage area for costumes used in some of the corporation's earlier programs.

CANADIAN CANOE MUSEUM

- Box 1338, Lakefield, Ontario, KOL 2HO
  PRESENT LOCATION: Haliburton, north of Hall's Lake
  FUTURE LOCATION: Little Lake, Peterborough on the Trent Canal
- (705) 652-3002
- Admission fee and hours to be determined

The Canadian Canoe Museum, formerly The Kanawa International Museum of Canoes, Kayaks, and Rowing Craft, contains an incredible collection of over 1,000 artifacts representing the first five thousand years of water transport on the North American continent as well as items from all over the world. The museum boasts "bark canoes, kayaks, baidarkas, umiaks, bull boats, dugouts and even rush floats . . . canvas canoes, cedar strip and cedar plank canoes, and craft representing virtually all the new technology that the [European] newcomers applied to construction." It is the largest collection of its kind in the world and the result of over forty years of collection and documentation, launched by Professor Kirk Wipper of Toronto, with the aid of many dedicated donors and volunteers. The museum also has an archives and library, now located at Trent University, and volunteers occasionally stage historical recreations of canoe launches. The Canadian Canoe Museum will be portaging to a permanent site in Peterborough over the next few years, but the old site in Haliburton is still accessible by appointment.

Canadian Museum of Caricature

* c/o National Archives of Canada, 395 Wellington Street, Ottawa, Ontario, KIA ON3
  LOCATION: 136 St. Patrick Street, Ottawa, Ontario
* (613) 995-3145
* Open daily, 10:00 – 6:00, Wednesday – Friday, 10:00 – 8:00
* Free admission

The Canadian Museum of Caricature is the official repository of Canada's funny, sarcastic, and sometimes downright nasty side. A project of the National Archives of Canada, the museum's mandate is to "acquire, preserve and make accessible political caricature and cartoons about Canada and by Canadians." The museum's holdings include over 30,000 items, starting from the 18th century. Themed exhibits of political cartoons, caricatures, humorous sculpture, and other media are regularly rotated in the spacious two-storey gallery in Ottawa's trendy Byward Market area. Recent features included work by Lynn Johnston, creator of the *For Better or for Worse* cartoon, and *Green and Bear It,* satirical sculpture on environmental issues by four Canadian "Mirth Scientists." Public access to the archives, children's programs, workshops, and school visits are also up for grabs. In the future the museum will be expanding to include a wider variety of materials, not specifically caricature-related, from the National Archives collection, and may be changing its name.

CANADIAN MUSEUM OF CIVILIZATION

* 100 Laurier Street, P.O. Box 3100, Station B, Hull, Quebec, J8X 4H2
* (819) 776-7000
* Open daily May 1 – June 30, 9:00 – 5:00; July 1 – September 5, 9:00 – 6:00; September 6 – October 10, 9:00 – 5:00; October 11 – April 30, Tuesday – Sunday, 9:00 – 5:00; open Thursdays, 9:00 – 8:00; admission free from 5:00 – 8:00
* Admission fee

The Canadian Museum of Civilization is not actually in Ontario, but just across the bridge from Ottawa in Hull, Quebec. The museum building, designed by Native architect Harold Cardinal, is highly unusual, featuring a soft, sculptural composition. Inside there are three main levels including History Hall, exhibition halls, and the Grand Hall, the latter showcasing the cultural and artistic creations of Canada's aboriginal peoples through life-size reconstructions of Native dwellings and arts. The history of Canada from its earliest beginnings to the present is interpreted throughout the museum, set off by exciting temporary exhibitions on a variety of subjects. The museum's own theatre group performs regularly. Also on the premises is a combined IMAX/OMNIMAX theatre, and the famous children's activity centre with hundreds of fun things to see and do. The CMC holds a breathtaking variety of special events, workshops, and educational programs and has quality shops and restaurants.

CANADIAN CLAY AND GLASS GALLERY

* 25 Caroline Street North, Waterloo, Ontario, N2L 2Y5
* (519) 746-1882
* Open Wednesday – Saturday, 10:00 – 5:00, Sunday, 1:00 – 5:00
* Admission fee

The Canadian Clay and Glass Gallery is housed in an award-winning new building, designed by Vancouver architectural team John and Patricia Patkau, across from the Seagram Museum in Waterloo. It is the first museum of its kind in Canada and aims to be a focal point for Canadian as well as international artists, to document and interpret past and present histories of the clay and glass arts, and to be a display and collection space for 20th-century Canadian pieces. Permanent and special exhibits showcase spectacular examples of vessels and art objects in ceramics, glass, clay, and other media by artists from across Canada and the world. The gallery has a very active schedule of exhibitions, holds artists' lectures and demonstrations, stages special events, and has a quality gift shop to suit every taste. Group tours by appointment.

Canadian Museum of Contemporary Photography

- P.O. Box 465, Station A, Ottawa, Ontario, KIN 9N6
  LOCATION: 1 Rideau Canal
- (613) 990-8257
- Open Saturday and Sunday, 11:00 – 6:00; Thursday and Friday, 11:00 – 8:00; Wednesday, 4:00 – 8:00; closed Monday and Tuesday; Research Centre by appointment only
- Admission fee, free on Thursdays

The Canadian Museum of Contemporary Photography began in 1985 as an affiliate of Canada's National Gallery, and is now housed permanently in a reconstructed railway tunnel at number one Rideau Canal, between the elegant Chateau Laurier and the Rideau Canal. The museum's mandate is to "collect, interpret and disseminate contemporary Canadian photography as an art form and as a form of social documentation." It manages this in a roomy 354 square metres of exhibition space, set up specifically for the display of photographs. The collection includes over 158,000 images by Canadian photographers, and exhibits change quarterly. The Canadian Museum of Contemporary Photography also has a Travelling Exhibition Program, which takes Canadian photography across the country and abroad. Education and Publication Programs are designed to further promote Canadian photography, and the space also includes a theatre, research centre, and boutique.

CANADIAN FIREFIGHTERS' MUSEUM

* Box 325, Port Hope, Ontario, L1A 3W4
  LOCATION: 95 Mill Street South, Port Hope, Ontario (east side of Ganaraska River near harbour)
* (905) 885-8985
* Open daily, June – August, 10:00 – 4:00
* Free admission

The Canadian Firefighters' Museum was established in 1984 to create awareness of the historical development of firefighting in Canada, with a mandate to "collect, preserve and display artifacts and information pertaining to firefighting in Canada from earliest times to the present." The collection is comprised of Canadian firefighting equipment from 1830 to 1955, and follows technological progress from hand- and horse-drawn examples to more modern, motorized pieces. Smaller artifacts and photographs are also collected. The Canadian Firefighters' Museum does not yet have a permanent facility, but a temporary workshop and exhibit space is open to the public in June, July, and August of each year. Special events are also held during this time, including Pitch-Ball tournaments and a Pumping Competition.

Canadian Football Hall of Fame and Museum

- 58 Jackson Street West, Hamilton, Ontario, L8P 1L4
- (905) 528-7566
- Open June – November, Monday to Saturday, 9:30 – 4:30, Sundays and Holidays, noon – 4:30; December through May, Monday to Saturday, 9:30 – 4:30
- Admission fee

The Canadian Football Hall of Fame and Museum in Hamilton has been collecting and exhibiting football memorabilia and artifacts since 1962. Photos, playing gear, mementoes, trophies, souvenirs, and other significant football-related items from the late 1800s up to the last football season of each year can be enjoyed, and a 92-seat theatre continually shows highlights of Grey Cup games. The centre of attraction is the Hall of Fame including a steel bust and brief biography of each member honoured. The Canadian Football Hall of Fame and Museum is also the permanent home of the "Crown Jewels" of Canadian football: the Grey Cup, when it is not on loan to the winning team from November through January of each year, as well as the lovely Schenley trophy, awarded annually to the game's most outstanding players including Canadian, Defense, Rookie, and Offense. Special events are held year round, and there is a gift shop full of CFL souvenirs.

Canadian Forces Base Borden Military Museum and Archives

- Canadian Forces Base Borden, Borden, Ontario, LOM 1CO
- (705) 423-3531
- Open Tuesday – Sunday (closed day following a long weekend), weekdays, 9:00 – 12:00 and 1:00 – 3:00; weekends, 1:30 – 4:00
- Admission free, donations accepted

Since 1916 Camp Borden has played a significant role in Canadian military history as the headquarters for the first armoured school and the birth place of Canada's Air Forces. It also became a training centre for Infantry, Medical, Provost and Dental Corps, and Military Intelligence, training approximately half the Canadian soldiers sent overseas during World War II. Today Base Borden is the Canadian Armed Forces' largest training centre. Preserving Canada's military history and Base Borden's past is a museum complex centred around the Base's Worthington Park. The park, named after the late Major-General Worthington, houses an outdoor display of armoured fighting vehicles and artillery pieces dating from World War I near the airfield, as well as several post-World War II aircraft mounted on pedestals. Two buildings contain weapons, uniforms, nuclear, biological and chemical warfare artifacts, and other military items used by the Armoured, Service, Medical and Dental Corps, the Intelligence and Security Branches and the Air Force. Of note are the World War II MK 16 "Spitfire" Fighter Plane from 1943/44, a Japanese 75mm field gun with ammunition limber *circa* 1902, and a 30-calibre type MMG Browning Machine gun M 1917 made in 1933.

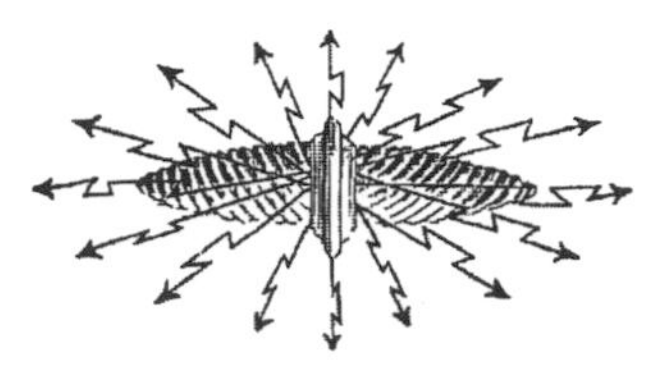

Canadian Forces Communications and Electronics Museum

* c/o Vimy Post Office, CFB Kingston, Ontario, K7K 5LO
  LOCATION: 4 kilometres east on Highway 2 in Vimy Barracks, Building B-16, Kingston
* (613) 541-5395
* Open all year, weekdays, 8:00 – 4:00; summer, weekdays, 8:00 – 4:00, weekends and holidays, 10:00 – 4:00; other times by appointment
* Free admission

The Canadian Forces Communications and Electronic Museum is a fascinating museum dedicated to the troops, times, and technology of the past, present, and future in Canadian military communications and electronics. It displays the "history of the integrated Canadian Forces Communications and Electronic Branch and its founding elements as well as aspects of our supporting defense electronics industry." Different rooms focus on various areas of military communication. To name a few: the Air Force Room, Corps Room, an early military communications classroom (reputedly authentic down to the cracks in the walls), and Modern Technology area. The museum boasts one of the world's best telephone collections, and also has a kit shop, theatre, and canteen facilities. Founded in 1961, the CFCEM has outgrown its present location and is slated to open in a more spacious and modern facility nearby in 1995. Tours available by request.

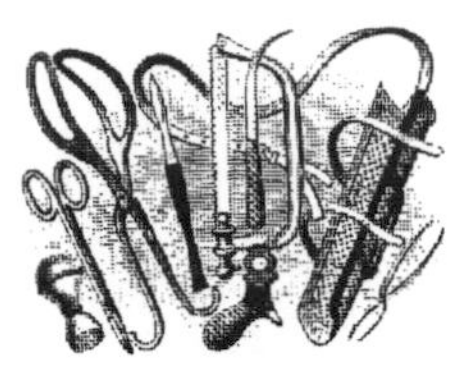

Canadian Museum of Health and Medicine

- Toronto Hospital/Western Division, Room MP 2-301, 399 Bathurst Street, Toronto, Ontario, M5T 2S8
- (416) 369-5444
- Hours, admission to be determined

The Museum of the History of Medicine had a fascinating collection of medical artifacts set up in the Academy of Medicine on the corner of Huron and Bloor in downtown Toronto for many years. In 1992 the collection was transferred to the Toronto Hospital where it will form the basis of the new Canadian Museum of Health and Medicine. This outstanding collection of approximately 8,000 artifacts was started in the early 20th century by the Academy of Medicine and includes mainly 19th- and 20th-century objects, with a focus on western medicine, although there are items from Asia, and other areas as well as an intriguing collection from the ancient world. Highlights include an Egyptian mummy, about 200 pap boats, silver soothers, teething rings and other elegant items for infants, tracheotomy sets, and a "birthing chair" from the mid-nineteen-eighties. One of the collections in the museum was started by the Canadian inventor of Pablum, Dr. T.G.H. Drake, and there is a considerable amount of mostly British medical caricatures from the late 18th and early 19th centuries. No date has been set for the opening of the new museum, although small exhibits will be featured in the hospital up until that time. Museum staff welcomes inquiries and research requests.

C L G A

Canadian Lesbian and Gay Archives

* Box 639, Station A, Toronto, Ontario, M5W 1G2
  LOCATION: 56 Temperance Street, Suite 201, Toronto, Ontario
* (416) 777-2755
* Open Tuesday – Thursday, 7:30 p.m. – 10:00 p.m., other times by appointment
* Free admission

The Canadian Lesbian and Gay Archives was founded in 1973 by members of *The Body Politic*, a gay liberation magazine, and has grown into an important repository, library, and research facility concerning all aspects of gay and lesbian culture. Holdings include books, a periodical collection of over 3,000 titles, Canadian daily newspaper clippings, papers of gay and lesbian individuals and organizations, a photograph collection of over 6,000 images, audio and video tapes, records, over 10,000 vertical files, and t-shirts, buttons, banners, posters, and other relevant artifacts. The archives welcomes both researchers and informal visitors. A limited reference service is available by telephone or mail, and there are photocopy facilities. The Canadian Lesbian and Gay Archives is run by volunteers who continue to actively collect materials, and organize and hold fundraising events.

CANADIAN NATIONAL EXHIBITION ARCHIVES

* Exhibition Place, Toronto, Ontario, M6K 3C3
* (416) 393-6135
* Open Monday – Friday, 8:30 – 4:30, by appointment
* Admission free

Step right up folks, and discover the history of a place that's been drawing crowds from all over Ontario since 1878. Through the years the Canadian National Exhibition, better known as the "Ex," has been the yearly centre of activity for all ages and interests including displays for agricultural, arts and crafts, and technological feats; a launching pad for boats, planes, trains, and all manner of automobiles; sports, communication, and music, and a midway for thrills, chills, freaks, geeks, eating, cheating, and overheating. Preserving the Ex's past is the Canadian National Exhibition Archives, home to printed materials, audio and video recordings, film, photographs, artifacts, and memorabilia dating from 1878 to the present. For researchers the archives also offers a reference service, photograph reproduction, book and poster sales, information packages, referrals, and photocopy facilities. Speaking engagements are occasionally held, and during the "Ex" an exhibition with interpretive staff is staged.

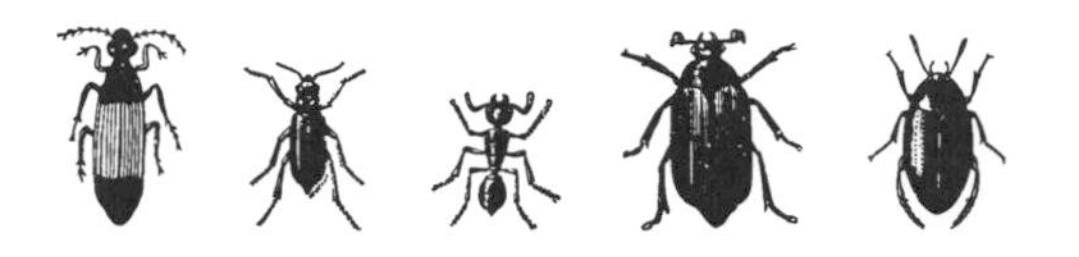

Canadian National Collection of Insects and Related Anthropods

- Biological Resources Division, Centre for Land and Biological Resources Research, K.W. Neatby Building, Central Experimental Farm, Ottawa, Ontario, KIA 0C6
- (613) 966-1665

- By appointment to researchers

The Canadian National Collection of Insects and Related Anthropods, part of the Centre for Land and Biological Resources Research, is a scientific research collection comprised of an incredible 15,000,000 insects, arachnids, and nematodes and is ranked as one of the best collections of its kind in the world. Specimens have been collected over the last century from across North America, the Canadian Arctic, and many other parts of the globe. The collection is used for research in systematics, biodiversity studies, faunistic inventories, ecology, evolution, and related biological studies, and supports research programs for Agriculture Canada, government research centres, and international universities. The Centre for Land and Biological Resources Research also has major herbaria for vascular plants and mycology and puts out a funky publication called *Fungi Canadenses*.

CANADIAN MUSEUM OF NATURE

* P.O. Box 3443, Station D, Ottawa, Ontario, K1P 6P4
  LOCATION: Victoria Memorial Museum Building, McLeod Street at Metcalfe, Ottawa
* (613) 996-3102 or 1-800-263-4433
* Open daily, summer 9:30 – 5:00, winter, 10:00 – 5:00, Thursdays to 8:00 p.m.; 1/2 price all day Thursday, free after 5:00
* Admission fee

The distinctive building that houses the Canadian Museum of Nature has had a long and unusual history. Construction began in 1905 and the resulting castle is a wild story-book mix of fantasy and influence. Constructed of sandstone on an unstable clay base, the 59,000-tonne stone structure eventually started to shift and sink, a problem ameliorated by the removal of three storeys of the tower. Many different museums and institutions have made the CMN building their home, including the National Gallery, and the Government of Canada in 1916 after the Parliament Buildings were burned. The Senate held meetings in the Hall of Invertebrate Fossils for four years and, after Sir Wilfrid Laurier's death in 1919, his body lay, wrapped in a flag, in the Auditorium. In 1988 the newly named Museum of Nature took complete control of the facilities. The Canadian Museum of Nature is the centre of a tremendous amount of important research in Canada, and the building holds exhibits on the Earth, life through the ages, birds, mammals, rocks and minerals, plant life, and dinosaurs. Other features include the Discovery Den for the very young, educational programs, and a gift shop.

Canadian Parliament Buildings

- c/o Public Relations, Parliament Hill, Wellington Street, Ottawa, Ontario, KIA OA6
- Centre Block: (613) 992-4793
  East Block: (613) 995-3960
- Hours are seasonal
- Free admission

The Canadian Parliament buildings offer all kinds of interesting things to see and do, like the changing of the Guard, carillon concerts, the firing of the Noon Gun throughout the summer, and tours and special events all year. There are five separate buildings, and the Centre Block is where most tours are conducted. Visitors will see interesting and impressive architecture and furnishings from gargoyles to the Speaker's Chair and see the House of Commons, Senate and Library, and the Peace Tower as they learn about the Canadian parliamentary system first hand. The East Block is the oldest building on Parliament Hill and is under separate management from the Centre Block, so tours here have to be arranged separately and have different hours. Equally as impressive as the Centre Block, the East Block features the Sir John A. Macdonald Office and the Governor General's Office, both furnished to period with original artifacts.

Museum of Canadian Scouting

- P.O. Box 5151, Station F, Ottawa, Ontario, K2C 3G7
  LOCATION: 1345 Baseline Road, Ottawa
- (613) 224-5131
- Open weekdays, 9:00 – 4:30
- Free admission

The Boy Scouts, founded early this century by Englishman Lord Baden Powell, is today the world's largest youth movement. Canada's national Boy Scouts office in Ottawa is the home base for Scouting in Canada and includes administrative offices, communications facilities, program headquarters, and the Museum of Canadian Scouting. The building's grounds feature a statue of a Boy Scout and a twenty-one metre Kwakiutl totem pole. Inside, murals depicting scenes from Kipling's *Jungle Books*, and Scouting themes can be enjoyed, along with ceramic tiles sporting Scout crests. Portable tape recorders can be borrowed at the front desk with information tapes in both English and French to give visitors more details on Scouting and on the building, and random access projectors and computers are located in various areas. The museum consists of over a dozen showcases displaying exhibits on Baden-Powell, interpreting how Scouting was established and developed in Canada through World War II, and up to the thriving present. Gifts from around the world to Canadian Scouts are displayed, and the trek ends with the Hall of Badges, featuring hundreds of badges and crests awarded to Scouts all over the globe.

Canadian Ski Museum

* 457A Sussex Drive, Ottawa, Ontario, K1N 6N4
* (613) 241-5832
* Open May 1 – September 30, Tuesday – Sunday, 11:00 – 4:00; October 1 – April 30, 12:00 – 4:00
* Admission fee

Canadians have been struggling across the snow for hundreds of years, and the ski, since its introduction here in about 1860, has seen many ups and downs. Canadians have distinguished themselves in skiing history, and the Canadian Ski Museum highlights this history, tributes famous ski personalities, showcases a variety of skis and related equipment, and discusses and explains their use. Early items like twisted birch bindings can be seen, followed by later developments up to and including modern ski equipment. The museum is home to the Canadian Skiing Hall of Fame, which honours greats like Nancy Greene and Steve Podborski, and also puts together the Honour Roll of Canadian Skiing. A library and archives are located on the premises. Not as slick or well-funded as many other sports museums and halls of fame, the Canadian Ski Museum is nevertheless a boon to all interested in the sport.

CANADIAN WAR MUSEUM

* 330 Sussex Drive, Ottawa, Ontario, K1A 0M8
* (613) 992-2774
* Open daily, 9:30 – 5:00; closed Mondays in winter, except holidays
* Admission fee

The Canadian War Museum, established in 1880, is an impressive institution offering a comprehensive look at Canadian military history. The extensive collection begins with artifacts of early aboriginal warfare and follows corresponding European conflict through art, photography, military equipment, documents, uniforms, vehicles, medals, and more. Artifacts are as diverse as a scarf knitted by Queen Victoria for a Canadian soldier who fought in the South African War to a Grosser Mercedes 7.7 limousine used by Adolf Hitler. Propaganda posters, audio effects, dioramas, and walk-in displays animate much of the setting. However, the museum's mandate firmly states that "the Canadian War Museum does not glorify war; rather, it serves to illustrate and commemorate the sacrifices and costs of freedom and independence." The museum is staffed primarily by retired officers, who proudly share their military knowledge with visitors. The museum also sponsors publications, film programs, workshops, ceremonies, and special events, and has a great souvenir shop.

Canadian Warplane Heritage Museum

- P.O. Box 35, Mount Hope, Ontario, LOR 1WO
  LOCATION: Hamilton Airport, Hangar 4
- (905) 679-4183
- Open daily, 10:00 – 4:00
- Admission fee

The Canadian Warplane Heritage Museum calls itself a "flying museum" and boasts Canada's biggest collection of flying, vintage, military aircraft. The museum's objectives are to preserve Canadian military aircraft flown by Canadians in World War II, to pay homage to those who were involved in the production, maintenance, and flying of them, and to create a fellowship with people interested in aircraft in general. The collection includes over forty planes for observation and communication, army cooperation, trainer and utility transport, bombers and fighters with highlights like the Avro Lancaster Bomber, the Fairchild Argus, and the Fairey Firefly. An aviation library and a resource centre are open to interested parties, and scheduled flying exhibitions and a theatre featuring continuously-running aviation films are available for viewing. And don't fly past the Aviation Shop and Art Gallery, Canada's largest emporium of aviation memorabilia.

Canadian Women's Movement Archives

* University of Ottawa, Library Network, Archives and Special Collections, 65 University, Room 603, Ottawa, Ontario, K1N 9A5
* (613) 564-8129
* Open Monday – Friday, 1:00 – 5:00; summer, 1:00 – 4:00
* Free admission

The Canadian Women's Movement Archives is located at the University of Ottawa, and consists of documents and artifacts related to the Canadian feminist movement after 1960. These include records, minutes, and reports produced by or written about various organizations, and periodicals, journals, conference records, audio recordings, posters, flyers and other visual materials. There are also badges, buttons and insignia, photographs and slides, t-shirts, banners, bookmarks and other artifacts, as well as lesbian and gay holdings. Over two thousand women's groups from across Canada are represented. Initiated by a coalition of feminist organizations, the Canadian Women's Movement Archives was handed over to the University of Ottawa in 1992, and now all service is offered in both French and English.

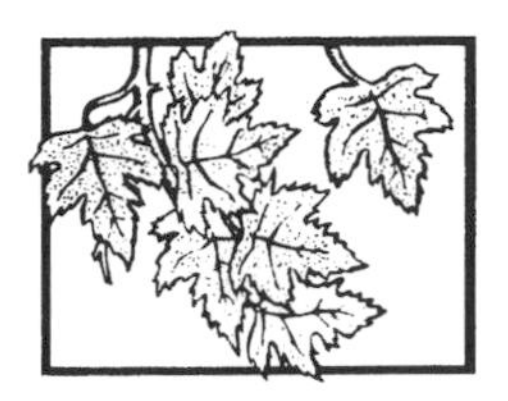

Canadiana Collection, North York Public Library

* Sixth floor, North York Public Library, 5120 Yonge Street, North York, Ontario, M2N 5N9
* (416) 395-5623
* Open Monday, 12:30 – 8:30; Tuesday – Thursday, 9:00 – 8:30; Friday, 9:00 – 5:30; Saturday, 9:00 – 5:00; Sunday, 1:00 – 5:00; closed Sundays May to Thanksgiving
* Admission free

The North York Public Library's Canadiana collection consists of over 130,000 documents important to Canadian history. These are in the form of books, magazines, pamphlets, catalogues, directories, maps, minutes, newspapers, letters, census records, and the list goes on. Areas of interest include North York and area history, Ontario and Canadian communities, genealogy, Canadian history, Canadian literature, art and architecture, and book arts, including works produced by small and private presses. They also have major Toronto newspapers on microfilm up to 1959 and more than 70,000 catalogued items from 1901 on microfiche. Materials are for use in the library only.

Casa Loma

* 1 Austin Terrace, Toronto, Ontario, M5R 1X8
  LOCATION: corner of Spadina Avenue and Davenport Road
* (416) 923-1171
* Open daily, 10:00 – 4:00
* Admission fee, tours are self-guided

A castle in downtown Toronto? It's true, and it's called Casa Loma, a fantasy mix of Gothic, Romanesque, and Norman architecture, complete with turrets, coats of arms, 2.4 hectares of grounds, stables, stained glass, oak panelled walls, a conservatory, library, and a 245-metre underground tunnel. Casa Loma was the dream home of the wealthy Sir Henry Mill Pellatt, a Canadian businessman and military officer. Built in his heyday, Casa Loma is a symbol of wealth and extravagance not normally seen in our rather modest country, although the castle was never completely finished, as Sir Henry's luck and funds ran out in the early 1920s. Talk about building castles in the air. However, the castle is now a fine heritage building, and visitors can take self-guided tours through Sir Henry's study, the Serving Room, the Great Hall, the Smoking Room, two towers, Sir Henry's Bathroom, which had a "surround spray" shower involving six taps, and stables with tiled floors and mahogany stalls. An exhibition in the Kiwanis Room discusses the Kiwanis Club's restoration of the building, and there is also a Girl Guides display in honour of Lady Pellatt's support of the organization. The Queen's Own Rifles Museum is also on the premises. There is a café and a gift shop and the lovely gardens are open in the summer.

Centennial Conservatory

* 500 Donald Street East, Thunder Bay, Ontario, P7E 5V3
  LOCATION: 1601 Dease Street, behind Chapples Park
* (807) 622-703
* Open daily, 1:00 – 4:00
* Free admission

The Centennial Conservatory is a botanical garden that was set up in 1967 as a Centennial project for the city of Thunder Bay. The Conservatory sits on two hectares of land and its construction required over 16 tonnes of glass, steel, and concrete. There are three viewing areas: the central area features tropical plants, trees, shrubs, and exotic flowers from the world over, while foot paths, a pool, and bridge enhance the tropical setting; the East Wing stages temporary flower shows, while the West Wing boasts 280 different species of cacti. Behind the main structure are facilities for the growing of plants to be distributed to the city's parks. Great for escaping the city and the cold, or for taking photographs. Tours are offered, and the space can also be reserved for weddings.

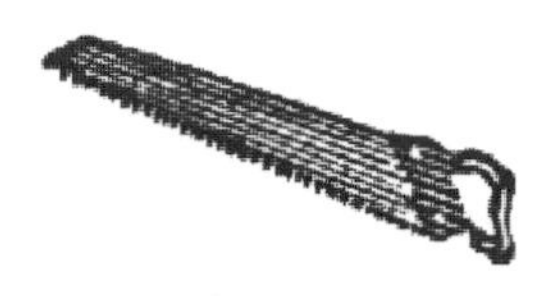

CENTENNIAL PARK 1910 LOGGING CAMP

- 950 Memorial Avenue, Thunder Bay, Ontario, P7B 4A2
  LOCATION: Centennial Park Road via Arundel Street, Hodder Avenue and Highway 17 – 11 East
- (807) 625-2351
- Logging Camp open during summer camping season, park open all year
- Free admission

Centennial Park was established in 1967, on the site of an old fox farm, to honour Canada's Centennial. In remembrance of the area's logging history, the site features a re-created logging camp, typical of the area *circa* 1910, with a bunkhouse, camp cookery, office, blacksmith shop, warehouse, stable, Finnish-style sauna, and outhouse, all in period. Documents, displays, and industry artifacts add to the logging experience. A fun wood playground and a small farm are open to children in the summer, and during the winter horse-drawn sleigh rides are offered, while cross-country ski trails and toboggan hills can be accessed throughout the park. Guided tours are conducted in season for groups and school classes.

The Central Experimental Farm

- CEF-2000, Building 86, Central Experimental Farm, Ottawa, Ontario, KIR OC6
  LOCATION: Prince of Wales Drive, Ottawa
- (613) 995-9554, toll-free 1-800-538-9110
- Farm open daily dawn – dusk; animal barns and greenhouses open daily, 9:00 – 4:00
- Free admission to farm

Known as Canada's premiere agricultural showcase and one of the National Capital's top five tourist attractions, is the Central Experimental Farm, established in 1886 as the headquarters and research centre for the Canada Department of Agriculture. Concerning itself with Canada's past, present, and future agricultural heritage and prowess, the farm covers 500 hectares and is open all year. The grounds include an arboretum featuring hundreds of trees both indigenous to Canada and from all over the world, a spectacular garden of annuals and perennials, plenty of livestock, showcase herds of cattle, swine and horses, a greenhouse, fountains and streams, and tours in a wagon pulled, from May – September, by powerful Clydesdales, weather permitting. The farm also holds entertainment and educational activities, sponsors lectures and courses, and is a great place to take a walk, ride a bike or have a picnic. The Agricultural Museum is also located on the Central Experimental Farm grounds.

Chippewa Park Wildlife Exhibit

* c/o 950 Memorial Avenue, Thunder Bay, Ontario, P7B 4A2
  LOCATION: City Road, east off Highway 61-B
* Camping season (807) 623-3912, other times (807) 625-2343
* Open camping season, mid-May to Labour Day
* Free admission

Chippewa Park, run by the City of Thunder Bay Parks and Recreation Department, is a 109-hectare park that follows the shoreline of Lake Superior and, open since 1921, is one of Thunder Bay's oldest parks. An original dance hall and pavilion, used by early visitors, is now the centre of Park activities, and log cabins and camping sites can be rented. Also on the grounds is the 4-hectare Chippewa Park Wildlife Exhibit. Overhead walkways allow visitors to view indigenous wild animals, including timber wolves, deer, coyotes, foxes, caribou, otters, cougars, and bears, in their natural environment. Waterfowl can also be seen in addition to an aviary featuring predatory birds. The Wildlife Exhibit is ongoing, and Parks and Recreation hopes to add many more birds and beasts to its ranks in the future.

C.H.P. HERITAGE CENTRE

* Box 498, Suite 100, 2 Bloor Street West, Toronto, Ontario, M4W 3E2
  LOCATION: Cumberland Terrace, Upper Level, Bay Street at Cumberland, Toronto
* (416) 515-7546
* Open Thursday – Saturday, noon – 4:00
* Free admission

The C.H.P. (Canadian Heritage Project) Heritage Centre is a focal point for a group of affiliated heritage groups such as the Canadian Railroad Historical Association, Clans and Scottish Societies of Canada, the Monarchist League of Canada, the Ontario Black History Group, and the Lincoln and Continental Owners Club. The downtown Centre location functions as an office and commercial space, and as an exhibit facility with wall displays from many of the Centre's affiliates. Small temporary exhibits put on by member groups and guest organizations are mounted in a room at the back of the Centre. Two recent displays included a feature on collectible toys like Matchbox cars and Trolls, and the history of local medicine from both Native and European traditions. An enormous selection of brochures advertising Ontario historical societies and institutions is available as well as a shop space, where all proceeds go back to the organizations involved. The Centre exists on a very thin shoestring budget with much office equipment recycled from cast-offs, so don't expect anything glamorous, but it is an interesting stop-off for historically minded shoppers in the Bay/Bloor area. A great information facility, and the volunteers really know their stuff.

CIRCULAR SAW MUSEUM

* R.R. 1, Cloyne, Ontario, KOH 1KO
  LOCATION: Highway 41, about 40 miles north of Highway 7
* (613) 333-2371
* Open June – October, Wednesday – Sunday, 12:00 – 5:00
* Free admission, donations appreciated

A name like the Circular Saw Museum might make visitors want to run away rather than cross the threshold, but it's not as scary as it sounds. The painting of circular saw blades is a folk art practised by museum co-founder Viola Seitz, and usually involves depictions of pastoral scenery or quaint rural cottages. The museum gets its name from Viola's *tour de force*, an enormous saw blade that reaches up to her light switches, on which she has painted houses from her home in Cloyne, Ontario. The sawblade is the centrepiece of a collection owned and displayed by Viola and her husband Glen, who were quoted in the local paper as saying, regarding their home, "we either had to build a museum or move out." Hence today the museum is located in two trailers, jam-packed with pioneer artifacts including spinning wheels, tools, glassware, barrels, pitchforks, tractor seats, milk bottles, a collection of 75 dolls, a silk display, butter churns, photographs, washboards, old advertisements, and, of course, a distinguished collection of circular saw blades, both painted and unpainted. Glen makes skillful carvings on rural themes, like miniature tractors with functioning steering wheels, and he and Viola have put together models of all the houses from Denbigh, 15 kilometres north of Cloyne, as they stood in the year 1920.

Cobalt-Coleman Firefighters Museum

* 50 Silver Street, Cobalt, Ontario, P0J 1C0
* (705) 679-5300
* Open seasonally, Monday – Saturday, 9:00 – 4:00; open Sunday during the Miners' Festival
* Free admission

The Town of Cobalt, famous for its silver mining industry, suffered five disastrous fires between 1906 and 1977, and the last destroyed one third of the town. These fires were brought under control by the Cobalt-Coleman Volunteer Fire Brigade, whose valiant efforts are commemorated in the Cobalt-Coleman Firefighters Museum. The museum opened in 1991 and displays equipment used by the local brigade going back to the 1930s, including fire extinguishers, nozzles, safety equipment, trophies, photographs, and ribbons. Information and artifacts related to Cobalt's major fires are also featured. The museum is located in an old mine shaft house from the town's more affluent period, which was later converted into a meat shop, benefiting from the cool underground air. This museum will be of special interest to Cobalt residents, children, and firefighters.

Cobalt's Northern Ontario Mining Museum/ The Heritage Silver Trail

- MUSEUM: 24 Silver Street, Cobalt, Ontario, P0J 1C0
- (705) 679-8301
- Open June 1 – September 30, daily, 9:00 – 5:00; October 1 – May 31, Monday – Friday, 9:00 – 12:00; other times by appointment
- Admission fee
- TRAIL: off Highway 11 at west entrance of Cobalt, open all year, free admission

Cobalt's Northern Ontario Mining Museum is located in the "town that silver built," Cobalt. Silver, cobalt, nickel, and arsenic-laden ores were discovered by accident in the area when the Temiskaming and Northern Railways were being built at the turn of the century, and the mining industry and town grew from there. The mere 8-hectare area saw 400 companies and 12,000 residents at its peak, and even had its own stock exchange. Cobalt's Northern Ontario Mining Museum is full of facts, figures, and artifacts relating to Cobalt's short but adventurous history and early hardrock mining, including the world's biggest native silver ores display. An exciting trip underground at the inactive Colonial Mine can be arranged through the museum. Free maps are also available for the self-guided Heritage Silver Trail, a project of the Ontario Ministry of Northern Development and Mines. This consists of a six-kilometre driving tour of five historical sites in "the world's most famous" silver mining camp including a mill site, a vein site, a lookout, and two mines.

Cochrane Railway and Pioneer Museum

* P.O. Box 490, 210 Railway Street, Cochrane, Ontario, POL 1CO
  LOCATION: north-east of Cochrane Union Station
* (705) 272-4361
* Open daily, mid-June to Labour Day
* Admission fee

The town of Cochrane began at the junction of two railways, originally a Native meeting ground called Little Lakes Camping Ground. White settlers soon moved in and by 1910 the town of Cochrane was incorporated. Because of its railway heritage, it is fitting that the Cochrane community museum be housed in cars of a train, including a steam locomotive, CN baggage car, CN coach, an "Interpretive" car and, of course, a caboose. On display in the T. & N.O. Locomotive No. 137, the Baggage Car and Caboose are the workings and many original fittings from various cars, First Nations and Inuit displays, logging, trapping, smithing and farming equipment, and exhibits and pioneer furniture. The CN coach holds exhibits on the railway, including a model train, seating, uniforms, photographs, and more. The museum also provides small classroom facilities and interpretive areas for educational visits.

COMBER PIONEER VILLAGE

* Route 3, Holland Centre, Ontario, NOH 1RO
  LOCATION: 3 kilometres north of Holland Centre and Highway 10
* (519) 794-3467
* Open summer, by appointment
* Donations appreciated

Robert Comber, retired Captain and instigator of Comber Pioneer Village, describes his museum complex as "a private hobby gone wild." The village's 1.8 hectares include five original and reconstructed buildings: the original Galbraith Cabin, *circa* 1841, which belonged to the area's first settlers; the first log school house in Holland Township, from the mid-1800s; a log barn and smoke house; and a reconstruction of Martin's Inn, which, in the last century, marked the end of the Toronto Sydenham Road, making it, as Comber puts it, "the last watering hole for man, beast and machine." Buildings are furnished with period artifacts, including furniture, tools, and housewares, such as an 1888 charcoal-heated iron. The upper level of Martin's Inn contains the Orange Lodge Collection, which displays flags, badges, record books, drums, swords, bibles, and other artifacts belonging to all branches of the Orange Lodge order. Guided tours are offered by appointment.

Commanda General Store Museum

* Commanda, Ontario, POH 1JO
  LOCATION: Hamlet of Commanda, Highway 522, 22 kilometres west of Trout Creek
* (705) 729-2113
* Open Victoria Day – Labour Day, daily, 8:00 – 6:00
* Free admission

The Hamlet of Commanda was once a small but thriving community boasting a smith and carpenter, a mill for flour and lumber, a hotel, livery, churches, schools, and the Commanda General Store. The store was started by a Toronto lawyer who saw the junction of east-west north-south roads as an excellent place to set up a business during the logging boom. The two-storey building, designed in High Victorian commercial style, sports an ornate gingerbread false front, with upper and lower verandahs, and was the place to get feed, medicine, food, clothing, and other items. Although it is the only commercial building left in tiny Commanda, the store still stands, thanks to the Gurd and Area Historical Corporation, who began an exhaustive restoration project in the late seventies. Now a delightful historic building, it shows the kinds of furnishings and goods that would have been available at the shop up to the mid-thirties. Future plans include transforming areas of the store into a tea room, gift shop, program centre, and archival resource library.

Conklin Collection of Vintage Carnival Equipment

* P.O. Box 31, Brantford, Ontario, N3T 5M3
* (519) 756-2111
* Location and admission fees vary

The Conklin Collection of Vintage Carnival Equipment is the private collection of Jim Conklin, who is the owner of Conklin Shows – a name long associated with fun and carnivals in Canada. Mr. Conklin calls it a "working museum" and visitors can actually go on the rides although, according to Conklin, the vintage equipment doesn't have the "thrill of today's more sophisticated rides." A ride is, however, a great jaunt into the past both for people who remember the old equipment, and for those who would like to know what their parents and grandparents used to do for kicks. The collection includes vintage Ferris wheels, merry-go-rounds, children's rides, illusion show gear, a mock guillotine, games of skill and chance, refreshment kiosks, tents, and trucks. There is also a lively collection of photos and memorabilia of the amusement industry where Conklin rides were featured. Exhibits vary in size, content, duration, and location, but tend to crop up near midways, so keep your eyes peeled if you want to catch a show. Recent exhibits were held in Simcoe, Ontario, and at Ontario Place, where the old favourites ran all summer.

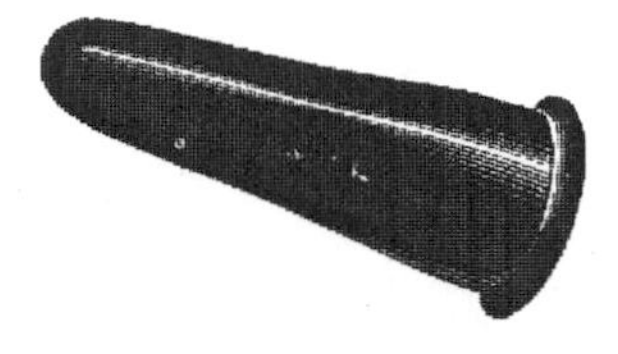

Museum of Contraception

* 19 Greenbelt Drive, Don Mills, Ontario, M3C 1L9
* (416) 449-9444
* The collection travels quite frequently and may be on loan for several weeks at a time
* Admission limited to health care professionals, by appointment only

Run by the pharmaceutical company Ortho Pharmaceutical, the Museum of Contraception is the only contraception museum in the world, and is a genuinely fascinating place. The collection was started in 1966 by the company's president, Percy Skuy – no easy task, as contraceptive devices, especially old ones, are not something people tend to keep. However, the museum collection includes some 270 artifacts, and traces contraceptive methods across cultures from 1850 B.C. through to today's high-tech methods. Early Egyptian use of crocodile dung as a pessary, ancient and modern sponges and condoms, the "random access" block pessary (known more as an instrument of torture than a contraceptive), dried beaver testicles, candy wrappers, and a bewildering selection of intra-uterine devices are interpreted and displayed in rows of wall cases. Important documents, paintings, and photographs of birth control activists are also presented. Truly a seminal collection, especially in light of the condom's newfound popularity.

Correctional Service of Canada Museum

- 555 King Street West, Kingston, Ontario, K7L 4V7
  LOCATION: take the Sir John A. Macdonald Boulevard exit from the 401 and proceed south
- (613) 545-8460 ext. 1104 or (613) 545-8686
- Open mid-May – Labour Day, Wednesday – Friday, 9:00 – 4:00; Saturday and Sunday, 10:00 – 4:00
- Admission fee

Fittingly located in the former Warden's residence constructed in the 1870s by inmate labour, the Correctional Service of Canada Museum can be found between Kingston's Prison for Women and the Kingston Penitentiary. The museum features four rooms full of artifacts used by staff and inmates from the Kingston Penitentiary's beginnings in the 1830s, and from other institutions throughout Canada. Staff uniforms, photos, important documents and historical information fill one room, while two others house objects both authorized and unauthorized, common throughout prison history. Ingenious fakes and home-made escape tools are displayed, including a false-bottomed paint can for transporting drugs, incredibly realistic imitations of pistols, picks, knives, confiscated tattoo guns, a series of dummy heads (used to dupe prison guards), liquor stills, false keys, and forged documents. The Corporal Punishment Room reminds visitors that physical punishment was practised in Canada between 1835 and 1968, and displays a number of fascinating and surprising artifacts. Archival facilities will be available in the future, and new exhibits will focus on modern prison life.

Criminals Hall of Fame Wax Museum

* 5751 Victoria Ave, Niagara Falls, Ontario, L2J 3L6
* (905) 374-3011
* Open summer 8:30 a.m. – 1:00 a.m. daily; other times vary
* Admission fee

Bonnie and Clyde, Charles Manson, Adolf Hitler, Lizzy Borden, Son of Sam, Jason, and many other hardened criminals and murderers await your company on the top of Niagara Falls' Clifton Hill. The Criminals Hall of Fame Wax Museum features wax effigies of the best of the bad, presented in cell-like modules along the walls, in appropriate settings and costume, including blood, sound effects, and all. This museum is not as fast-paced or slick as many of Niagara's other attractions, but its rather seedy interior actually complements its content. Of interest to museum buffs is a video at the ticket booth on wax model making, and a tiny display inside the museum on the company that does the work. Best of all is the opportunity for visitors to sit in a mock electric chair, setting off bells, electric charges, and frequently, an ear-piercing scream.

Crysler Farm Battlefield Park and Queen Elizabeth Gardens

* c/o The St. Lawrence Parks Commission, R.R. 1, Morrisburg, Ontario, K0C 1X0
  LOCATION: Crysler Farm Battlefield Park, Highway 2, Interchanges 750, 758, and 770 on Highway 401, 11 kilometres east of Morrisburg
* (613) 543-3704
* Park open daily
* Admission fees apply to some locations

In 1813 what is now Crysler Farm Battlefield Park was the site of a battle between American forces and British Regulars, who were aided by a Canadian contingent during the War of 1812. The area was later settled by Loyalists, and now the beautifully landscaped park, next to Upper Canada Village, stands to commemorate this important part of Canadian history. A Pioneer Memorial, Loyalist Memorial, and a Bicentennial Stone are located around the park as well as a marina, railway exhibit, beach, picnic area, and golf course. Queen Elizabeth Gardens, in the heart of Crysler Park, was created in the mid-eighties in tribute of a visit from Queen Elizabeth II. This beautiful area includes the sunken Rose Garden which, in season, showcases a wide variety of roses, and the Antique Rose Area with varieties dating from 1590 to 1850. The Native Materials and Wildflower Area contains Woodland species and an experimental wildflower section; the Exotic Area highlights dwarf trees and the Upland Area features dogwood, sumac, hemlock, and cedar.

Cullen Gardens and Miniature Village

- 300 Taunton Road West, Whitby, Ontario, L1N 5R5
  LOCATION: 40 minutes drive east of Toronto
- Whitby (905) 668-6606; Toronto (905) 686-1600; Ontario or Quebec call 1-800-461-1821
- Hours are seasonal
- Admission fee

During every season, Cullen Gardens' 10-hectare grounds have a variety of things to offer the visitor, including a playground for kids, tulip, rose, and chrysanthemum festivals, the Festival of Lights, a winter carnival, a historic house, and a village in miniature. The flowers, topiary, and sculpted grounds make a great place for a scenic afternoon, wedding, or special event, and children in particular will enjoy the special events, puppet shows, and flower sculptures. Also on the grounds is historic Lynde House *circa* 1856, hosted by costumed staff. The Miniature Village consists of about 180 miniature buildings, including shops and houses, a lake, and carnival built to 1/12 scale, and is complete with furniture, cars, boats, and tiny people strolling the streets. Cullen Gardens also has plenty of souvenir shops, restaurants, and there is even a bakery on the premises.

Currency Museum, Bank of Canada

* 245 Sparks Street, Ottawa, Ontario, KIA OG9
* (613) 782-8914
* Open Tuesday – Saturday, 10:30 – 5:00, Sunday, 1:00 – 5:00, all year; open Mondays, May 1 – Labour Day
* Admission fee, free on Tuesdays

The comprehensive, well-planned Currency Museum is truly worth its weight in gold. Located inside the Bank of Canada building in downtown Ottawa, the museum traces the history of currency in Canada and throughout the world from its diverse beginnings and many manifestations. Eight galleries present artifacts and information in a dramatic setting, with stimulating features like plaster hands holding coins and multi-level displays. Visitors will learn how shells, beads, arrowheads, playing cards, elephant hair, compressed tea, cigarettes, beaver pelts, and even stones at the bottom of the sea have been, and in some cases still are, used as money. There is a great "hands-on" room for children and a 7,000 volume research library. The museum also sponsors travelling exhibits based on themes such as the use of birds on coins and bills, and the history of the "love token."

DANCE COLLECTION DANSE

- 145 George Street, Toronto, Ontario, M5A 2M6
- (416) 365-3233
- By appointment only
- Free admission

The Dance Collection Danse calls itself a "living museum" and its primary mandate is "the promotion and celebration of Canada's theatrical dance history." The D.C.D. began in 1983 as a series of projects attempting to restage works, and to pay tribute to dances and dancers, from Canada's past. These included the reconstruction of six historical Canadian dance productions, the formation of the ENCORE! Dance Hall of Fame, and multimedia presentations. Today the Dance Collection Danse functions as an archive, both preserving physical documents and recording them electronically; as the home to the special collections of late choreographer and dancer Judy Jarvis and the Ballet Russe's Nesta Toumine, and as a choreographic library, preserving the works of Canadian choreographers. It continues to actively accumulate and document information, artifacts, and papers. The collection boasts over 2,000 photographs dating back to 1915, films, scrapbooks, costumes, reviews, props, backdrops, set and costume designs, programs, and more. Dance-related videos and publications are available through the D.C.D. and they also produce a regular newsletter. The D.C.D. is a non-profit organization and membership is free. The archives are open by appointment to the general public, students, scholars, and schools.

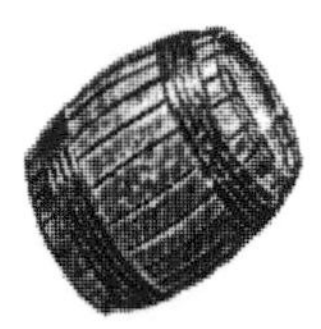

The Daredevil Adventure

* 6170 Buchanan Avenue (adjacent to the Skylon tower) Niagara Falls, Ontario, L2G 7J8
* (905) 358-3611
* Call for show times
* Museum can only be accessed during IMAX show times; there is a separate admission fee for the museum or admission is free with purchase of an IMAX ticket

Dare to enter the Daredevil Adventure and learn about the many who have plunged over raging Niagara Falls – some who made it, some who didn't. Visitors can see the museum after watching *Niagara: Miracles, Myths and Magic*, in impressive IMAX, or just catch the adventure on its own. Learn about Annie Taylor, a middle-aged schoolteacher, who was the first person and so far the only woman ever to intentionally brave the Falls. She went over in a barrel and actually survived to tell her tale. Her comments? "No one ought ever to do that again." Charles Blondin walked tightrope over the Falls in 1859 while cooking breakfast in a wheelbarrow and Dave Mundy took a video camera in his barrel in 1985; the resulting video is shown continuously in the museum. The museum's claim to fame is "the largest" (presumably in the world) collection of Niagara daredevil artifacts, from simple barrels to something called a Plunge O'Sphere, all used by various people who have taken the leap. A sensational but interesting tribute to the bizarre compulsion of throwing oneself into Niagara Falls.

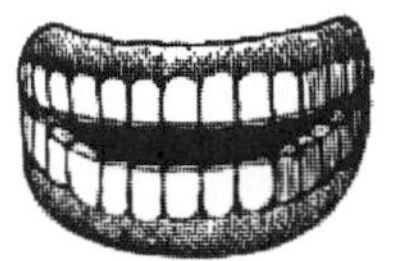

Dentistry Museum

- Faculty of Dentistry, University of Toronto, 124 Edward Street, Toronto, Ontario, M5G 1G6
- (416) 979-4900
- By appointment only
- Free admission

You'll be flapping your gums when you leave this crowded museum which follows the incredible history of dentistry, with a focus on Canadian and Ontario artifacts. Paintings, prints, books, and old texts document the history of dentistry and glorify great moments and discoveries. Chairs, tools and equipment used throughout the years follow the profession's progression and make a distinct contrast with the technology, ethics, and materials of today. Most notable are a bristly collection of historical toothbrushes (including a hand-turned plastic rotary model), a set of homemade dentistry tools made of waste metals by a soldier in a prisoner of war camp to treat fellow inmates, and "Waterloo" dentures, made from teeth plucked from corpses on the wargrounds of the Battle of Waterloo and sent to dentists in North America in barrels. The Dentistry Museum is part of the University of Toronto's Faculty of Dentistry, but because of limited staff and space regular tours and hours are not offered. However, it is an absolute must for dentists and medical history enthusiasts, and a visit is nothing like a trip to the dentist.

DIONNE QUINTS MUSEUM

* P.O. Box 747, North Bay, Ontario, P1B 8J8
  LOCATION: North Bay Bypass and Seymour Street
* (705) 472-8480
* Open mid-May – mid-October, daily, 9:00 – 5:00; July and August, 9:00 – 7:00
* Admission fee

On May 28, 1934, the Dionne quintuplets – Annette, Yvonne, Cecile, Emilie, and Marie – conceived without fertility drugs, were born against incredible odds, and survived against even higher odds. Their home in North Bay, now the Dionne Quints Museum, was to become an object of pilgrimage for over three million visitors. Much of the early life of these five girls was spent dressed up and on display for droves of tourists who flocked to North Bay to see this quirk of nature first hand. The Quints' family life was fraught with politics and conflict, and the museum stands, in some ways, as a memorial to exploitation and human curiosity. However, the Dionne Quints were born in a different social climate, and their birth was a symbol of hope and fecundity amid the Depression's poverty and despair. The "Quints Industry" also gave employment to thousands of people. Either way, the Dionne Quints Museum, through Quints artifacts and memorabilia, including the butcher's basket the newborns used as a cradle, shows the human side of five little girls who lived a very unusual life, and preserves a unique part of Canadian history.

Discovery Harbour

* P.O. Box 1800, Penetanguishene, Ontario, L0K 1P0
  LOCATION: follow Highway 93 through Penetanguishene, turn right at the water and follow the ship logo
* (705) 549-8064
* Open daily, Victoria Day weekend – Thanksgiving; call for hours of operation
* Admission fee

Discovery Harbour, formerly Penetanguishene Historic Naval and Military Establishments, is an exciting heritage site in and around the shores of lovely Penetanguishene Bay. The area's naval history began in 1793 when John Graves Simcoe marked the spot for a naval base where ships could be maintained and protected. The British Navy began building the area up during the War of 1812 and, after 1817, it was home to war and supply ships. In 1825 Penetanguishene Bay was even a stopover for Sir John Franklin's second polar expedition. By 1834 the Navy shipped out and the base became fully military. Today the establishments are preserved and run by the Ministry of Tourism and Recreation. Two dozen buildings, staffed by guides and costumed interpreters, include a charthouse, dockyard, barracks, cemetery, kitchen, surgeon's house, and boatshop. In the Bay are fully-rigged replicas of the vessels *Bee* and *Perseverance.* Historic sail training is offered along with a great range of special events and summer programs, and dining, theatre, and shopping can be enjoyed throughout the season.

Doon Heritage Crossroads

* R.R. 2, Kitchener, Ontario, N2G 3W5
  LOCATION: corner of Homer Watson Boulevard and Huron Road, Kitchener
* (519) 748-1914
* Open daily, May – September, 10:00 – 4:30; early September – late December, Monday to Friday, 10:00 – 4:30
* Admission fee

1914 was an important time of change in Waterloo County: the end of a traditional way of life, and the dawning of a new era. The creators of the 24-hectare Doon Heritage Crossroads chose this year to create a "frozen moment" for visitors, by recreating a small village of that period when modern technology and attitudes were in their infancy. The site includes a country lane, covered bridge, railway station, farm, weavery, dry goods and grocery store, harness, butcher, print, repair, and blacksmith shops, a firehall, and resident houses, many of which are staffed by costumed interpreters. Early model cars, sewing machines, cash registers, bicycles, and the occasional sighting of an ankle make this historic village a little off the beat of the usual butter-churn and spinning wheel circuit. The village is also home to the Waterloo County Hall of Fame. Souvenirs can be purchased at the Presents from the Past shop, a wide range of school programs is offered, and the Church and Willow Green are available to rent for special occasions.

Doris Lewis Rare Book Room, University of Waterloo

* University Library, 200 University Avenue West, Waterloo, Ontario, N2L 3G1
* (519) 885-1211
* Open Monday – Friday, 9:00 – 12:00 and 1:00 – 4:00
* Free admission

The Doris Lewis Rare Book Room at the University of Waterloo, named after the Library's first librarian, is home to an important collection of rare books from the era of hand printing to the modern private press. Holdings include early editions of Euclid, books on the history of dance and ballet, local history materials, the Library of George Santayana, and the Rosa Breithaupt Clark Architecture Collection, to name a few. Archival collections include the Kitchener-Waterloo Record Photographic Negative collection, the archives of the Kitchener Waterloo Oktoberfest Incorporated, the University of Waterloo archives, and papers, manuscripts, and correspondence of notable Canadian women. The Doris Lewis Rare Book Library is open to the general public, although identification must be shown and standard archival practices apply.

Dracula's Museum of Horrors and the Castle Village Gift Shop

* P.O. Box 144, Midland, Ontario, L4R 4K6
  LOCATION: Balm Beach Road, off Highway 93, Midland, Ontario
* (705) 526-9683
* Open mid-March – December, Tuesday – Saturday, 10:00 – 5:30, Sunday, noon – 5:00; Victoria Day – Labour Day, also open Mondays
* Admission fee

In deepest darkest Midland visitors will find what looks suspiciously like a genuine replica of a medieval castle, a cheesy mix of Roman, Greek, and Norman styles, with thirty towers, a dragon spewing water, and a moat guarded by creatures of the underworld. Of course, a place like this needs a dungeon, and this particular one is full of animated versions of all the hairy, scary creatures of your worst nightmares, including Frankenstein, Dracula, Jack the Ripper, Wolfman, and the Mummy. After being terrified beyond the powers of restoration, visitors will certainly be in the mood for a little shopping and can head upstairs to the Castle Village Gift Shop, where they will find the largest gift shop north of Toronto.

Dressler House

- 212 King Street West, Cobourg, Ontario, K9A 2N1
- (905) 372-5831
- Open Monday – Friday, 9:00 – 5:00; Saturday, 9:00 – 2:00; July and August, daily, 9:00 – 5:00
- Free admission, donations welcome

Actress Marie Dressler, born Leila Koerber in 1869 in Cobourg, Ontario, was best known as the feisty lead in *Tugboat Annie.* Her role in *Min and Bill* made her one of the first Canadian actresses to win an Oscar. The daughter of an Austrian immigrant, Leila changed her name to avoid family conflict when she went into show business. She started out in an opera chorus, moved on to comic opera, vaudeville, theatre, and eventually got her first movie role in 1914 in *Tillie's Punctured Romance,* in which she co-starred with newcomer Charlie Chaplin. Marie made several movies in her lifetime, leaving the world a "legacy of laughter" after her death of cancer in 1934. The house where Dressler was born was built in the 1840s in the Regency Cottage style, and was used as a restaurant from the 1930s to 1989 when it suffered a fire. A group of local residents interested in preserving Cobourg's Dressler heritage formed the Marie Dressler Foundation, purchased the house and had it renovated and restored. It is now home to the Cobourg and District Chamber of Commerce, a tourist information centre, and Dressler memorabilia. Life-size wax figures of Dressler and Wallace Beery on the original set of *Min and Bill* is a highlight, as are Marie's will and an Edison phonograph with five original wax cylinders of the actress singing.

Dundurn Castle

* Dundurn Park, York Boulevard, Hamilton, Ontario, L8R 3H1
* (905) 546-2872
* Open June 1 – Labour Day, daily, 10:00 – 4:00; Labour Day – May 31, 12:00 – 4:00, Tuesday – Sunday
* Admission fee

Dundurn Castle, a walloping great 35-room mansion in the Italianate style, is a National Historic Site. The mansion was constructed as the home of then prime minister of pre-confederation Upper Canada, Allan Napier MacNab, between 1832 and 1835, over an earlier structure. MacNab led an interesting life, serving loyally in both the War of 1812 and the Rebellion of 1837, for which he was knighted by Queen Victoria. Dundurn is a living history museum, and the costumed interpreters bring to life the rooms furnished in the Regency, mid-Victorian style. They offer a range of educational and special programs such as the Tea-and-Tour. The Castle is surrounded by beautiful grounds and has a gift shop.

Ed's Theatre Museum

- 276 King Street West, Toronto, Ontario, M5V 1H9
- (416) 974-9378
- Open Saturday and Sunday, 12:00 – 9:00
- Free admission

Ed Mirvish, Toronto's wackiest millionaire, is best known for his showbiz theatres, restaurants, and Canada's most light bulb-encrusted department store, Honest Ed's. That means it won't be a surprise to anyone familiar with Ed that he also has his own museum, or that his museum has the distinction of being "the only museum in the world where everything is for sale." The collection is made up of a surplus of items from Ed's private holdings, as well as leftover bits and pieces from various theatre productions. But this is no junk pile – the 1,860 square metre space upstairs from Old Ed's Restaurant is a funhouse of weird and wonderful artifacts priced from 5¢ to $50,000. Humdingers include vintage penny arcade machines like loonie-gobbling mechanical fortune tellers, music boxes and peep shows, three 4.5-metre cuckoo clocks, cigar-store wooden Indians, Peter O'Toole's boots, furry chairs backed with moose antlers, a six-foot rabbit, a mechanical grand piano, and innumerable props, costumes, posters, programs, photos and, of course, stacks of Ed memorabilia.

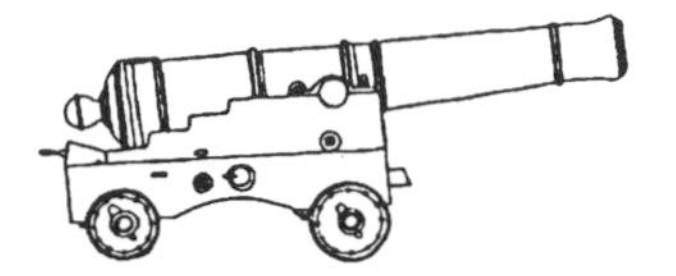

Elgin Military Museum

- 30 Talbot Street, St. Thomas, Ontario, N5P 1A3
- (519) 633-7641
- Open all year, Tuesday – Friday, 1:00 – 5:00; Saturday, 10:00 – 12:00 and 2:00 – 5:00; Sunday 2:00 – 5:00
- Admission fee

Through the display of artifacts, photos, memorabilia, and personal accounts, the Elgin Military Museum commemorates the many Elgin County natives who participated in the War of 1812, the Rebellion of 1837, the Fenian Raids, the Riel Rebellions, the Boer War, World Wars I and II, and the Korean, Vietnam, and Gulf Wars. According to the museum, "Elgin County people served ashore and at sea on everything from small torpedo boats to mighty battleships." The Elgin Regiment, whose origins can be traced back 125 years, is also celebrated. Housed in an historic building *circa* 1848, museum highlights include a convoy display and a replica periscope. Veterans' records can be accessed on site, and the Elgin Military Museum also offers interpretive programs and a gift shop.

Elliot Lake Nuclear and Mining Museum

- 45 Hillside Drive North, Elliot Lake, Ontario, P5A 1X5
- (705) 848-2287
- Summer, weekdays, 8:00 – 8:00, weekends 9:00 – 5:00; other times, 9:00 – 4:30 weekdays, and by appointment on weekends
- Admission fee

The Elliot Lake Mining and Nuclear Museum describes itself as a "jewel in the wilderness," and with its many fascinating facets, it certainly is a gem. A miniature antique car collection, an aboriginal feature, logging exhibits, a mineral collection, a mini art gallery, and, oddly, an L.B. Pearson and J.F. Kennedy memorial corner, are all mixed together at this museum. The history of the Elliot Lake area, being rich in logging and mining lore, is the most prominent feature, with exhibits on how uranium is mined and milled, from the raw product to the final "yellow cake." And thanks to the Atomic Energy Commission and Ontario Hydro, information on nuclear energy, including use, storage, disposal, and a model refinery and reactor are also displayed. For young children there is a hands-on wildlife feature with local birds and beasts and visitors will want to catch the yearly Uranium festival. The museum has a gift shop and ore samples are available to the public.

Elvis Museum

* c/o Pyramid Place, 5400 Robinson Street, Niagara Falls, Ontario, L3G 2A6
  LOCATION: next to IMAX, base of Skylon Tower
* (905) 357-4442
* Open all year, times vary
* Admission fee

The all new Elvis Museum, in a new location and under new management, has recently reopened and is ready to love your tender (legal, that is). The collection belongs to members of the Royal Family (the Presleys), and consists of about 500 artifacts, including all kinds of King memorabilia as well as items owned and used by His Majesty. See the black plastic hairdryer used to coif the King's 'do, bestudded, bellbottomed, and berhinestoned clothing and stage costumes he wore, and even vehicles he rode, including his now-famous three-wheeled motorcycle. Of course, there are lots of records, photos, mementoes, souvenirs, newspaper clippings, and a life-sized portrait to which fans can pay homage. There is also the Elvis shop where visitors can stock up on King souvenirs, t-shirts, tapes, and highly sought after replicas of Presley's jewellery.

Enoch Turner Schoolhouse (1848)

* 106 Trinity Street, Toronto, Ontario, M5A 3C6
* (416) 863-0010
* Open year round, 10:00 – 4:00, by appointment only
* General admission free, charge for groups, donations welcome

Enoch Turner was a prosperous Toronto brewer of English descent, and an advocate of education who funded the building of the Enoch Turner Schoolhouse, designed in the Gothic Revival style, which was completed in 1848. His was the only free school of its time in the area and was large enough to accommodate 240 children. After falling out of use as a school, the building saw many incarnations, including a recruiting centre during the Boer War, a soup kitchen during the Great Depression and later an artists' workshop and studio space. Saved from the wrecker's ball in the 1970s, the schoolhouse was recognized as an important historic and architectural building, and turned into a museum. Naturally the museum focuses on education and the area's history, and houses a schoolroom, period artifacts and a research library. Today the Enoch Turner Schoolhouse is still known for its school programs which include slide shows and role-playing of a typical school day *circa* 1851. Many special events are held throughout the year, including fashion shows, concerts and fairs. Enoch Turner is not a drop-in museum, and appointments for tours and special programs must be arranged in advance.

ERLAND LEE MUSEUM HOME

* 552 Ridge Road, Stoney Creek, Ontario, L8J 2Y6
  LOCATION: off Highway 20 via Mud Street
* (905) 662-2691
* Open April 1 – November 30, Monday – Friday, 10:00 – 4:00, Sundays, 1:00 – 5:00; November – April by appointment
* Admission fee

The Lees were United Empire Loyalists from Maryland who emigrated to Canada in the late 1800s. Here they built their Neo-Gothic home in 1801, with later additions in the 1860s. Erland Lee, a son of the original settlers, was a broadminded farmer who, after hearing an address by a prominent woman speaker of the time, decided, with his wife Janet, to found the world's first Women's Institute. Women's Institutes are still in existence today, worldwide, and the museum is owned and maintained by the Ontario branch. According to the Institute, it is "an educational organization for women who, by working together can expand their skills, broaden their interests and work to improve conditions in homes, communities, the nation and around the world." Artifacts from the 1850s to 1900s are displayed as they would have been used by the Lee family, and the Drive House outside features farm tools and rotating displays. Guided tours are offered as well as use of a special children's room. Women's Institute days, Victorian Tea, and a harvest festival can be enjoyed yearly.

The Exotarium

* Old Athol School, County Road 10, Cherry Valley, Ontario, K0K 1P0
* (613) 476-7710
* Open daily, mid-June – Labour Day; weekends beginning early May – Thanksgiving, 10:00 – 5:00
* Admission fee

Come and see the "animals you love to hate" in this educational emporium full of live reptiles, amphibians, and invertebrates. The Exotarium is housed in an old, picturesque two-room schoolhouse: one room is dedicated to species indigenous to the area, while the second is crawling with exotic creatures from all over the world. The Exotarium contains more than 70 displays and 150 creatures, all live, including a 5-metre python, tarantulas, hissing cockroaches, turtles, all sorts of lizards, and a slimy assortment of snakes. And if visitors get out alive, they won't want to miss the gift shop, where they can stock up on books on all kinds of scaly, hairy, and slithery creatures, t-shirts, and rubber and candy creepy-crawlies. Originally a project of the Reptile Breeding Foundation, the Exotarium is now privately run, but is still an important breeding facility dedicated to the preservation of endangered reptiles.

FANSHAWE PIONEER VILLAGE

- R.R. 5, London, Ontario, N6A 4B9
  LOCATION: off Fanshawe Park Road, east of Clarke Road
- (519) 457-1296
- Open daily, May 1 – October 10, 10:00 – 4:30; October 11 – December 20, Monday – Friday, 10:00 – 4:30; open weekends for special events
- Admission fee

The Fanshawe Pioneer Village was founded in 1957 by Dr. Wilfrid Jury and today the two-hectare site holds over 22 restored rural buildings complete with furniture, knick-knacks, tools, and textiles appropriate for a pioneer crossroads community of the 19th century. The buildings include a log house, church, school, trades shops, and barn, among others, all brought to life by costumed staff: blacksmiths forging iron implements, printers preparing text, bakers making bread, weavers, woodworkers, farmers, and more. Visitors can take hay and wagon rides and won't want to miss the village shop offering a wide assortment of Canadiana, the village tea room, or the picnic facilities. Special events such as a Pumpkin Party, Strawberry Social, and Apple Cider Festival are held annually.

Fashion Resource Centre

- Seneca College of Applied Arts and Technology, 1750 Finch Avenue East, North York, Ontario, M2J 2X5
- (416) 491-5050
- By appointment only
- Admission fee

The Seneca Fashion Resource Centre is the home of over 8,000 items of apparel and accessories made or worn in Canada dating from about 1840. Collected from a fashion standpoint, artifacts are almost exclusively from the Euro-Canadian tradition and include men's, women's, and children's clothing, a few uniforms, underclothes, footwear, hats, and other accessories. The Centre, begun in 1988 as a teaching resource for Seneca College students, describes itself as a "working library" and is a hands-on facility where students can get a close-up look at how historical garments were made, what they were made of, how they move and feel, what signs of wear can tell about a garment, how they are stored, and have survived through time. A typical visit to the Centre might include a classroom discussion and viewing of various pieces from the collection and temporary exhibitions are staged in and beyond Seneca College walls. Run exclusively by volunteers, the Seneca Fashion Resource Centre hopes to "further the appreciation and recognition of the historic value of Canadian fashion" and staff hope it will eventually grow into a museum.

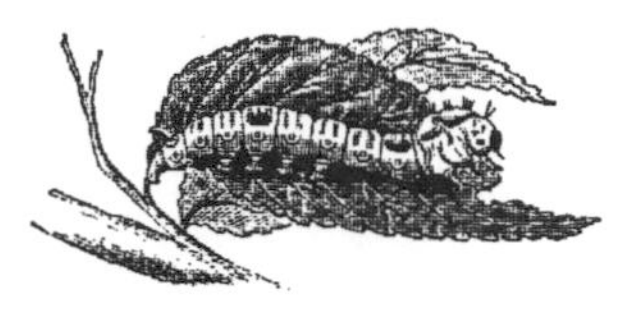

Forest Pest Management Institute

- 1219 Queen Street East, Sault Ste. Marie, Ontario, P6A 5M7
- (705) 949-9461
- Tours daily, Monday – Friday, late June – late August; call for hours
- Free admission

Forestry Canada is a government agency whose mission is "to promote the sustainable development and competitiveness of Canada's forest sector for the well-being of present and future generations of Canadians." An important part of this has to do with the control of forest pests, hence the advent of the Forest Pest Management Institute, a division of Forestry Canada, which shares facilities with Forestry Canada, Ontario Region in Sault Ste. Marie. The Institute's goal is "responsible forest pest management through science" and 7 million insects from some 20 species are produced there annually, allowing the Institute to supply its clients with massive shipments of creatures like Eastern Spruce Budworm and Hemlock Looper which help control forest pests naturally. For the general public, summer tours are offered at the Institute, which is Canada's biggest forest research complex. Tours include audiovisual presentations, laboratory demonstrations, greenhouse visits, and live insect displays.

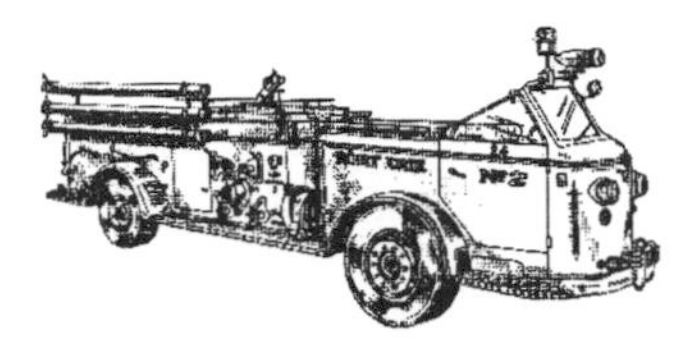

Fort Erie LaFrance Firefighting Museum

- 1118 Concession Road, Fort Erie, Ontario
- (905) 871-1271
- Open July – Labour Day weekend, Wednesday – Sunday and holiday Mondays, 10:00 – 5:00
- Free admission

The 1983 purchase by thirteen volunteer firefighters in Fort Erie of a 1947 open cab LaFrance fire engine, in use from 1947 to 1977, sparked the beginning of a museum now dedicated to the preservation of firefighting history across North America. The collection has grown like wildfire with the addition of a closed-cab LaFrance from New York, also from 1947, a Ford Model T from 1924, and a 1915 Ford Model T chief's car. These are now displayed in pristine condition in a 372-square-metre building, alongside hand pumpers from the 1800s, a steamer *circa* 1905, fire hoses, nozzles, clamps, extinguishers, and other firefighting apparatus from across the continent. Parades are held yearly and group tours are available by request.

Fort Erie Railroad Museum

- P.O. Box 339, Ridgeway, Ontario, LOS 1NO
  LOCATION: off the Niagara Parkway at Central and Gilmore Streets, Fort Erie
- (905) 871-1412
- Open late May – Labour Day, daily, 9:00 – 5:00
- Admission fee

Opened in 1973, the Fort Erie Railroad Museum has been going full steam ahead displaying, collecting, and preserving important buildings, vehicles, and artifacts from Canada's golden age of steam. The museum is actually a complex of buildings and walk-through engines, dating back to the late 1800s. Two original railway stations, one from 1910, the other from 1873, were relocated to the current museum site. The 1910 Ridgeway station still has a working station clock, telegraph office, and cast iron stove while the earlier station houses the admissions desk and gift shop. The steam Locomotive #6218, built in the 1940s and retired in 1973, was the last steam engine in Canada to carry passengers and a rudely furnished caboose vividly portrays the rustic living conditions endured by railway workers of earlier times. A railroad reference library can also be accessed on the site and contains books, manuals, guides, timetables, and magazines.

Fort George National Historic Site

- P.O. Box 787, Niagara-on-the-Lake, Ontario, LOS 1J0
  LOCATION: south edge of town, Niagara-on-the-Lake
- (905) 468-4257
- Open daily, July 1 – Labour Day, 9:00 – 6:00; mid-May – June 30, 9:00 – 5:00; day after Labour Day – October 31, 10:00 – 5:00; by appointment rest of year
- Admission fee

Fort George was established in 1796 at the heart of the Niagara frontier, and played an important role in the war of 1812. The fort was briefly captured by American forces in 1813, but after being won back by the British, it fell to ruin until restoration efforts began in 1937, based on the original plans of the Royal Engineers. Today Fort George is a National Historic Site, restored to its earlier glory, and includes an artillery park, guardhouse, officers' quarters and kitchen, artificers' building, powder magazine, blockhouse, a cottage and other buildings with furnishings, equipment, weapons, field artillery, and textiles that bring them all to life. Historical reenactments, special events, and self-guided tours are offered.

Fort Henry

* P.O. Box 213, Kingston, Ontario, K7L 4V8
  LOCATION: junction of Highways 2 and 15, east of Kingston
* (613) 542-7388
* Open Victoria Day weekend – Thanksgiving weekend, 10:00 – 5:00
* Admission fee

Fort Henry, once known as the "citadel of Upper Canada," is the most impressive and famous of Ontario's forts. Begun during the summer of 1812 and completed in 1816, the original fort served various military functions, but was demolished and rebuilt in the 1830s. Over the years Fort Henry served as a storehouse, stable, and prisoner of war and internment camp. The Fort eventually fell to ruin until, during the Great Depression, a massive job-creation project saw the employment of 1,000 people to help restore the facilities. At this time it also developed one of the first historical reenactments or "animations," now a common feature in similar establishments. Today the restored fortification, with 125 rooms, is largely furnished to depict life as it would have been when occupied by British garrisons. It also features over 30 rooms with displays of historic military and naval artifacts. The Fort is staffed by costumed interpreters, including the Fort Henry Guard, and holds guided tours, drills, musical and special events, and salutes. A gift shop and refreshment facilities are located on the premises.

FORT MALDEN NATIONAL HISTORIC SITE

* P.O. Box 38, Amherstburg, Ontario, N9V 2Z2
  LOCATION: 1 block west of Highway 18 at 100 Laird Avenue, Amherstburg
* (519) 736-5416
* Open May 1 – December 24, 10:00 – 5:00; December 27 – April 30, 1:00 – 5:00 weekdays, 10:00 – 5:00 weekends
* Admission fee

Fort Malden, originally Fort Amherstburg, was established in 1796 along the Detroit River. Its functions were to control shipping along the river, to act as a base for the Provincial Marine and to uphold the presence of the British military. It also served as part of the Indian Department, keeping up good relations with the Native peoples of the northwest area. The Fort saw its military peak during the War of 1812, although it was involved in later conflicts. By the 1840s Fort Malden was handed over to the Royal Canadian Rifle Regiment who "held the fort" until it again changed hands and went to the provincial government. The Fort became the first lunatic asylum in northern Ontario in 1859 and later a planing mill. Restoration began in the 1930s and now the National Historic Parks and Site Branch of Parks Canada has full control of the 4.5-hectare site, which includes remains of the 1840 earthworks and several buildings. Today period rooms and buildings, military, marine, and Native exhibits can be viewed. Fort Malden staff offer educational programs, guided tours, and reenactments and there is a gift shop and research facilities on the premises.

Fort St. Joseph National Historic Park

* P.O. Box 220, Richard's Landing, Ontario, POR 1J0
  LOCATION: south tip of St. Joseph Island via Highway 548
* (705) 246-2664
* Open daily, Victoria Day weekend – July 1st, 10:00 – 5:00; July 2nd – Labour Day, 10:00 – 6:00; Labour Day – Thanksgiving, 10:00 – 5:00
* Free admission

Fort St. Joseph was built in 1796 and served as a British fur-trading centre, as home to the Indian Department, and as a military post situated to protect the territory north of the Great Lakes. The most westerly outpost in British North America, isolation and hardship endured there earned it the epithet of "The Military Siberia of Upper Canada." Important to the British during the War of 1812, Fort St. Joseph was destroyed in 1814 by the Americans. The stabilized ruins are maintained today by the Canadian Parks Service. Archaeological research begun in 1963 unearthed many important details about the site, as well as significant artifacts which are displayed in the Visitor Centre along with tools, furs, uniforms, and other items intended to illustrate the Fort's history. The 372-hectare site also includes nature trails into the rich maple forest, and a lovely view of the islands of the St. Mary's River.

Fort Wellington National Historic Site

* P.O. Box 479, Prescott, Ontario, KOE 1TO
  LOCATION: Dibble Street East
* (613) 925-2896
* Open daily, mid-May – Labour Day, 10:00 – 5:00; daily, day after Labour Day – September 30, 10:00 – 5:00; by appointment rest of year
* Free admission

Fort Wellington was built to serve the British military during the War of 1812, primarily to protect the supply line between Montreal and Kingston along the Upper St. Lawrence. The Fort was never besieged, and was abandoned not long after the war. The buildings fell to ruin, but a second fort was built on the site of the first, for use in the Canadian Rebellions of 1837 and later border raids. Garrisoned by the British until 1854, it became the centre of a militia camp in the mid 1860s during the Fenian threat. By 1940 the area had been named a National Historic Park, and today the Fort has been furnished with historical artifacts and is staffed by costumed interpreters *circa* the 1850s. The four standing original structures are surrounded by earthworks, a palisade, and a ditch and contain a guard room, armory, powder magazine, barracks, and officers' quarters. The Fort offers guided tours, school programs, and reenactments.

FORWARDERS' MUSEUM

* P.O. Box 2179, Prescott, Ontario, KOE ITO
  LOCATION: Centre and Water Streets, Prescott
* (613) 925-5788
* Open mid-May – Labour Day, Monday – Saturday, 10:00 – 4:00, Sunday noon – 4:00
* Admission fee

Prescott pays homage to the forwarding, or shipping trade of early Canada at its Forwarders' Museum. Forwarders transported goods in and out of inland Canada and the early forwarders braved rapids and extreme weather conditions while dealing with literally tons of equipment and goods on the job. Things got easier with technological and engineering advances, and the museum claims that through its exhibits, "the story unfolds to tell of the coming of the first roads, the stage coaches and wagon transportation, the ferries which served Prescott and Ogdensburg for over 200 years, the building of the canals to bypass the St. Lawrence Rapids, the railways, which brought the greatest transportation advances, the transport and distribution of the mails." The museum building, constructed in the 1800s, was once the office and warehouse of Capt. William Gilkison, an early forwarder, and was later used as a post office and as the United States Consulate. The museum features displays and commemorative plaques, and items like oak timbers retrieved from the bottom of the St. Lawrence, which were used as rafts by early forwarders.

CENTRE FRANCO-ONTARIEN DE FOLKLORE

- Maison D'Youville, 38 Xavier Street, Sudbury, Ontario, P3C 2B9
- (705) 675-8986
- Open all year, 8:30 – 4:30
- Admission fee

The goals and objectives of the Centre franco-ontarien de folklore, established in 1972, are the "research and interpretation of Franco-Ontarian culture by way of collecting, preserving, publishing and 'exhibiting' its oral traditions; surveying and archiving its material, spiritual, symbolic and historic heritage." As well as being a centre for social, cultural, and historical activities, the centre holds symposia and festivals, puts out publications, conducts surveys, holds workshops and conferences, and has a sound room, office and meeting rooms, a library, and folklore archives. Three exhibit areas focus on music, tools, and machinery, and household objects relating to French Canadian folklore and culture. Plans for the future include a permanent exhibit devoted to French Canada's oral traditions and the renovation of the Maison d'Youville, an historical house built in 1894. Guided tours of current exhibits are offered by appointment.

Centre for Research on French Canadian Culture

* University of Ottawa, Lamoureux Hall, Room 274, 145 Jean-Jacques Lussier Street, Ottawa, Ontario, K1N 6N5
* (613) 564-6847/8
* Open Monday – Friday, 8:45 – 12:00 and 1:00 – 4:45, or 3:45 from June – September
* Free admission

The Centre for Research on French Canadian Culture was founded in 1958 and its primary objective is to promote research on all aspects of French Canadian culture. It functions as an archive and research facility and produces relevant publications. Holdings include 750 linear metres of documents, manuscripts, photographs, tapes, newspapers, periodicals, and artifacts relating to French Canadian life and literature, the humanities, social sciences, history, religion, and popular culture. Recent and ongoing projects include a dictionary of North American French and a publication on the arts in French Ontario. The Centre is in close contact with other research and cultural groups and associations, and receives visits from all over the world. Standard archival practices apply.

French Perfume Factory Outlet and Museum

* 393 York Road, Niagara-on-the-Lake, Ontario, LOS 1J0
  LOCATION: on QEW and Highway 55 exit
* (905) 685-6666
* Open daily, May – end of December, 10:00 – 5:00; February – end of April, 12:00 – 4:00
* Free admission

Ahh, the sweet smell of success – and who would think you'd find it on the side of Highway 55? The French Perfume Factory Outlet and Museum is a fragrant shop accompanied by perfumery displays and artifacts which comprise the only perfume museum in North America. Conditioning rooms, manufacturing facilities, raw materials, perfumery utensils, equipment, antique labelling, and perfume profile charts are exhibited and explained at the outlet. Visitors will find out what a "perfumer's organ" is, how scent is extracted from flowers, and follow the perfume-making process through enfleurage, maceration, fat processing, distillation, and the solvent extraction process. Demonstrations are held, and visitors can enjoy a variety of aromas. Although the site's prime function is to sell its scented wares, The French Perfume Factory Outlet and Museum is definitely worth a stop along the highway.

Museum and Archive of Games

* Burt Matthews Hall, University of Waterloo, Waterloo, Ontario, N2L 3G1
* (519) 888-4424
* Open weekday afternoons, one or two evenings a week, and Sunday afternoons
* Free admission, tours by appointment

Everyone who visits the Museum and Archive of Games comes out a winner. This exciting collection includes ancient and antique games from a multitude of cultures to present day electronic games, and features gambling games, pub games, carnival games, puzzles, war games, and scores of other mind benders and time wasters. Although the collection is multicultural, it focuses on Canada, and houses many unique Aboriginal Canadian and Inuit games. Artifacts are made of wood, bone, stone, plastic, metal, paper, and micro-chips and the documentation of game-related behaviour is also ongoing. Exhibits put games into their cultural and historic context, and explain the social and political climate in which they were played. The museum includes what is naturally a great hands-on area, features regular changing exhibits, and houses an archive of about 2,000 items. Educational kits are available, and the museum's state of the art computer cataloguing system makes it childsplay for researchers.

GARDEN FOR THE BLIND

* The Round Garden, Inc., Sunset Boulevard, grounds of Lanark County Administration Building, adjacent to Lanark Lodge, Perth, Ontario
* (613) 267-3200
* Open daily, early summer – early fall
* Free admission

The Garden for the Blind is a place where the vision- and mobility-impaired and the elderly can touch, smell, hear, and taste a variety of plants, flowers, shrubs, vegetables, and herbs, from chrysanthemums to cucumbers. A self-guiding system helps visitors make a comfortable transition from one area to another, and there is often an interpreter on site to answer questions or to discuss the gardens. Shady shelters and a fountain can be enjoyed on the premises, and sanitary facilities can be accessed in the nearby Lanark County Administration Building from 9:00 – 5:00 during the week. The Garden for the Blind is wheelchair accessible.

The George R. Gardiner Museum of Ceramic Art

* c/o Royal Ontario Museum, 100 Queen's Park, Toronto, Ontario, M5S 2C6
  LOCATION: 111 Queen's Park, Toronto, Ontario
* (416) 586-8080
* Open Tuesday – Sunday, 10:00 – 5:00; Tuesday until 7:30, Victoria Day – Labour Day; Sunday, 11:00 – 5:00; free Tuesdays after 4:30, or all day for seniors
* Admission fee or free with admission tag from the ROM

The George R. Gardiner Museum of Ceramic Art, now under the auspices of the Royal Ontario Museum (located across the street), is the collection of Canadian businessman George R. Gardiner and his wife Helen. The spacious, specially designed two-storey museum building contains an impressive collection of ceramics from the world over, and it is North America's only specialized ceramics museum. Ancient pottery vessels from Central and South America, English 17th-century Delftware, Meissen porcelain, Italian Maiolica, and other significant collections reflect the technology and tastes of different cultures and eras. Fuddling cups, pap boats, tea sets, chocolate cups, crude vessels, decorative objects, and gorgeously painted plates fill the display cases. Highlights include porcelain figures from the Commedia dell'arte, delightfully tiny 18th-century perfume bottles, and 16th-century Italian Maiolica plates decorated with multicoloured grotesques. The museum regularly sponsors travelling exhibits, holds lectures, workshops, and educational programs, and offers guided tours. There is also a smashing gift shop.

German Canadian Heritage Museum

* 37 Eglinton Square, P.O. Box 51087, Postal Outlet Scarborough, Scarborough, Ontario, MIL 4T2
  LOCATION: 6650 Hurontario Street, Mississauga
* (905) 759-8897
* Open Sundays, 11:00 – 5:00
* Admission fee

Located in a white house with a green roof just north of Mississauga is the German Canadian Heritage Museum, set up to preserve and pay tribute to the German peoples' contribution to Canada. Settlers of German stock began arriving in Canada in the late 18th century, and their numbers were sufficient to warrant a German-Canadian press and later, a German language newspaper. After the American War of Independence, many German loyalist troops remained in Canada as settlers, cultivating the land and helping to build up Canada's cities and towns. Many German-speaking people also immigrated from the U.S. in the 19th century, particularly from Pennsylvania. A number of artifacts from the early periods of German settlement are shown in the German Canadian Heritage Museum, including very early examples of German-Canadian language books and newspapers, Bibles, pictures, certificates, a model of a Contestoga wagon of the type used for immigration from Pennsylvania, and models of a grist and sawmill and a blacksmith shop with miniature tools and equipment.

GINGERBREAD DOLL MUSEUM

* P.O. Box 91, Wroxeter, Ontario, NOG 2XO
  LOCATION: Howick Street, Wroxeter, Ontario
* (519) 335-3830 or (519) 357-2498
* Open May – October, 12:00 – 6:00, days vary, appointments appreciated
* Admission fee

Eileen Hamilton and Virginia Newell's private army of dolls is constantly bringing in new recruits. The mother-daughter team started doll collecting seriously in the mid seventies, until the collection outgrew both their houses and they set up shop in an old school portable. This is now the Gingerbread Doll Museum, and extensions are in the works here too, as the collection is also outgrowing this space. The museum features over 3,000 dolls from all over the world, dating back to 1840, and includes pieces collectors would die for. Eaton's Beauties, a Ronald Reagan doll, a Loblaws "Miss Lucky Green Stamp" doll, Royal Family dolls, Dionne Quints dolls with a signed picture of the famous five, and dolls made of everything from walnuts to paper mâché and porcelain to plastic make up the Gingerbread ranks. Furniture, accessories, and other dolly items are also displayed. Hamilton and Newell prefer to collect dolls with a past, like a Second World War Canadian Army Medical Corps nursing sister doll, who has her early history written on her body under her dress. One story came directly from a visitor who recognized a doll she owned as a child smiling back at her from a museum shelf. Appointments are appreciated. Expect to spend a few hours.

Girl Guides of Canada Archives

* 50 Merton Street, Toronto, Ontario, M4S 1A3
* (416) 487-5281, ext. 276
* Open by appointment, Monday – Friday, 9:00 – 4:00; Fridays before a long weekend and during July and August, 9:00 – 3:00
* Free admission

The Girl Guides of Canada Archives exists to preserve and promote Guiding in Canada. Its mandate is to "provide resources for research in its role as a tangible memory, helping to celebrate and publicize achievements, past and present, while pointing the direction for future accomplishments." Holdings include textual records, publications, minutes, handbooks, guidebooks and photographs, going back to about 1912. Films, slides, and tapes form part of the collection, and uniforms and insignia are also stored on the premises. An exhibit at Casa Loma, Toronto, set up to commemorate Lady Mary Pellatt's contribution to Girl Guides in Canada, is the closest thing the Girl Guides of Canada have to a museum, but the archives will be of use to researchers. Standard archival practices are in effect.

THE GRANGE

* Entrance through The Art Gallery of Ontario, 317 Dundas Street West, Toronto, Ontario, M5T 1G4
* (416) 977-0414
* Open Wednesday – Sunday, 12:00 – 4:00, Wednesday also 6:00 – 9:00
* Fee included with admission to the AGO

Built in 1817, when Toronto was still the town of York, the Georgian brick home now known as the Grange became the social and political centre of the upper crust of Upper Canada. The Grange was built and inhabited by D'Arcy Boulton Junior, whose son William Henry became Mayor of Toronto. William Henry's widow later married an Oxford scholar and the couple entertained people like the Prince of Wales and Winston Churchill. The Grange's greatest distinction, however, was being the first home of the Art Gallery of Ontario, originally the Art Museum of Toronto, and it played an active role in the gallery's growth between 1911 and 1970. Today the house has been restored to its original beauty, *circa* 1835, and is run as a living history museum staffed by costumed guides. The main and upper floors display elegant period furnishing and relevant artifacts, and the kitchen gives a feeling of what life was like behind-the-scenes at the original Grange. Interpreters occasionally bake bread for visitors, and will gladly discuss the history and furnishings of the house. A reference library on the Decorative Arts from 1800 to 1914 can be accessed by appointment, and group tours and school visits can be arranged.

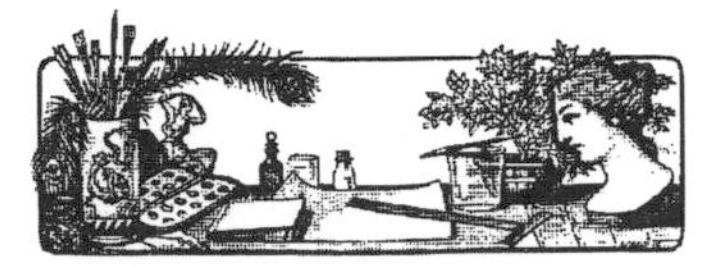

THE GUILD

- 191 Guildwood Parkway, Scarborough, Ontario, M1E 1P5
- Tours (416) 266-4449
- Open all year, 24 hours
- Free admission

The Guild of All Arts was the all-encompassing name of an artists' colony started by Rosa and Spencer Clark in 1932 on 16 hectares of land, just a stone's throw from the Scarborough Bluffs near Toronto. Their workshops produced textiles, ceramics, and visual arts and encouraged projects in drama and music. A building on the site, erected in 1914, served as a focal point for the colony, and grew into a resort hotel as the grounds expanded. During the Second World War the Guild became an official naval base for women, and later a veterans' hospital. Although many artists and artisans returned after the war years, the Guild never returned to its former creative glory. However, a unique legacy of the Guild's creative past lives on at the Guild's grounds, through Spencer Clark's collection of sculpture and significant architectural pieces from buildings in and around the Toronto area. Corinthian columns, wrought iron gates, enormous archways, decorative panelling, monuments, sculpture, a grindstone, a belfry, an early log cabin, a Greek-style theatre, and other architectural delights have been saved from the wrecker's ball and allowed to stand at the Guild for all to admire. The Clarks' contribution to Canadian arts is worth carving in stone, and the operators of the Guild are setting up an archive and making plans for a possible museum to preserve Guild heritage. Guided tours can be arranged by appointment.

Guinness World of Records

* 4943 Clifton Hill, Niagara Falls, Ontario, L2G 3N5
* (905) 356-2299
* Hours are seasonal
* Admission fee

See for yourself if the Guinness World of Records, completely revamped in the last few years, lives up to its claim as the "World's Greatest Museum." This commercial enterprise combines actual objects with recreations and representational displays of record-breaking animals, vegetables, and minerals familiar to most visitors through the *Guinness Book of World Records.* Life-size reproductions of monstrosities like a giant carrot, the tattooed lady, revolting North American eating habits, and the world's tallest and fattest man revel in the extremes of our world. Displays on achievements in space and sports, the mechanical world, architecture, literature, arts and entertainment, the natural world, and lots of human and animal oddities are presented in a loud, glossy, easily digestible and delightfully overblown setting.

Guy Lombardo Music Centre

- 205 Wonderland Road South, London, Ontario, N6K 3T3
  LOCATION: off Highway 2E
- (519) 473-9003
- Open daily, May – September, 1:00 – 5:00
- Admission fee

Guy Lombardo and his Royal Canadians were one of the most successful groups of the Big Band Era and beyond, selling 300 million records in fifty years. Guy Lombardo (1902 – 1977) accomplished much during his career, including staging extravagant musical productions, playing at seven Presidential Inaugural Balls, receiving an honorary Doctorate from the University of Western Ontario, and winning the Gold Cup for speedboat racing in 1942. Lombardo and his band, the Royal Canadians, however, were most famous for their broadcasts of *Auld Lang Syne* on New Year's Eve. A centre dedicated to the memory of Guy Lombardo, built by his friends in his hometown of London, Ontario, displays Lombardo photographs, posters, trophies, records, and memorabilia, and a documentary on Lombardo's life is also screened for visitors. Future plans for expansion of the Centre include exhibits on other Big Bands.

HALTON COUNTY RADIAL RAILWAY MUSEUM

* R.R. 2, Rockwood, Ontario, NOB 2KO
  LOCATION: north of Highway 401 on the Guelph Line
* (519) 856-9802
* Open Saturday, Sunday, and holidays mid-May to late October, 10:00 – 5:00; daily, July and August; closed Monday and Tuesday in June
* Admission fee

The Halton County Railway Museum is dedicated to preserving the history of Canadian rail transportation and is the biggest museum of its kind in Canada. One ticket buys unlimited rides on historical streetcars, radial cars, and work cars from Toronto and Southern Ontario, over a mile of scenic track. The museum's 15.4 hectares feature 60 vehicles dating from the 1930s to the 1960s, all in operating condition. Inside visitors will see the leather seats, cast-iron stoves, stained glass, and gold-leaf embellishments that were once a common sight to riders trundling along Ontario's main streets. The old Rockwood Station has been preserved in its original state and workshops can be visited where vehicles are stored and restorations are in progress. Founded in 1953 in an attempt to save two historic vehicles, and staffed by volunteers, the Halton County Railway Museum has never stopped rolling. Educational programs and kits are available and a gift shop stages a railway nostalgia gallery and offers streetcar-related items for purchase.

HAMILTON CHILDREN'S MUSEUM

* 1072 Main Street East, Hamilton, Ontario, L8M 1N6
* (905) 549-9285
* Open Tuesday – Saturday, 10:00 – 4:00, Sunday 1:00 – 4:00
* Admission fee

"Learning can be fun" is the motto of this wonderful hands-on museum for kids. Started in 1978, the Hamilton Children's Museum is intended especially for children ages 2 to 13 and features both historical and contemporary artifacts. Kids are encouraged to learn by experiencing objects: discovering how they operate, grow, move, and function using role-playing, games, interaction, and exploration. The Children's Museum offers a great variety of interactive displays, and has different educational features throughout the year designed for various age groups. A recent exhibit was called "Me and My Body," and answered many questions children ask about their own bodies, such as "why do I sneeze?" and "why do I have freckles?" Activity and curriculum kits and educational packages are available for teachers, group leaders, and parents. Outside the museum visitors can take advantage of picnic facilities, a playground, and wading pool.

HAMILTON MILITARY MUSEUM

- Dundurn Park, York Boulevard, Hamilton, Ontario, L8R 3H1
  LOCATION: Dundurn Park
- (905) 523-5681
- Open daily, June – Labour Day, 11:00 – 5:00; Labour Day – May 31, 1:00 – 5:00, closed Mondays
- Admission fee or free with admission to Dundurn Castle

The Hamilton Military Museum, on the grounds of Dundurn Castle, showcases Canadian military history and traditions through displays and artifacts from the late 1700s to the 20th century, and focuses on Hamilton's distinguished military history. But unlike other military museums, the Hamilton Military Museum tries to focus on the social history of war and military life rather than strategy, victories, and equipment. How soldiers lived, spent their spare time, washed, how they ate, and what they kept in their pockets will more likely be the subject of a tour than will the names and calibres of guns or vehicles. But that doesn't mean the museum won't appeal to the military enthusiast, as the collection holds many rare and interesting artifacts among its weapons, uniforms, medals, paintings, photographs, and other military paraphernalia. A trench typical of the First World War has been recreated and a display area about the Hamilton Scourge Project, which involves the upcoming underwater excavation of two American ships from the War of 1812, will also be of interest to visitors. Educational programs, tours, and special events are offered and there is a gift shop on the premises.

HAMILTON-SCOURGE PROJECT

* c/o City Hall, 71 Main Street West, Hamilton,
  Ontario, L8N 3T4
  LOCATION: 10 kilometres off Port Dalhousie
* (905) 546-4615

During the War of 1812, on August 8, 1813, two schooners were waiting, with eleven other American-owned ships, for first light to renew action against a British-Canadian squadron. The schooners, the *Hamilton* and the *Scourge*, capsized in Lake Ontario due to a squall, taking with them 53 sailors, and leaving only 19 survivors. The schooners are still in the bottom of Lake Ontario, exquisitely preserved with all they held on the day of the tragedy, thanks to the ideal preservation conditions of total darkness, low temperatures, and fresh water. The schooners were discovered in 1973, after a premeditated search, and the site was visited by Jacques Cousteau in 1980. The Hamilton-Scourge Foundation was set up to initiate a conservation project and plans for removal and display of the ships. Naturally, the ships cannot be seen by the public, but Hamilton's Military Museum has a display which keeps the public abreast of project activities, and where written materials, and posters are available. Hamilton's Confederation Park has a memorial garden featuring 53 headstones dedicated to the sailors who lost their lives in the tragedy. This site is also slated as the tentative home of the future Hamilton-Scourge Museum.

HAMILTON MUSEUM OF STEAM AND TECHNOLOGY

- 900 Woodward Avenue, Hamilton, Ontario, L8H 7N2
- (905) 549-5225
- Open daily (closed non-holiday Mondays), June – Labour Day, 11:00 – 4:00; Labour Day – May, 12:00 – 4:00
- Admission fee

Hamilton's Waterworks Pumping Station, built in 1859 and topped with a tall Victorian chimney, is now the home of the Hamilton Museum of Steam and Technology. The all-Canadian 19th-century architecture of the pump house is one of the highlights of the museum, as well as two towering Gartshore steam-powered walking beam engines, the first of their magnitude in Canada, now restored to their former steamy glory. Occasionally the steam engines are fired up for visitors to see how this old-fashioned type of power works. Satellites include waterworks buildings from 1859 and 1913. The old boiler house, now the Keefer Gallery, stages both permanent and temporary displays on industrial and technological developments in and around Hamilton. Educational programs are offered, special events are held year-round, and there is a gift shop on site.

Her Majesty's Royal Chapel of the Mohawks

- Six Nations Tourism, General Delivery, Ohsweken, Ontario, NOA 1MO
  LOCATION: 184 Mohawk Street, Brantford
- (519) 445-4528
- Open late May – Thanksgiving; hours vary
- Admission by donation

The Six Nations People have been living in the Grand River region since the American Civil War when they were forced to leave their homeland in the Mohawk Valley. Six Nations of the Grand River is the only place in North America today that represents each of the six Iroquois nations and it offers many interesting attractions, including the Chiefswood Museum, currently undergoing renovations, Six Nations Veterans' Memorial Park, and Her Majesty's Royal Chapel of the Mohawks, the first Protestant Church and probably the first Christian church in Ontario. Known as the Mohawk Chapel, this delightful, simple, spired white chapel was built in 1785, and today the building features eight stained glass windows depicting Iroquois history and is the only Royal Chapel in the world owned by Native North Americans. The Chapel is surrounded by beautiful grounds and the Mohawk Chief Joseph Brant is buried nearby. Informal "step in" tours with Native guides are offered at many of the Six Nations of the Grand River sites.

Highland Cinema Collection

* P.O. Box 85, Kinmount, Ontario, KOM 2AO
  LOCATION: Town of Kinmount, north of Main Street
* (705) 488-2107
* Open nightly, mid-May to Labour Day, then weekends until Thanksgiving
* Museum admission only with purchase of movie ticket

The Highland Cinema Collection of movie paraphernalia and equipment is housed in a three-theatre first-run cinema in the tiny town of Kinmount and the adventure begins just trying to find the place. Standing on the top of the Highland hill, all you can see is someone's house – certainly not a movie theatre – because a large part of the theatre is hidden underground. And the architecture inside is quite the movieland memory lane, as just about everything in the cinema, including seats, curtains, screens, and walls, has been made from the leftovers of closed-down movie theatres all over Ontario – even the toilet seats used to sit in the Mustang Cornwall, and the urinals stood in Toronto's Willow Theatre. But the best part is the 45-metre lobby, starring a wonderful wall-to-wall collection of movie paraphernalia and projection equipment. Literally hundreds of image and movie projectors going back to 1890 are displayed, supported by original movie posters, lobby cards from 1922, 150 glass advertising slides, old Photo Play magazines, catalogues, theatre signs, and even a cloud machine once used for atmospherics. And all this is just the hobby of local construction worker Keith Stata, who's been staging his own productions in various formats since the age of six. Two thumbs up, Keith.

HISTORIC FORT ERIE

- 350 Lakeshore Road, P.O. Box 1044, Fort Erie, Ontario, L2A 5N8
- (905) 871-0540 or 1-800-263-2558 for group tours, U.S.A. and Canada
- Open daily, early May – late September
- Admission fee

The original Fort Erie was built by the British in 1764, destroyed by flood and ice in 1779, rebuilt and again destroyed by a storm in 1803. A third Fort was begun in 1804 but was incomplete by the War of 1812 when it endured the fierce Siege of Fort Erie. In 1814 Fort Erie was captured by 4,500 Americans under General Jacob Brown, strengthened, and used in one assault. Later abandoned, the Fort fell to ruin as the thriving town of Fort Erie grew up around it. In the 1930s American trenches which had served as mass graves for soldiers were discovered, and graves continued to be found in the area until 1987. Now restored, Fort Erie is an interesting historical site featuring a ditch, drawbridge, bastions, and guns, and including an impressive collection of military artifacts and relics of the War of 1812 from both British and American forces. Demonstrations and reenactments are staged in the summer by guards in period uniform who perform drills, use muskets, and fire cannons. Tours are offered and there is a gift shop.

Historic Fort Sainte-Marie II

* c/o Cedar Point Post Office, Christian Island, Ontario, L0K 1C0
  LOCATION: Highway 27 to Elmvale, then turn onto County Road 6, and travel 25 kilometres to Tiny Township Concession 16; turn left to village of Lafontaine, and follow the signs to Cedar Point Ferry Landing
* (705) 247-2051
* Open all year, dawn to dusk
* Free admission, fee for ferry ride

Christian Island is one of three islands which are part of 2,200 hectares on Georgian Bay now inhabited by the Beausoleil First Nation people, who have lived there since 1856. Historic Fort Sainte-Marie II is the remains of a fort built on the island in 1649-50, a testament of the Jesuit missionaries, 60 Frenchmen and up to 8,000 Huron people who fled their homes, villages, and the original Sainte-Marie-Among-the-Hurons, and came to the island to avoid Iroquois war parties. Most of the Huron people there died over the winter, and the island was abandoned in 1650. This was the final dispersal of the Huron people as an organized nation. Excavations began in 1965, disclosing a well, a portion of a Huron burial area, European living quarters, and many artifacts including nails, beads, Huron pottery, French finger rings, and other items. Visitors can enjoy several sites on the island, and may even catch archaeologists at work. The Administration Office provides self-guided tour brochures. Regular round-trip ferry rides from Cedar Point to Christian Island are offered year-round, as long as the water is not frozen, and take about 15 minutes.

Historic Fort York

- Toronto Historical Board, Marine Museum, Exhibition Place, Toronto, Ontario, M6K 3C3
  LOCATION: Garrison Road off Fleet Street, 2 blocks east of the CNE
- (416) 392-6907
- Open daily, 9:30 – 5:00
- Admission fee

Fort York was first established by Colonel John Graves Simcoe in 1793. It began with a group of huts, which later developed into a lodgment, palisade, and blockhouse, and by the War of 1812, a worthy fort had been established, around which the city of Toronto eventually grew. Several of the original buildings have survived including a barracks, blockhouses, gunpowder magazines, and officers' quarters and are preserved as a National Historic Site, living history museum, and display facility run by the Toronto Historical Board. Buildings contain period furnishings, equipment, and personal effects mixed with models and formal displays. Costumed staff dressed as soldiers and their wives bring the fort to life playing penny whistles, doing chores, performing military reenactments, talking to visitors, and giving guided tours. Fort York sponsors educational programs, teacher training, lectures, workshops, and special events and exhibits. Gifts, souvenirs, and light refreshments are available at the gift shop.

Archives on the History of Canadian Psychiatry and Mental Health Services

- Queen Street Mental Health Centre, Room 1010, 1001 Queen Street West, Toronto, Ontario, M6J 1H4
- (416) 535-8501, ext. 2172
- Open by appointment only, Tuesday and Thursday, 9:00 – 12:30 and 1:30 – 5:00
- Admission free, appointment recommended

The mandate of the AHCPMHS (how's that for an acronym!) is to "preserve, and make available for study, material concerning the history and development of psychiatry and mental health services in Canada, especially Ontario." Housed in one of Ontario's most famous Mental Health facilities, the Queen Street Mental Health Centre, formerly the Toronto Asylum, the archives has many holdings of interest to mental health workers, researchers, and patients. These include publications, such as community programs, legislation, and reports from various hospitals, institutions, and clinics involved in mental health. Also included are biographies, references, research papers, various arts media relating to mental illness, Canadian Mental Health Association records, and early 20th century case files from the Toronto General Nervous Ward. Services include a research room, reference staff and document reproduction. The archives is also closely affiliated with the Museum of Mental Health Services Foundation, which is hoping to have a permanent space sometime in the near future.

H.M.C.S. HAIDA NAVAL MUSEUM

* 955 Lakeshore Boulevard West, Toronto, Ontario, M6K 3B9
  LOCATION: Ontario Place, Lakeshore Boulevard
* (416) 314-9755 or (416) 314-9869
* Open daily, Victoria Day – Labour Day, 10:30 – 7:00; Labour Day – Thanksgiving, weekends, 10:30 – 5:00; other times by appointment
* Admission fee

The H.M.C.S. *HAIDA*, named after the Haida people of British Columbia, is one of two survivors of over 300 ships used by the Royal Canadian Navy in World War II. Built just before that war, she also saw action in Korea, and would have been sold for scrap in the mid-sixties if it wasn't for the efforts of various Torontonians who recognized the historical value of what the H.M.C.S. *HAIDA* Naval Museum now calls the "most famous ship in the Canadian Navy." Today the *HAIDA* is permanently berthed at Ontario Place on Lakeshore Boulevard, functions as a museum, a memorial, and provides weekend Sea Cadet training. The museum also offers school programs and visits, self-conducted tours, and stationed interpreters to answer any questions. Relevant naval artifacts are displayed and there is a gift shop on the premises.

HOCKEY HALL OF FAME

- BCE Place, 30 Yonge Street, Toronto, Ontario, M5E 1X8
  LOCATION: northwest corner of Yonge & Front Streets, Toronto, Ontario
- General Information: (416) 360-7765
  Special Events Bookings: (416) 360-7735
- Open all year, Monday – Wednesday, 9:00 – 6:00; Thursday and Friday, 9:00 – 9:30; Saturday, 9:00 – 6:00; Sunday, 10:00 – 6:00
- Admission fee

The stunning Hockey Hall of Fame, recently opened in the new BCE Place, is a great source of pride for Canadians. Unveiled with much pomp and ceremony in the summer of 1993, the Hall features state-of-the-art technology and methods to fulfill its three goals of excellence, entertainment, and education. "In short," organizers claim, the new Hall "will be a unique 21st Century family entertainment attraction where the spiritual essence of the game is honoured and celebrated." Thirteen different areas, covering 4,740 square metres of hockey, hockey, and more hockey, completely fulfill the mandate. Innovative visual and interactive exhibits, many sponsored by large corporations such as the *Toronto Sun* and Coca-Cola, cover all aspects of Canada's national sport. The heart and soul of the Hockey Hall of Fame, however, is the awesome Bell Great Hall, a grand space with a domed stained glass ceiling, which pays tribute to Hall of Famers, and is home to a complete collection of NHL trophies, including the Stanley Cup, which is displayed with religious reverence. And of course, the Hall scores big with "the world's greatest hockey store."

Holocaust Education and Memorial Centre of Toronto

- 4600 Bathurst Street, Willowdale, Ontario, M2R 3V2
- (416) 635-2883, ext. 144
- Open Monday – Thursday, 9:00 – 3:00, Friday 9:00 – 1:00, Sunday 11:00 – 4:30
- Free admission, donations welcome, group visits by appointment

The Holocaust Memorial Centre of Toronto is a space dedicated to the memory of six million Jews who were annihilated during the Holocaust and serves as a centre for education about this tragedy. The entrance and exit areas display a multitude of photographs depicting Jewish life before and after World War II. The Memorial Centre also contains a large theatre space, and has on display a few poignant artifacts like an empty can of Zyclon B, the poisonous gas used in gas chambers. The Hall of Memories is an enclosed space in the middle of the Centre reserved for reflection, remembrance, and prayer, and tiles with the names of Holocaust victims cover the walls. For school groups a special educational program can be arranged, which may include an introduction to the centre, a slide show on the Holocaust, and a lecture by a Holocaust survivor, so students can hear a first-hand account and ask questions. A moving and informative place, a trip to the Holocaust Memorial Centre will leave visitors with a better understanding of the dangers of racism and prejudice.

Houdini Hall of Fame

* 4983 Clifton Hill, Niagara Falls, Ontario, L2G 3N5
* (905) 356-4869
* Hours and times vary according to season
* Admission fee

Worth the climb up to the top of Niagara's wonderfully commercial "museum row" is a trip to the sensational Houdini Hall of Fame, a museum dedicated to the feats of "Master Mystifyer" Harry Houdini. Inside its dark and ominous halls visitors can follow Houdini's legendary career and see an exciting collection of artifacts used not only by the man himself but also by other great illusionists such as Thurston, Kellar, LeRoy, and Dunninger. Original Houdini posters, challenges, theatre programs, and photos are displayed, as well as video clips of Houdini's legendary acts. Not to be missed are the $100,000 Houdini Handcuff Collection, equipment for "Cutting a Girl in 8," and a myriad of magical, mystifying materials. Try your hand at the museum's test for Psychic Ability and you could win $31,000. Or enter the Transformation Chamber yourself and be metamorphosed into a hideous werewolf. Just don't forget to change back before you leave.

House of Frankenstein Wax Museum

* 4973 Clifton Hill, Niagara Falls, Ontario, L2G 3N5
* (905) 357-4330
* Open daily, April – October, 9:00 a.m. – 1:00 p.m.; November – March, weekends only, 9:00 a.m. – 12:00 p.m.
* Admission fee

Another one of Niagara Falls' cheesy main-drag attractions, the House of Frankenstein Wax Museum boasts the best gargoyles on the street. Inside you'll meet Frank, the wife, and all their cronies, in life size, waxy splendor, and get to watch a bite-sized version of the 1931 classic. Scary stuff.

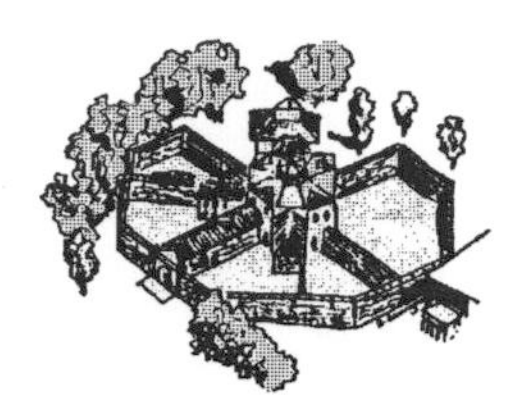

Huron Historic Gaol

* 110 North Street, Goderich, Ontario, N7A 2T8
  LOCATION: Highway 21 and Gloucester Terrace
* (519) 524-2686
* Open Monday – Saturday, Victoria Day – Labour Day, 9:00 – 4:30; Sunday, 1:00 – 4:30; Labour Day – November 30, Monday – Saturday, 10:00 – 4:30, Sunday, 12:00 – 4:30
* Admission fee

When it first opened in 1842, the Huron Gaol's unusual octagonal shape and interior design were considered the utmost in humanitarian prison design. The building has undergone many changes and improvements throughout the years, and seen use as a courthouse, an old-age home, an insane asylum, a poorhouse, a hospital, and as offices for Children's Aid. One of the last public hangings in Canada is believed to have taken place outside its gates in 1865, and James Donnelly, of the murderous Black Donnelly clan, did time there. A spiral staircase runs through the centre of the building, and cells, a library, gaoler's apartment, bathroom, kitchen, and other special-purpose rooms can be seen along with the rude furnishings they would have held. The Governor's House, also on site, was built in 1901, and, with its fine furniture and luxurious trimmings, is a telling contrast to the utilitarian setting of the gaol.

Huron Indian Village and Huronia Museum

* P.O. Box 638, Midland, Ontario, L4R 4P4
  LOCATION: Little Lake Park, King Street South, Midland
* (705) 526-2844
* Open Monday – Saturday, 9:00 – 5:00, Sunday, 12:00 – 5:00
* Admission fee

The Huron Indian Village and Huronia Museum claim to cover about 11,000 years of history in Central Ontario. Built in 1955/56 and based on archaeological evidence and surviving documentation, the village was the brainchild of archaeologist Wilfrid Jury in conjunction with a museum from the University of Western Ontario, and was Canada's first recreated Indian village. Representing one of hundreds of similar villages that would have dotted Huronia before European contact in 1610, the site includes a palisade, corn field, longhouses, a sweat lodge, drying racks, canoes, furnishings, tools, and other items typical of pre-contact Huron life. Adjacent to the village is the Huronia Museum, which displays an interesting and lively collection of Native and European artifacts, spanning 9,000 B.C. to the present. Clothing, tools, pottery, maps, glassware, cradles, stoves, pioneer furnishings, baby carriages, water vessels, and Huron artifacts of the area fill the space. Artwork of local importance, including pieces by local artists and members of the Group of Seven, are also displayed and there is a great gift shop. Both the Huron Indian Village and the Huronia Museum have outstanding educational programs including tours, slide shows, tie-ins with the Wye Marsh Wildlife Centre, resource kits, and hands-on opportunities.

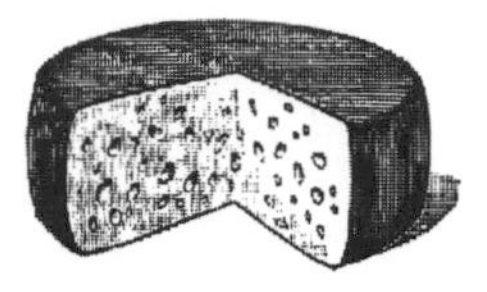

Ingersoll Cheese Factory Museums and Sports Hall of Fame

* Box 340, Ingersoll, Ontario, N5C 3V3
  LOCATION: Highway 19 and Canterbury Street in Centennial Park
* (519) 485-0120, or (summer only), (519) 485-5510
* Open May–Thanksgiving, weekends only, 1:00 – 5:00; July and August, daily, 10:00 – 6:00; other times by appointment
* Free admission

What a combination – sports and cheese! The Ingersoll Museums consist of five buildings housing exhibits on local agriculture, cheese making, and sports, all of which have made Ingersoll the delightful place it is today. The Agricultural Museum and blacksmith shop are housed in reconstructed barns, and contain early blacksmithing and farming equipment and related exhibits. The Cheese Factory Museums explain, through various media and artifacts, the importance of cheese making to the area, starting in the mid 1800s. Visitors will learn about a "Mammoth Cheese," made in 1866 in Ingersoll, which weighed 3,310 kilograms. It was displayed in England and New York, but eventually got cheesed off by a much larger cheddar made in Perth, Ontario, in 1893. The Sports Hall of Fame commemorates important people and events in Ingersoll's sports history, displaying photos and memorabilia, as well as a 10.4 metre mahogany speedboat, raced 1948-50. A gift shop, camping and picnic facilities, group tours, teaching kits, and special events are also featured.

International Ice Hockey Federation Museum

- P.O. Box 82, York and Alfred Streets, Kingston, Ontario, K7L 4V6
  LOCATION: on the fairgrounds at York and Alfred Streets, Kingston
- (613) 544-2355
- Open daily, mid-June to mid-September, 10:00 – 5:00; by appointment rest of year
- Admission fee

The International Ice Hockey Federation Museum interprets and preserves the history of the sport of ice hockey all over the world. Operated under the auspices of the International Ice Hockey Federation, the museum exhibits trophies and memorabilia from A and B groups in Europe, and has international displays of hockey cards, trophies, sweaters, sticks, skates, photographs and memorabilia relating to the players, executives, and referees of amateur and professional hockey. The museum also boasts the oldest hockey sweater on record, from Queen's University in Kingston, Ontario, in the late 1800s. Important hockey players are also remembered here, and the museum is the proud home of the Bobby Hull collection. An historic hockey series, which reenacts early Kingston hockey games, is held annually at Kingston Harbour. Guided tours are offered by appointment and gifts and memorabilia can be purchased on the premises.

Irving E. and Ray Kanner Heritage Museum

* Baycrest Centre for Geriatric Care, 3560 Bathurst Street, North York, Ontario, M4K 2E1
  LOCATION: main floor, northeast corner of the Silverman Garden Court
* (416) 789-5131, ext. 2802
* Open every day except Saturday, 9:00 – 9:00
* Free admission

The Irving E. and Ray Kanner Heritage Museum, at the Baycrest Centre for Geriatric Care in North York, regularly displays a permanent collection of Judaica and artifacts pertaining to local Jewish life. Exhibits include religious objects such as Torah crowns, breastplates, pointers and scrolls, as well as domestic artifacts like textiles, candleholders, dishware and table ornaments. In addition, there are personal belongings such as jewellery and clothing and historical photographs, documents, and books. There is also a display on the history of the Baycrest Centre for Geriatric Care, originally the Toronto Jewish Old Folks Home, which has been in operation since 1918. Temporary displays focusing on Jewish life include subjects like a recent exhibition highlighting the Jewish community of downtown Toronto, specifically Kensington Market, from 1920-50.

JACK MINER'S MIGRATORY BIRD SANCTUARY

- Kingsville, Ontario, N9Y 2E8
  LOCATION: north of town off Highway 3, Kingsville
- (519) 733-4034
- Open Monday – Saturday, dawn – dusk Museum open Monday – Saturday, 9:00-5:00
- Free admission

Jack Miner was a simple God-fearing Canadian whose early discoveries and pioneering efforts in naturalism have made international contributions to wildlife preservation. Miner's original sanctuary idea was copied all over the world, his techniques of banding and tracking migration routes have influenced laws, and the week of his birthday, April 10th, was declared International Wildlife Week in Canada. The Sanctuary is still staffed by Miner's descendants, and Miner's incredible career and philosophies are commemorated in a small museum on the grounds which also displays a map showing the migratory flight route of the birds. And of course, every year during the migration seasons thousands of wild geese, swans, and ducks can be seen coming and going. The best time for viewing is from 3:00 p.m. to sunset during the last three weeks of March to early April, and the last three weeks of October and all of November. Feeding and banding is demonstrated by guides, an activity that has been going on since 1909. To date, over 100,000 migratory geese and 100,000 wild ducks have been tagged.

J.F.K. Assassination Exhibit

* 5950 Hillcrest Crescent, Niagara Falls, Ontario, L2J 2A7
* LOCATION: 2nd Floor of Maple Leaf Village, Niagara Falls
* (905) 357-5372
* Open summer, 10:00 a.m. – midnight; winter weekends only, hours vary
* Admission fee

The J.F.K. Assassination Exhibit was opened in 1992 in Niagara Falls' Maple Leaf Village to help feed the never-ending fascination of what is commonly known as the "J.F.K. Conspiracy." The Exhibit is owned and operated by two brothers with a genuine fascination and zeal for the J.F.K. "thing," and their aim is to present the evidence, some of which they claim as *bona fide* "scoops," and let visitors decide for themselves what happened, who was guilty, and why. And they certainly provide a wealth of juicy artifacts and information. It all begins in the theatre area with a 20-minute synopsis of the entire ordeal from J.F.K. and Jackie's arrival at Love Field to the President's burial. Next is the impressive 1.8 by 1.2 metre model of the "Kill Zone" made for the set of Oliver Stone's *J.F.K.* film. Seven TV sets around the exhibit area play film footage, witness reports, discussions of the "magic bullet" theory, doctors' opinions, and more, continuously. Cases full of assassination "memorabilia" line the walls, presenting newspaper clippings, colour photos, a reproduction of Jack Ruby's pistol used to kill Oswald, a replica of Oswald's rifle from the movie *J.F.K.*, and the original handcuffs used to arrest Ruby, among other items, all displayed in chronological order. Plans for the future include a library and research facility. Books, t-shirts, pens, key chains, and photos can be purchased on the premises.

Joan Baillie Archives of the Canadian Opera Company

- 227 Front Street East, Toronto, Ontario, M5A 1E8
- (416) 363-6671
- By appointment Monday, Wednesday, and Thursday from 9:30 – 3:00
- Free admission

The Canadian Opera Company Archives bears the name of Joan Baillie, the archives' Founding Archivist, who has run the whole show from its inception in 1974. The archive was set up to "provide the resources necessary for future generations to trace the progression of Canada's first permanent opera company," which began in 1950 as the Opera Festival Association of Toronto. Holdings include periodicals, press clippings, company records, tapes, production videos and cassettes, programs and posters, 25,000 photographs, 5,000 slides and design materials, all relating to the C.O.C. Also under the auspices of the C.O.C. Archives is the Canadian Opera Archives, which documents Canadian opera unrelated to the C.O.C., dating back to 1825. These materials are from the private collection of Joan Baillie, and feature programs, playbills, including some rare examples in silk, reviews, photographs, and other articles. Exhibit space in the front area of the archives diplays posters, set models, and other visually interesting items. Upstairs, in the Company's music library, books, 5,000 operatic recordings, and videotapes of productions can be accessed.

JOSEPH BRANT MUSEUM

* 1240 North Shore Boulevard, Burlington, Ontario, L7S 1C5
* (905) 634-3556
* As of July 1, 1995, open all year, Monday – Saturday, 10:00 – 4:00, Sunday 1:00 – 4:00
* Admission fee

Joseph Brant, a Six Nations war chief, was an important military figure in Upper Canada (now Ontario) in the late 1700s, as he and his Six Nations troops supported the British during the American Revolution. In 1800 King George III granted Brant a 1,400-hectare tract of land, and a house, for his services. Several decades later the house was turned into a summer resort, and in 1900 the Hotel Brant was created. In 1927 these buildings were destroyed, but the present reconstruction of the original Brant house was built in 1937/38. The house now serves as a museum and displays a mixture of artifacts from both European and Native traditions. The Woodland Indian Gallery pays homage to Brant's Mohawk heritage, and showcases Native artifacts found locally. The Joseph Brant Gallery displays items owned by Brant, including gifts from King George III, and a portion of a parlour furnished according to the style Brant would have enjoyed. A further gallery features the history of Burlington, including part of a 9,500-year-old mastodon's tusk.

JOSEPH SCHNEIDER HAUS MUSEUM & GALLERY

* 466 Queen Street South, Kitchener, Ontario, N2G 1W7
* (519) 742-7752
* Open daily, May – September, 10:00 – 5:00; rest of year Tuesday – Saturday, 10:00 – 5:00, Sunday, 1:00 – 5:00, other times by appointment
* Admission fee

The Joseph Schneider Haus is a local history museum with a focus on the German Mennonite community in the Kitchener area. The Georgian home, which once belonged to Mennonite Joseph Schneider and his family, has been restored to *circa* 1856, and features furnishings and textiles common to a Mennonite family of the period and the work of Waterloo County Germanic carpenters and cabinetmakers. Costumed interpreters perform daily tasks, such as gardening and cooking, and sheep-shearing and apple-schnitzing bees are held regularly. The Heritage Gallery, housed in a modern museum wing, features the Canadian Harvest Collection of Germanic Folk Art and relevant temporary exhibits. There is a gift shop on site and educational programs and special events are offered.

JUMBO

- c/o St. Thomas and District Chamber of Commerce, 538 Talbot Street, St. Thomas, Ontario, N5P 1C4
  LOCATION: 65 Talbot Street West, St. Thomas
- (519) 631-1981
- Accessible all year
- No charge

Jumbo is not a museum, but a monument to a big celebrity and an untimely event. Jumbo the elephant was (quite literally) the biggest star of P.T. Barnum's circus in the late 1800s, and his name is now a household word (think of the Jumbo Jet). Jumbo, reputedly the biggest elephant ever held in captivity, was born in Kenya, and lived in England for 17 years before being sold to Barnum and shipped to America. Here he toured with the circus, often accompanied by the relatively tiny clown elephant Tom Thumb. On September 15, 1885, during a visit to St. Thomas, Jumbo and Tom were being led to their railway car along the tracks, when they were hit by a train. Tom survived, but Jumbo's brain was impaled by one of his own tusks. As he died Jumbo tenderly wrapped his trunk around his lifelong companion and trainer. Ever the showman, Barnum had Jumbo's skin and skeleton mounted and, in this incarnation, Jumbo continued to travel with the circus for two more years. A century later the steel and concrete monument to Jumbo, slightly larger than life, was erected in St. Thomas in memory of Jumbo's gentle nature and fateful accident. Adjacent to the statue is a former Grand Trunk Railway caboose, which serves as an info booth in the summer.

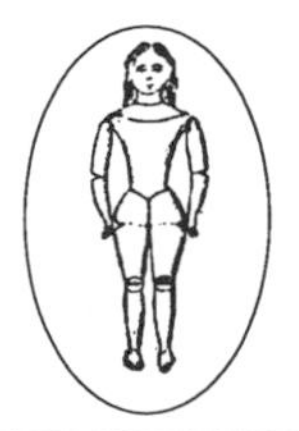

Kleinburg Doll Museum

* The Antique Junction, 10489 Islington Avenue North, Kleinburg, Ontario, L0J 1C0
* (905) 893-1358, Kleinburg, or (416) 248-9469, Toronto
* Open Tuesday – Sunday and holiday Mondays, 12:00 – 5:00
* Free admission

Housed in the Antique Junction antique shop in Kleinburg is a collection of about 170 historical dolls from the 1870s to the present. The bulk of the collection comes from Germany, France, Italy, and Japan, with various pieces from Canada and the United States. Bisque and porcelain dolls, wax dolls, folk dolls, and character dolls fill the cases, including turn-of-the-century Penny Wooden dolls, Italian Lenci dolls, *circa* 1920, Eaton's Beauties, a ventriloquist's Charlie McCarthy dummy, Barbara Anne Scott, and a Gibson Girl. Kewpies, Howdy Doody, and even an eighties Barbie can also be admired. This little doll community is part of a private collection which has been amassed over the last two decades. Visitors to this delightful and interesting display are also welcome to browse through the many treasures of the antique shop.

KOMOKA RAILWAY MUSEUM

- 133 Queen Street, P.O. Box 22, Komoka, Ontario, NOL 1RO
  LOCATION: 8 miles west of London on Middlesex County Road 14
- (519) 657-1912
- Open June 1 – September 30, Tuesday & Thursday, 7:00 – 9:00 p.m., Saturday 9:00 – 12:00 a.m., Sunday 1:00 – 4:00 p.m.
- Admission fee

The Komoka Railway Museum is a lively museum dedicated to the preservation of Ontario's railroad history. The museum building is the former Grand Trunk Station, which was moved, by rail of course, from Gobles, Ontario, to its present location in 1939. It was moved again to the other side of the tracks in 1974 when it was purchased for use as a museum. Today it boasts many interesting artifacts including a three-wheel velocipede, telegraph keys, spike hammers and pullers, uniforms, switch lanterns, steam gauges, a railroad safe, a baggage sleigh, and the museum's pride and joy, a 1913 Shay Steam Logging Locomotive, now undergoing restoration. There is an HO gauge model railroad based on the Komoka area tracks and videos on railway themes. On-site archives are open to researchers and modellers, and educational materials for children are also available.

Kortright Centre for Conservation

* Metropolitan Toronto & Region Conservation Authority, 5 Shoreham Drive, Downsview, Ontario, M3N 1S4
  LOCATION: City of Vaughan, north of Metro Toronto: take Highway 400 North to Major Mackenzie Drive, go west to Pine Valley Drive and south one kilometre to entrance
* (905) 661-6600
* Open all year, 10:00 – 4:00, call for tour times
* Admission fee

"If you want to become better acquainted with the world around you, then Kortright's the natural place to be." So reads the motto of the Kortright Centre for Conservation, 162 hectares of natural, preserved land on the Humber Valley. The adventure begins in the Woodland building, where visitors can decide on things like hiking, bird-watching, following a guided tour, joining one of the Kortright's many educational programs, seeing the exhibits and the theatre, taking the boardwalk into the marsh, visiting the "Renewable Energy Demonstration Cottage," or renewing their own resources in the café. Staff include naturalists trained in dealing with all age groups and on a variety of subjects, with hands-on public programs. Special events throughout the year feature workshops and happenings like the "Fall Forest Festival" or maple syrup festivities. Night life includes exciting events like a hike in search of bats, or the seasonal "Mysteries of Halloween."

Kortright Waterfowl Park

* 305 Niska Road, Guelph, Ontario, N1H 6J3
  LOCATION: South West corner of Guelph, Kortright Road West of Highway 6
* (519) 824-6729
* Open Saturday, Sunday, and holidays, March 1 – October 31, 10:00 – 5:00
* Admission fee

The Kortright Waterfowl Park was opened in 1965 by the Niska Wildlife Foundation, a private, non-profit organization dedicated to wildlife conservation. The word "Niska" is Swampy Cree for "gray or Canada Goose" and the park is named after Francis Kortright, an important Canadian conservationist. The park covers 47 hectares and an area of Hanlon Creek on the park site is an habitual winter refuge for scores of wild geese and ducks. It plays home to Green and Blue Herons, songbirds, rabbits, fish, and hundreds of other forms of plant and animal life as well, including a herd of White-Tailed Deer. Also on the grounds is the Niska Propagation and Research Centre, which produces up to 1,000 ducklings, goslings, and cygnets annually, and houses wintering facilities and a clinic for sick, injured, or orphaned wildlife. This part of the park is closed to the public during the spring and summer for obvious reasons, although research facilities and birds are made available for students and scholars. Visitors are most welcome during regular hours, but are asked to "take nothing but pictures, leave nothing but footprints."

Lang Pioneer Village

* c/o 470 Water Street, Peterborough, Ontario, K9H 3M3
LOCATION: 16 kilometres southeast of Peterborough, 3.2 kilometres north of Keene at Lang
* (705) 295-6694
* Visitor Centre open year-round, village open early May – mid-October, Monday – Friday, 11:00 – 5:00, Saturday and holiday Mondays, 1:00 – 5:00, Sunday, 1:00 – 6:00
* Admission fee

Lang Pioneer Village is a 10-hectare site run by the County of Peterborough that was opened in 1967 for the centennial of Canada's Confederation. The main focus is the Visitor Centre, which houses a multipurpose room, a gallery for special exhibits, a gift shop, and research centre. The actual village is home to about 20 Peterborough County buildings from the 1800s and a collection of artifacts, many of which were donated by local residents. Settlers' houses, log cabins, a carpenter's shop, print shop, blacksmith's shop, hotel, church, city hall, school, mills, a general store, and barns, furnished and equipped to period, are brought to life by historical interpreters, creating the charming rural atmosphere of another century. Special events are held throughout the year, including sheep shearing, corn roasts, folk dancing, crafts making, and special tours and school programs. The delightful Lang Pioneer Village lives up to its claim as a "living monument to the faith, endurance, and ingenuity of the pioneers and to the generosity and interest of their descendants and those who came later to Peterborough County."

Laura Secord Homestead

- Pen Centre Highway 406 & Glendale Ave, St. Catharines, Ontario, L2P 2K9
  LOCATION: Queenston, corner of Queenston and Partition Streets
- (905) 684-1227
- Open Victoria Day weekend to Labour Day, 10:00 – 6:00
- Admission fee

Laura Secord is one of few recognized heroines in Canadian history. Laura Ingersoll was born in Massachusetts, and moved with her family, who were United Empire Loyalists, to Upper Canada in 1795. She married James Secord and they settled with their five children into what is now the Laura Secord Homestead in about 1803. During the war of 1812, Laura learned from an American soldier of a surprise attack on a significant British outpost. As her husband lay wounded, Secord walked across more than 30 kilometres of harsh terrain, braving rough weather and military threat, to carry the news to Lieutenant James Fitzgibbon, leader of the targeted British outpost. Her news lead to the interception of American troops and their forced surrender at the Battle of Beaver Dams. Today her homestead is owned by the Laura Secord Candy Shops, who had the home restored and sponsored an archaeological excavation. The result is a significant monument to Secord, and an up-close look at her private life. Recreations of significant moments, period furnishings, and archaeological artifacts are displayed, as well as a lovely rose garden, reflecting Secord's own love of the flower. Guided tours are by appointment, and of course, there is a gift shop on the premises.

Laurier House

* 335 Laurier Avenue East, Ottawa, Ontario, K1N 6R4
* (613) 692-2581
* Open April – September, Tuesday – Saturday, 9:00 – 5:00; Sunday, 2:00 – 5:00; Tuesday – Saturday, 10:00 – 5:00, Sunday 2:00 – 5:00, rest of year
* Free admission

Stately Laurier House, in Ottawa's Sandy Hill, was built in 1878 in the Second Empire style and served as the home of two of Canada's Prime Ministers, Sir Wilfrid Laurier and the Right Honourable William Lyon Mackenzie King. Laurier and his wife lived in the house from 1896 until both their deaths, his in 1919 and hers in 1921. In 1923 Mackenzie King moved into the house, which had been extensively renovated, including the addition of a study in the attic from where King dealt with many of the affairs of the nation. King was Prime Minister for an unprecedented 21 years and remained in the house until his death in 1950. The King period dominates the furnishings of the house, and many of the rooms are virtually identical to King's day, although Laurier is well represented, as King retained several portraits and furnishings used by his predecessor. Items from all over the world decorate the house, many with interesting histories of their own, including Winston Churchill's cigars, busts, photos of the Royal Family and other famous people, knick-knacks, books, portraits, lavish furnishings, and the crystal ball King used for spiritual encounters. A recreation of Lester B. Pearson's study is also featured and tours of the house are offered.

Leslie M. Frost Natural Resources Centre

- Highway 35, Dorset, Ontario, POA IE2
  LOCATION: 12 kilometres south of Dorset on Highway 35
- (705) 766-2451
- Open 7 days a week by reservation for organized groups
- Free admission

The Leslie M. Frost Natural Resources Centre, comprised of 24,000 hectares of Crown land, describes itself as a "residential natural resources education and demonstration facility" and is operated by the Ministry of Natural Resources. Here teachers, students, the general public, and people in the natural resources fields can enjoy and use the surroundings and learn all about how natural resources such as land, water, wildlife, and forests are used, managed, respected, and preserved. From 1945 to 1968 the centre was the Ontario Forest Technical School but in 1974 it became the Leslie M. Frost Natural Resources Centre, named after the late Premier who initiated the opening of the centre. Today education is still the main focus and a variety of programs and activities, like "Moose Mania" and a study of firefighting history in the area, are offered to all ages and interest groups by well-trained staff. Other features include canoe, hiking, snowshoeing, and cross-country ski trails, a working sawmill and maple syrup operations, dormitory facilities and a cafeteria.

London Museum of Archaeology and Lawson Prehistoric Indian Village

* Lawson-Jury Building, 1600 Attawandaron Road, London, Ontario, N6G 3M6
  LOCATION: Off Wonderland Road North, 2 blocks south of Highway 22
* (519) 473-1360
* Museum open daily, May – September, 10:00 – 5:00; Tuesday – Sunday, September – December, 10:00 – 5:00; Wednesday – Sunday, January – April, 1:00 – 4:00; village open May – September, 10:00 – 5:00
* Admission fee

An affiliate of the University of Western Ontario since its opening in 1933, the London Museum of Archaeology functions as both a museum and an archaeological research centre. A permanent exhibition gallery features changing displays and artifacts and information on southwestern Ontario going back 11,000 years. Adjacent Lawson Prehistoric Indian Village is both a recreation of a Neutral village of approximately 500 years ago, and an ongoing excavation site for archaeologists who can be seen in action. The village includes a palisade, earthwork mound, garden of cultivated crops, longhouses, storage pits, and other buildings and equipment typical of the pre-contact Neutrals. The London Museum of Archaeology offers a wide array of school programs, tour packages, festivals, lectures, and tie-ins with other museums. Also on site, the Quill Box Gift Shop has an impressive variety of First Nations arts and crafts.

London Regional Children's Museum

- 21 Wharncliffe Road South, London, Ontario, N6J 4G5
- (519) 434-5726
- Open daily, 10:00 – 5:00
- Admission fee

The London Regional Children's Museum bills itself as "Canada's First Children's Museum," where the "children are the stars." It is a lively, educational, colourful place where kids can learn through hands-on participation and play. There is a cave/maze to crawl through, a sandy pit in which to find dinosaur bones, a space gallery which somehow manages to hold the entire universe, and the Science Hall where wonders of the world can be explored. The "Child Long Ago" area features a street of a century ago, where kids can discover the past by visiting, pretending, and playing in an old-time schoolroom, house, drygoods store, and other fun places. Then they can compare with the "Street Where You Live," a modern street complete with a gas station and a restaurant. A terrific, educational experience designed from a child's perspective. The museum also features an outdoor sculpture playground, a gift shop, and picnic area.

Lorne Scots Regimental Museum

* The Armory, 48 John Street, Brampton, Ontario, L6W 1Z3
* (905) 451-2144 or (905) 459-5153
* Open first and third Sunday of each month, from 2:00 – 4:00, and first and third Monday evenings from 7:30 p.m. – 9:30 p.m., other times by appointment
* Free admission

The Lorne Scots, including the Peel, Dufferin, and Halton Regiments, was formed in 1866 for local defense, later made part of the Canadian Militia, and continues to serve Canada today through armouries in Brampton, Georgetown, and Oakville. The regiment has served Canada with distinction and includes five cadet corps and a band of pipes and drums. The Lorne Scots Regimental Museum was opened in the Brampton Armory in 1980 to pay tribute to the regiment; its mandate is "to display, for all to view, as many artifacts as possible which will perpetuate the memories and illustrate the past histories of our forces and communities." The museum accomplishes this by exhibiting photos, pictures, weaponry, badges, medals, uniforms, historical documents, and other items of historical significance. The museum welcomes researchers and offers tours by appointment.

Louis Tussaud's Waxworks

* 4915 Clifton Hill, Niagara Falls, Ontario, L2G 3N5
* (905) 374-6601 or 374-4534
* Open Labour Day to mid-March, 10:00 a.m. – 5:00 p.m.; other months, 10:00 a.m. – 9:00 p.m.; mid-May to Labour Day 9:00 a.m. – 1:00 a.m.
* Admission fee

Known locally as "Two Sods," Louis Tussaud's Waxworks is a Niagara Falls-style waxworks museum in the tradition of Madame Tussaud's in England. It is located at the bottom of Niagara's sublimely cheesy Clifton Hill, in a big, glitzy fake Tudor building. Inside, of course, is a waxy army of famous people, and some who are not so famous, like the museum's "security guard." John Lennon, Sir John A. Macdonald, Queen Victoria, Michael Jackson, George Burns, Pablo Picasso, and Queen Elizabeth I, all appear in period attitude, costume, and frequently, an appropriate setting. Some displays are better than others, but when they are good, they are really good, spelling serious photo opportunities. Don't miss the "Chamber of Horrors" downstairs – a genuinely scary place where werewolves howl and bleeding victims hang from meat hooks.

LOYALIST CULTURAL CENTRE

- Box 112, R.R. 1, Bath, Ontario, KOH 1GO
  LOCATION: Adolphustown Park, Adolphustown
- (613) 373-2196
- Open Tuesday – Saturday, 10:00 – 4:00; Sunday, 1:00 – 5:00; open holiday Mondays
- Admission fee

In 1784 Joseph Allison was among the first bands of Loyalists who came from the U.S. to what was then Upper Canada, a place where he could freely serve the British Empire. A century later one of his descendants, David Wright Allison, had become one of the most prosperous men in Adolphustown, building an elegant brick house in 1876, with luxuries practically unheard of at the time in Adolphustown, including hot running water, indoor bathrooms, and a fountain outside. Glamorous furniture including a white grand piano adorned the lovely house, which became the local centre of society and social life of the period. Great dinners and balls were held there, and in 1884 a three-day long celebration of the Loyalist Landing, one hundred years earlier, was held. The house is now the Loyalist Cultural Centre, where important artifacts and exhibits relevant to Loyalist heritage and the Allison legacy are displayed, along with an archive and facilities for genealogical studies. Nearby is a Loyalist burial ground. Afternoon teas are held every day except Mondays from 2:00 to 4:00 p.m.

Lundy's Lane Historical Museum

- 5810 Ferry Street, Niagara Falls, Ontario, L2G 1S9
  LOCATION: 1.6 kilometres from Niagara Falls on Highway 420
- (905) 358-5082
- Open daily, May – November, 9:00 – 4:00; other months Monday – Friday, noon – 4:00
- Admission fee

The Battle of Lundy's Lane, fought near Niagara Falls on July 25, 1814, was one of the most ferocious battles of the War of 1812. The Stamford Townships Hall, an impressive cut stone building erected in 1874 on the battlefield of Lundy's Lane, is now a museum dedicated to this battle, the people who fought it, and its importance to Canadian history. The first floor has exhibits on the War of 1812 and the Fenian Raids, and discusses early settlement and tourism in the Niagara region. Native artifacts, pistols, flags, and uniforms, among other items, are displayed. The second floor conveys the lifestyle of settlers in the area of the last century, featuring a Victorian parlour and kitchen outfitted with homey period furnishings, toys and dolls, costumes and textiles, tools and utensils, Native artifacts, and a collection of Niagara Falls prints, engravings, watercolours, and souvenirs. The museum has seasonal displays, sponsors travelling exhibits, and provides educational kits and programs.

Mackenzie House

- 82 Bond Street, Toronto, Ontario, M5B 1X2
- (416) 392-6915
- Open Monday – Saturday, 9:30 – 5:00, Sundays and holidays, noon – 5:00
- Admission fee

Mackenzie House is the 1857 home of William Lyon Mackenzie, political reformer, newspaper publisher, leader of the 1837 Upper Canada Rebellion, and Toronto's first mayor. The house was a gift to Mackenzie from his friends in recognition of and gratitude for his reform efforts. Mackenzie House reflects a mid-Victorian middle-class Toronto lifestyle, restored and furnished to commendable detail, including gas lamps, horsehair parlour furniture, paintings, tableware, textiles, and floor coverings. A period print shop, to reflect Mackenzie's zealous production of various political newspapers, has also been set up in the house including a hand-operated flat bed Washington press. Visitors will be lucky to catch a demonstration of these facilities in use, and can even purchase a paper hot off the press. Daily demonstrations in the Victorian kitchen are also held. The house is one of five sites run by the Toronto Historical Board, and is staffed by costumed interpreters.

MacLachlan Woodworking Museum

* c/o Township of Pittsburgh, P.O. Box 966, Kingston, Ontario, K7L 4X8
  LOCATION: Grass Creek Park on Highway 2, 16 kilometres east of Kingston
* (613) 542-0543
* Open daily, Victoria Day weekend – Labour Day, 10:00 – 5:00; March 1 – Victoria Day weekend and Labour Day – October 31, Wednesday – Sunday, noon – 4:00; November – February, group visits by appointment
* Admission fee

The MacLachlan Woodworking Museum's mandate is "to preserve, interpret, document, and acquire artifacts in the theme of 'wood in the service of mankind.' " Certainly, visitors will leave the museum knowing more about and appreciating wood better than they could have imagined. There are two buildings. The first is a two-storey white cedar log house, built in the 1850s, now home to Canada's most extensive collection of woodworking tools, including over 2,000 planes, and a comprehensive collection of mostly Canadian saws, axes, chisels, augers, and braces. Reconstructions of cooper, wheelwright, blacksmith, and cabinetmakers' shops, a pioneer farmer's workshop, and wife's kitchen display the tools in an historical context. The new building has special displays, such as "Understanding Wood," which discusses trees, and a gallery space for temporary exhibits showcasing works by important woodcrafters. The Museum offers great tours and significant school programs.

Maple Syrup Museum of Ontario

- Spring Street South, St. Jacobs, Ontario, NOB 2NO
- (519) 664-3626
- Hours vary and the museum may be closed for long stretches
- Admission by donation

Maple syrup is one of the most truly Canadian things, and how sweet it is! Opened in the spring of 1985, the Maple Syrup Museum of Ontario was started to "preserve the heritage of the people and industry through a collection of artifacts, to educate the population about the development of the syrup industry and to promote the industry of maple syrup." The museum includes industry artifacts and equipment such as old and new sap buckets and evaporators, and displays and information on both historical and modern maple syrup industry techniques, addressing how sap is collected, processed, graded, stored, maintained, and best of all, consumed. A five-minute video on maple syrup industry history is available for viewing and the museum offers instructional courses and sugar bush tours in season. Visitors can also take a trip to the Farm Pantry store nearby, where a delicious range of maple products is available.

MARINE MUSEUM OF THE GREAT LAKES

* 55 Ontario Street, Kingston, Ontario, K7L 2Y2
* (613) 542-2261
* Open January – March, 10:00 – 4:00, Monday – Friday; daily, April – December, 10:00 – 5:00
* Admission fee

Launched in 1975, the Marine Museum of the Great Lakes exists to preserve and educate the public about the marine heritage of the Great Lakes. The museum is housed at the 19th-century Drydock, along the historic waterfront, which is now a National Historic Site. The original Engine House, still holding steam engines and pumps, is part of the museum, as are a blacksmith shop, a sail and steam gallery, shipbuilding gallery, displays on shipbuilding and shipwrecks, a space for special exhibitions, and a great selection of Canadian marine artifacts. The 2,720 tonne ice breaker Museum Ship *Alexander Henry*, docked next door, can be toured or used for its bed and breakfast facilities. The Marine Museum also has an impressive marine library and archives containing thousands of books, photographs, and other printed matter, and maintains a close relationship with related marine institutions. Impressive membership and educational programs, and a salty variety of special events are offered year-round.

MARINE MUSEUM OF UPPER CANADA

* Toronto Historical Board, Stanley Barracks, Exhibition Place, Toronto, Ontario, M6K 3C3
  LOCATION: Exhibition Place, west of the Princes' Gates entrance at Lakeshore Boulevard
* (416) 392-6827
* Open Tuesday – Friday, 9:30 – 5:00; Saturday and Sunday, 12:00 – 5:00
* Admission fee

The Stanley Barracks in Toronto's Exhibition Place was built in 1841, and is the only surviving building of seven which were constructed to replace Fort York. Now the Barracks is home to the Marine Museum of Upper Canada, one of five sites operated by the Toronto Historical Board. The museum focuses on Toronto Harbour and the marine heritage so important to the city's growth. Exhibits cruise through marine aspects of the fur trade, warships of the Great Lakes, Toronto Harbour's ferries, and other significant themes. Artifacts include diving equipment, model ships, marine art, and beyond the museum walls, the 1932 steam tug the *Ned Hanlan* and a working steam engine can be closely examined. The Marine Museum also has an impressive archival and photographic collection. Visual materials and audio-visual presentations will enhance visitors' knowledge of local marine history, and group tours and educational programs are offered year-round.

Mariners' Park Museum

- Box 54, Milford, Ontario, KOK 2PO
  LOCATION: South Bay, South Marysburgh, Prince Edward County, County Road 9-13
- (613) 476-8392
- Open weekends, late May – Thanksgiving weekend; daily, July and August, 9:00 – 5:00, closed Fridays
- Admission fee

Mariner's Park Museum includes a museum and a lighthouse in a park, which are closely tied to local marine history. Displays follow the earliest local European contact to the period around World War II, which saw the end of the marine era in Prince Edward County. Many artifacts are on view, including a map locating wrecks offshore, ships' logs, anchors, fishermen's nets and similar equipment, and relevant pictures. Many of these have been donated by local families whose ancestors ran the trade routes and ports, handled passengers, agricultural products and other goods, were fishermen, ship owners, shipbuilders, sailors, and generally had a hand in the water. The lighthouse, physically separate from the museum, has its own history. The original was built in the late 1820s, on a place called False Duck Island, towering 19 metres above high water, with a beacon visible at 21 kilometres. The light was extinguished for the last time in 1965 and the iron superstructure, lantern, and light were handed over to the South Marysburgh Council, who built the existing lighthouse in the Park as a Centennial project for the township. Here it serves as a memorial to sailors of the county, and a special service is held annually on the second Sunday of every August.

Marten River Provincial Park Logging Camp

- c/o General Delivery, Marten River, Ontario, P0H 1T0
  LOCATION: Highways 11 and 64, Marten River Provincial Park
- (705) 474-5550 or (705) 892-2200
- Days and hours of operation are seasonal
- Free admission

Rich in white and red pine, the Marten River area was important for logging at the early part of the 20th century. Today the Marten River Provincial Park is home to a re-created logging camp which brings to life the logging industry and lifestyle of the turn of the century. Buildings, tools, and equipment along the self-guided route are explained by an anecdotal and informative brochure, full of original photographs, which visitors can find at the Orientation Centre at the entrance of the camp. At the first stop an office, bunkhouse, cookery, meathouse, scaler's shack, stables, and blacksmith shop can all be seen and entered. Further on visitors will see square timber, logs, and equipment like wooden plows, sleighs, a "Crazy Wheel" for braking bundles of logs going downhill, and a log boom. A truly interesting place to visit while staying at Marten River Provincial Park, the logging camp is a very good overview of an important Canadian industry and lifestyle now completely changed by the tractor and chainsaw.

Martyrs' Shrine

- Midland, Ontario, L4R 4K5
  LOCATION: Highway 12, east edge of Midland
- (705) 526-3788
- Open long weekend in May to Thanksgiving weekend in October, daily 9:00 – 9:00 Groups and pilgrimages by reservation
- Admission fee to grounds

The Martyrs' Shrine is one of four shrines in Canada, and the only one outside the province of Quebec. It is dedicated to the memory of eight Jesuit missionaries who lost their lives in Huronia and district in the period between 1625 and 1650. These eight martyrs, Brébeuf, Lalemant, Daniel, Garnier, Chabanel, Jogues, Goupil, and de Lalande, with a handful of others, came to Canada to make converts of the Huron people living there. All led lives of deprivation, disease, and hardship, and the eight featured at the Shrine all met violent deaths for their cause. The imposing stone shrine, near Midland, Ontario, has witnessed impressive events, such as the beatification of the martyrs and a visit by Pope John Paul II, and it is the site of pilgrimage and ritual for thousands of followers of the Catholic faith. The history of the martyrs is depicted throughout the shrine, and relics are occasionally displayed, including items like Brébeuf's skull. The surrounding grounds include a miniature of the Lourdes Grotto, and a lookout offering an impressive view of Georgian Bay, the Wye River, and the lake nearby. A cafeteria, picnic table, and a religious articles and souvenir shop are also on the premises.

McCrae House

* 108 Water Street, Guelph, Ontario, N1G 1A6
* (519) 836-1482
* Open daily, 1:00 – 5:00, all year
* Admission fee

McCrae House, a site of Guelph Museums, is the birthplace of John McCrae, a military officer, physician, and professor of medicine who became famous through his poem "In Flanders Fields." The poem first appeared in 1915, and struck a chord with soldiers and their loved ones everywhere. Today, thanks to McCrae, the poppy, mentioned in his poem, is used as a tributary symbol for those who served and died in the First World War. McCrae House, a limestone cottage built in 1858, is now a National Historic Site and has been restored to *circa* 1870, which was when John McCrae's parents first inhabited it. Visitors will enjoy period rooms, a memorial park, and grounds blooming with several species of poppy when in season. Displays focus on Remembrance, World War I, Scottish traditions, and items of local interest while changing exhibitions, guided tours, lectures, outreach and educational programs are offered all year. Truly a place to remember.

McLaughlin Planetarium

* 100 Queen's Park, Toronto, Ontario, M5S 2C6
* Bookings (416) 586-5736
  Astronomical Events Hotline (416) 586-5736
  Courses and workshops (416) 586-5797
* Call in advance for hours and special events
* Admission to Astrocentre free with admission to ROM, Star Show tickets extra, discount with ROM admission

Ask for the moon at the McLaughlin Planetarium and they'll give you the entire universe. The McLaughlin Planetarium came about through a donation from Colonel Robert Samuel McLaughlin (1871-1972), Chairman of the Board of General Motors Canada, whose only stipulation was that the planetarium be the best of its kind. So far, it's been doing a darned good job of living up to this request. The building opened in 1968, and has three floors and a basement, including a workshop area, lecture theatre, rooms for business, the Astrocentre, and the Star Theatre. The Astrocentre is a permanent display area featuring spacey wall panels, hands-on exhibits, slide shows, and the Stellarium, a three-dimensional walk-in exhibit, which makes the visitor the centre of 800 stars. In the Star Theatre, inside the Planetarium's domed ceiling, light shows are projected with the phenomenal Zeiss Jena Star Projector, worth some 1.5 million dollars. Star Shows are held year-round in both French and English, as are various workshops and programs for all ages. Regularly scheduled 3-D laser light shows such as "Laser Grunge" offer stellar entertainment for the musical set.

McMichael Canadian Art Collection

- Islington Avenue, Kleinburg, Ontario, L0J 1C0
  LOCATION: Islington Avenue north, off Highway 7
- (905) 893-1121
- Open November 1 – May 31, 10:00 – 4:00, Tuesday – Sunday; June 1 – October 31, daily, 10:00 – 5:00; Wednesday until 9:00 all year
- Admission fee

A visit to the McMichael Canadian Art Collection gallery makes a great day trip, combining art, history, entertainment, and nature. The collection includes thousands of works by contemporary Inuit and Aboriginal North Americans and famous Euro-Canadian artists, most notably the Group of Seven. The spacious gallery complex, made of logs and natural stone, holds 14 galleries, the larger ones featuring spectacular views through window-walls. The McMichael is located on over 40 hectares of conservation land made up of woods and meadows overlooking the Humber River valley, where visitors can enjoy nature walks, hikes, skiing, or relaxing. The wilderness setting is a nice complement to the gallery, demonstrating the type of environment that inspired, influenced, and often hindered the artists featured inside. A shack used by Tom Thomson, one of the Group of Seven, and containing some of his personal effects, is also on the grounds. Special events include movies, lectures, and jazz performances, and there is a restaurant and gift shop.

The Meetingplace

- 33 King Street, St. Jacobs, Ontario, NOB 2NO
- (519) 664-3518 or (519) 664-2103
- Open summer, Monday – Friday, 11:00 – 5:00; Saturday 10:00 – 5:00; Sunday 1:30 – 5:00; winter, Saturday 11:00 – 4:30, Sunday 2:00 – 4:30
- Admission fee

The Mennonites are a Protestant, Christian sect who reject violence, church organization, and mostly lead simple lives as close to their interpretation of the life as Christ as possible. Because they do not practise infant baptism, they are know as "Anabaptists." Anabaptism began in Zurich, Switzerland, in the early 1600s, and has since spread all over the world. Approximately 774,000 Mennonites, including the Amish and the Hutterites, exist worldwide, and almost half live in North America. In order to educate the public about their faith and lifestyle, local Mennonites have set up an interpretation centre in St. Jacobs, Ontario. It is called the Meetingplace, and includes a multi-media exhibit on Mennonite history, beliefs, and lifestyle brought to life through photos, storylines, displays, slide presentations, and a 28-minute documentary called *Mennonites of Ontario*. Recreations of a Mennonite meetinghouse and a Swiss Cave also add to the experience.

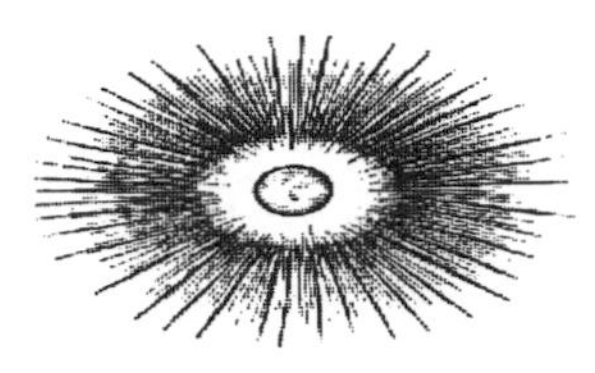

MUSEUM OF MENTAL HEALTH SERVICES TORONTO, INC.

- c/o 1001 Queen Street West, Toronto, Ontario, M6J 1H4
- (416) 535-8501, ext. 2172
- Hours, admission to be determined

The Museum of Mental Health Services is a museum without a home at present. Run by volunteers, and closely associated with the archives on the History of Canadian Psychiatry and Mental Health Services, the museum is waiting for more funds so it can set up a permanent home in the Queen Street Mental Health Centre. Its aim is to educate the public about mental illness, while "recovering a fascinating aspect of medical history and making it available for future generations." At present, a catalogue is available featuring information, artifacts, and photographs to be used in the museum's first exhibition, and if the catalogue is a good indication of what to expect from the museum, it will certainly be a remarkable and moving place. Artifacts and documents include a trepanned skull (perforated to let evil spirits escape) *circa* 1600, advertisements and sketches of horrifying medical instruments, first-hand accounts by early visitors of squalid conditions and practices, the history of the Toronto Asylum (now the Queen Street Mental Health Centre) all juxtaposed with modern, humane health care and philosophies from the perspective of both the patient and the establishment. The first phases of the museum should materialize within the 1994/95 period. Funds are being raised through membership and the catalogue is available through the above address.

MERRIL COLLECTION

- 40 St. George Street, 2nd floor, Toronto, Ontario, M5S 2E4
  Moving to 239 College Street in 1995
- (416) 393-7748
- Open Monday – Friday, 10:00 – 6:00; Saturday, 9:00 – 5:00; closed Sunday
- Free admission

Founded in 1970 as the result of a donation by well known science fiction author Judith Merril, the Merril Collection, under the auspices of the Toronto Public Library, is one of the world's major popular culture collections and the largest science fiction collection held in a public library. The Merril is primarily a research collection focusing on science fiction, fantasy, magic realism, and criticism pertaining to areas of speculative fiction. It consists of 56,500 items, mostly periodicals and books, but also plays home to games, videos, and original science fiction and fantasy art. Highlights include a first edition of *A Clockwork Orange* and James DeMille's *Strange Manuscript Found in a Copper Cylinder*, and the collection is particularly strong in the works of Jules Verne. The Merril Collection is intended primarily for research although it does offer over 8,000 circulating paperbacks and photocopying of non-circulating material is permitted.

METRO TORONTO ZOO

* P.O. Box 280, West Hill, Ontario, M1E 4R5
  LOCATION: Scarborough, just north of Highway 401 on Meadowvale Road Exit 389, 16 kilometres east of Don Valley Parkway
* (416) 392-5900
* Open daily, year round, summer 9:00 – 7:30; winter, 9:30 – 4:30
* Admission fee

The Metro Toronto Zoo is truly the king of Ontario's jungle, with an incredible, international array of birds, beasts, activities, and facilities for its visitors. The zoo is home to over 4,000 animals, including mammals, reptiles, fish, and invertebrates of every size, shape, and origin, like Hairy Nosed wombats, polar bears, tree frogs, pygmy hippos, zebras, meerkats, penguins, gnus, emus, and Lesser-Pied hornbills. The area is divided into six geographic regions: Africa, Australasia, Eurasia, the Americas, Indo-Malaya, and Canada. Trails include the "Round the World" tour, the Lion Trail, Camel Trail, and Grizzly Bear Trail, which can be accessed by foot, monorail, and sometimes even camel. Special activities include Meeting the Keeper, and Public Animal Feedings; animal demonstrations such as free flights of birds like the red-tailed hawk; and "touch tables," operated by volunteers, where visitors can handle various animal-related objects. The zoo is open all year, and animals are housed in dwellings as close as possible to their natural habitats. Refreshment facilities are on site, and don't miss the "zoopermarket" where visitors can buy mementoes.

Metropolitan Toronto Police Museum and Discovery Centre

- Metropolitan Toronto Police Headquarters, 40 College Street, Toronto, Ontario, M5G 1K2
- (416) 324-6201, for tours (416) 324-6200
- Open daily, 9:00 – 9:00, tours by appointment
- Free admission

Just on its feet, the new Metropolitan Toronto Police Museum is intended as an educational facility explaining and paying tribute to the police profession in the Metropolitan Toronto area. A fun and fascinating place, displays go back to the 1850s, and include restraining equipment, communications devices, photographs, case evidence, uniforms, and all manner of things lawful and unlawful. A re-creation of a prisoner's cell and a turn-of-the-century police station show how far crime-fighting standards and technology have advanced in Toronto. Police vehicles are a big draw, including hands-on exhibits of a Harley Davidson police motorcycle and a cruiser cut in half. A crash car with a video on impaired driving and a 1914 Paddy Wagon can also be seen up close. The museum is located in the Metropolitan Toronto Police Headquarters, and tours conducted by a police officer can be arranged by appointment for large groups. Otherwise, tours are self-guided, and there is a gift shop on the premises.

METROPOLITAN TORONTO REFERENCE LIBRARY ARTS DEPARTMENT

* 789 Yonge Street, Toronto, Ontario, M4W 2G8
* (416) 393-7000
* Hours are seasonal
* Free admission

The Arts Department of the Metropolitan Toronto Reference Library contains a wonderful collection of books and related materials on Canadian arts, and its historical theatre collection, started in 1961, is now Canada's largest and foremost. The department holds over 100,000 books related to the arts, including reference materials, indexes, bibliographies, catalogues, and rare books. There are over 800 current periodical titles, 25,000 recordings of classical, jazz, Broadway, and other types of music from 78s to CDs, and an enormous collection of printed music. More than 3,000 stage designs, a manuscript collection, documentation files of newspaper clippings, pamphlets, thousands of programs and playbills and posters for primarily Canadian productions, and over 800,000 picture clippings can also be accessed. An exciting collection and unlimited resource, the Metropolitan Toronto Reference Library Arts Department is open to researchers, scholars, and the general public, although restrictions may apply to some materials, and reference service is available in person, or by mail or telephone. Advance notice is required for the use of non-book collections.

Mildred M. Mahoney Silver Jubilee Dolls' House Gallery

* 657 Niagara Boulevard, Fort Erie, Ontario, L2A 3H9
* (905) 871-5833
* Open daily, May 1 – December 31, 10:00 – 4:00; other times by appointment
* Admission fee

Fort Erie's Mildred M. Mahoney Silver Jubilee Dolls' House Gallery is the world's biggest, and possibly the world's finest, collection of historical dolls' houses. The collection, worth over 1.5 million, spans the last 200 years, and holds more than 200 miniature houses and thousands of pieces of dollhouse furniture from all over the world. Mildred M. Mahoney has been researching, collecting, and restoring dolls' houses for more than four decades, and her expertise, knowledge, and skill show in every piece. The museum started off as a private collection in Mahoney's house, but is now located in Bertie Hall, a red brick Greek Revival mansion built in 1826, which was used during the Civil War by the Underground Railroad. Now it houses houses – lots of them, some as big as three or four metres in length, all delightfully displayed and exquisitely and accurately furnished. A replica of the Ancient House of Ipswich inhabited by a tiny gold statue of Queen Elizabeth II, a Dutch sea-captain's house with a biffy in the closet under the stairs, and a mansion from England *circa* 1780 with the windows painted black – a reflection of the avoidance of a window tax being charged on real houses of the time – are just a few of the exquisite treasures to be seen at Bertie Hall.

Mill of Kintail Museum and Conservation Area

- R.R. 1, Almonte, Ontario, KOA 1AO
  LOCATION: 8 kilometres west of Almonte, off Highway 15 and follow signs
- (613) 256-3610
- Visitor Centre and museum open May 15 – October 15, Wednesday – Sunday and holidays, 10:30 – 4:30; Visitor Centre also open winter Wednesday – Sunday, 12:00 – 4:00
- Admission fee

The Mississippi Valley Conservation Area is a lovely 63-hectare expanse of natural grounds which have been preserved by the Mississippi Valley Conservation Authority since 1972. On this site is the Mill of Kintail Museum, once the summer home of Robert Tait McKenzie (1867-1938), an outstanding Canadian sculptor, scholar, physician, physical education activist, writer, athlete, and collector. McKenzie pioneered many medical practices and helped to establish the tenets of physical education in North America. The Mill of Kintail was originally a grist mill, built in the 1830s, but McKenzie later made it into his summer residence and studio. The museum features items used and made by McKenzie, including memorabilia, pioneer artifacts, and a fine collection of his detailed sculpture. At the entrance of the conservation site is the Gatehouse, originally a grain storage building which McKenzie later used as a lodge. It is now an information centre about the Conservation Area, containing a library with books on local history and McKenzie and a gallery space for changing exhibitions. Special events are held throughout the year.

Miller Museum of Geology and Mineralogy

- Miller Hall, Queen's University, Dept. of Geological Sciences, Kingston, Ontario, K7L 3N6
- (613) 545-6767
- Open weekdays, 8:30 – 4:30, tours by appointment
- Admission free

The Miller Museum of Geology and Mineralogy is run by geologists from Queen's University, which is famous for having the best university geology department in Canada. The collection is named after W.G. Miller who was the first Provincial Geologist for Ontario, and although the museum was founded in 1930, its roots go back to the 1850s. Two large rooms, covering about 230 square metres, focus on rocks and minerals, but also contain fossils, dinosaur bones, including parts of a duck-billed lambeosaurus, a working seismograph which monitors ground movement and local earthquakes, and a recreated mineralogist's lab, which features historical equipment *circa* 1900. The Miller Museum provides educational services and facilities for both undergraduate and graduate students, as well as educational programs for school groups.

Mississippi Valley Textile Museum

- P.O. Box 784, Almonte, Ontario, KOA 1AO
  LOCATION: 3 Rosamond Street East, Almonte, Ontario
- (613) 256-3754
- Open May – October, Wednesday – Saturday, 12:00 – 4:30; Sunday, 11:00 – 4:30
- Admission by donation, tours by appointment

Located on the banks of the Mississippi River, in the former Rosamond Textile Mill, the Mississippi Valley Textile Museum is an appropriate centre for the history of Canada's early wool manufacturing industry. In the late 1880s at least 16 textile mills were located in Almonte thanks to the area's abundant waterfalls, so necessary to run the mills. The museum features period business offices, equipment, visual materials, tools, textiles, and displays to create awareness about and in remembrance of the Mississippi Valley Textile Industry. Temporary exhibitions on relevant subjects, such as the recent "Textiles from Afghanistan," are held, and special events and programs are offered. The museum is relatively new, but already has plans for expansion, including an "eco-museum," involving a large portion of the community, which will combine static displays with activities and events of local and historic interest. There is a gift shop on the premises.

Mounted Animal Nature Trail

- Terry Gordon's Taxidermy, R.R.1, Highway 6, Tehkummah, Manitoulin Island, Ontario, P0P 2C0
- (705) 859-2470
- Open daily, June 1 – Labour Day, 10:00 – 4:30
- Admission fee

Throw out your Roadkill Cookbook, folks, because Terry and Rita Gordon are raising the dead at the Mounted Animal Nature Trail. A romp through their hardwood forest trails will give the visitor a close-up look at mounted wildlife, 97% of whom are roadkills, including eagles, peacocks, ducks, partridges, hawks, and other birds, foxes, deer, porcupines, mink, weasels, skunks, owls, and a black bear. The Gordons describe their outdoor adventure as a "backyard museum, rich with nature, history and geology" and there are three trails to cover, including Mother Nature (1.2 kilometres) which winds around a pond; Porcupine Trail (2.4 kilometres), which extends to high rock area and through various rock outcrops, fields, woods, and vegetation; and Fossil Lane (5.8 kilometres), rich in fossils and wildflowers. Visitors will also see the beech that won the "Biggest Tree" title in the Great Tree Hunt Contest on Manitoulin Island. Washrooms, swings, a picnic area, and pop and ice cream are available.

MOVIELAND WAX MUSEUM

* 4950 Clifton Hill, Niagara Falls, Ontario, L2G 3N4
* (905) 358-3061
* Hours vary according to season
* Admission fee

A trip up Clifton Hill, Niagara Falls' glitzy, outrageously commercial main drag, just wouldn't be complete without a visit to the Movieland Wax Museum. Marilyn Monroe, in her famous subway-breeze-and-white-dress scene from *The Seven Year Itch* will catch your eye outside the museum, staged as if filming is in progress. Inside are wax replicas of stars from the silver screen in life-size splendour, set in classic scenes from the classics. Sets and stars from favourites like *The Wizard of Oz*, *Batman*, *The African Queen*, and *Fatal Attraction* are recreated along with contemporary television personalities and recording artists. Life-like animations of Snow White and the Seven Dwarfs are more real than Disney could hope for, and the Teenage Mutant Ninja Turtles are a blockbuster with kids. New displays featuring what's hot in Tinsel Town are mounted each year, and visitors are encouraged to take photographs. Getting autographs, however, may be more difficult.

MUSKOKA PIONEER VILLAGE

* Box 2802, Huntsville, Ontario, POA IKO
  LOCATION: accessible via Brunel Road, following signs to Pioneer Village
* (705) 789-7576
* Open daily, July 1st – Thanksgiving; summer, 11:00 – 4:00; fall, 11:00 – 4:00; other times Monday – Friday 9:00 – 4:00 by appointment
* Admission fee

Muskoka Pioneer Village is a reconstructed pioneer village reflecting local life during the period of 1860-1910, and to date includes about 20 historic buildings. The village started as a small collection of artifacts, and grew to include several structures such as a church, barn, houses, village inn, general store, maple sugar shack, sawmill, workshop, and craft house, all of which were donated and moved to their present location. Pioneer tools, furniture, equipment, and household items are displayed and put to use by the Village's costumed staff. Also on site is a separate museum building with educational exhibits on Muskoka's past, reflecting the Village's hopes "to provide insight into the lives of the early settlers . . . to instill a feeling for what pioneer life was like, to provide a place where history can come alive." Special events are held every few months, such as the Strawberry Social, which opens the Village for the summer, Market Day, featuring the sale of arts and crafts, and Victorian Christmas which offers old fashioned family festivities. The Shop-in-the Barn gift shop is located at the entrance of the Village.

Nancy Island Historic Site

- Wasaga Beach Provincial Park, Box 183, Wasaga Beach, Ontario, LOL 2PO
  LOCATION: 119 Mosley Street, corner of Mosley and 3rd Streets
- (705) 429-2728 (Island), (705) 429-2516 (Park Office)
- Open Victoria Day weekend – 3rd Friday in June, weekends 10:00 – 6:00; weekdays, groups by appointment only; 3rd Friday in June – Labour Day weekend, daily, 10:00 – 6:00; Labour Day – Thanksgiving, groups by appointment only

In the summer Wasaga Beach's main attraction is its big, sandy 14-kilometre beach complete with hot dog joints, beachwear kiosks, ice cream vendors and, of course, lots of young people. It seems like an unlikely place for a museum, but just around the corner is an interesting historic site with an unusual origin. During the War of 1812 a British ship called the *Nancy* was burned by the Americans and sank in the Nottawasaga River, where it remained for over a century collecting sand and silt and helping to form Nancy Island. In 1928 the hull of the *Nancy* was recovered and is now on display in the Nancy Island Historic Site Museum, located on the island. The museum and adjacent theatre offer a unique architectural interpretation of sails straining in the wind. Inside, educational displays and artifacts can be viewed. Close to the museum are two more historic facilities, the Schooner Town Parkette, which has an educational exhibit and walkway, and the Van Vlack Display Court, describing Wasaga Beach's logging history. Special events are held throughout the summer on the Nancy Island site.

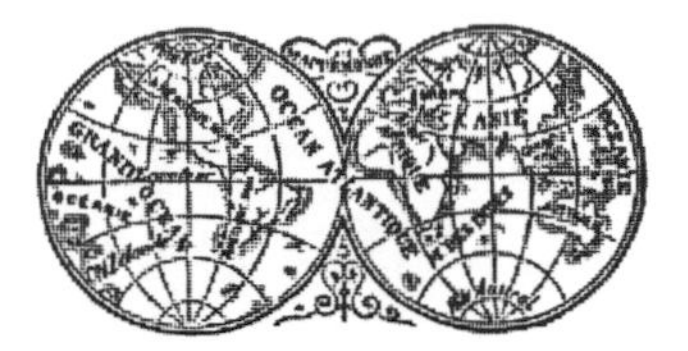

National Archives of Canada

* 395 Wellington Street, Ottawa, Ontario, K1A 0N3
* (613) 995-5138
* Staff available for research requests between 8:30 a.m. and 4:30 p.m., Monday – Friday, except statutory holidays; main reading room open daily, 7:00 a.m. – 11:00 p.m.; main exhibit room open 9:00 a.m. – 9:00 p.m.
* Admission free, although a pass must be obtained

The National Archives of Canada was established in 1872, and since then has been serving as "the collective memory of the nation, by acquiring, preserving and making available to the public Canada's documentary heritage." Holdings include written materials of every kind, thousands of kilometres of government records, and 10,000 private collections of unpublished documents. There is also documentary art like portraits, landscapes, commercial designs, posters and postcards, medals, buttons, seals, publicity materials, maps, atlases, globes, architectural blueprints and plans, stamps and other philatelic records, computer generated data, and countless other documents. The National Archives of Canada also plays an active role in the Canadian Archival community by sharing its expertise, and through its documentation centre on archives. An excellent resource facility, the archives also regularly stages special exhibitions and events throughout the year.

NATIONAL AVIATION MUSEUM

* P.O. Box 9724, Ottawa Terminal, Ottawa, KIG 5A3
  LOCATION: 1 Aviation Parkway, Rockcliffe Airport, Ottawa
* (613) 993-2010
* Open May 1 – Labour Day, 9:00 – 5:00, Thursday until 9:00; Labour Day – April 30, closed Mondays, except public holidays
* Admission fee, free on Thursdays from 5:00 – 9:00

The National Aviation Museum contains a world-class collection of historic flying craft and is a tremendous source of pride for Canadians. The spectacular museum building was designed specifically for the collection, which currently displays about 50 aircraft (from a collection of over 100), with related artifacts. These come from all over the world, although the museum focuses on Canadian aviation history. Visitors will be greeted in the lobby by *The Falcon,* a spectacular sculpture of a winged man, created by Robert Tait McKenzie. Next is the Hall of Tribute, an awe-inspiring walk-in monument to members of the Royal Canadian Air Force, then it's on to the "Walkway of Time," which is both a chronological look at flight history and a journey through various aviation themes such as pioneer aviation, the wars, and bush flying. Highlights include a reproduction of the Silver Dart – the first heavier-than-air machine to take flight in Canada, the Avro Lancaster X, and the famous barnstormer Curtiss JN-4 "Canuck." Theatres, interactive displays, information consoles, and other media help convey aviation facts and figures. Group tours can be arranged, and don't fly past the great aviation gift shop.

National Ballet of Canada Archives

* 157 King Street East, 2nd Floor, Toronto, Ontario, M5C 1G9
* (416) 362-1041
* Open Monday – Friday by appointment only
* Free admission

The National Ballet of Canada began in 1951, and today is one of the few professional Canadian dance companies that can boast an on-site archives. The archives was set up in 1971 to preserve the company's rich history. Holdings include files, programs, photographs, production notes, books, musical scores, cast lists, budgets, press clippings, videos, films, and annual reports of the company although the archives also contains dance related materials from all over the world. In the early 1970s a fire destroyed many of the National Ballet's costumes, although several costumes, going back to the earliest performances, have survived as well a few pairs of pointe shoes from former dancers, all of which are held in the archives. Design sketches, awards, medals, and set models also form part of the holdings. The National Ballet of Canada Archives is open by appointment to researchers, and standard archival practices apply.

NATIONAL LIBRARY OF CANADA

* 395 Wellington Street, Ottawa, KIA ON4
* (613) 992-9988, public programs
* Open daily, 9:00 a.m. – 9:00 p.m.; exhibitions open 9:00 a.m. – 10:30 p.m.
* Admission free, except for some special events

The National Library of Canada contains the biggest collection of Canadiana in the world and bills itself as the "home of Canada's published heritage." Its music collection is particularly noteworthy, including sheet music, recordings, and memorabilia surrounding Canada's musical heritage, and its children's collection, literary, and rare book holdings and Canadian and pre-Confederation literature areas are also very strong. The National Library of Canada shares facilities with the National Archives, and the building itself is something to see, with its lovely murals, sculpture, and etched glass. Special events and programs are offered throughout the year, including readings, concerts and rotating displays. The Library also stages special exhibitions that occasionally travel, including a recent feature on Glenn Gould. Tours are offered at set hours during the summer and at other times by request.

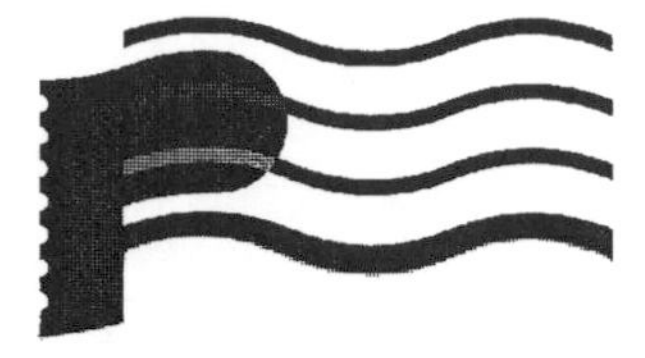

National Postal Museum

- c/o The Canadian Museum of Civilization, 100 Laurier Street, P.O. Box 3100, Station B, Hull, Quebec, J8X 4H2
  LOCATION: The Canadian Museum of Civilization, 100 Laurier Street, Hull, Quebec
- (819) 776-7000
- Open May 1 – September 3, 9:00 – 5:00, Thursday, 9:00-9:00; early September – late April, closed Mondays
- Admission fee, free on Thursdays

Believe it or not, the National Postal Museum has no fixed address, but resides temporarily at the Canadian Museum of Civilization building in Hull, Quebec, which, as it's just over the bridge from Ottawa, we'll include here. The National Postal Museum's mission is "to preserve and interpret the material heritage of postal communication within the context of global and societal communications, especially, but not exclusively, in Canada." Special exhibitions cover themes in Canadian postal history, with a recent feature following postal progress from when sailors would pick up and leave letters to and from Europe under specially marked stones, through mailboxes from centuries past to our own, and another exhibition on postal scales. Holdings include uniforms, mail equipment, stamp dispensers, scales, and lots of wonderful mailboxes as well as Canadian and international philatelic collections. Of note is the Postal Museum's emphasis on children's participation, especially through a lively publication called *Youthletter*, which tells kids as much about how and why museums exist and collect as it does about the postal system.

National Museum of Science and Technology

- 1867 St. Laurent Boulevard, Ottawa, Ontario, K1G 5A3
  LOCATION: 2 kilometres south of the Queensway
- (613) 991-3044
- Open daily, May 1 – Labour Day, 9:00 – 5:00, Thursdays 9:00 – 9:00; Closed Mondays, Labour Day – April 30, except public holidays
- Admission fee

The great big, fun, exciting, and educational National Museum of Science and Technology introduces visitors to Canada's technological and scientific history, explains how and why things were and still are used, and looks toward what science may hold for the future. Reproductions, artifacts, and participatory exhibits on science, methods of transportation, broadcasting, astronomy, space, computers, agriculture, graphic arts, and much more are all interpreted. Visitors can participate in live experiments, climb in, on, and use various vehicles and equipment, activate displays, and use multi-media exhibits. Steam locomotives, railway coaches, carriages, antique automobiles, vintage fire engines, and farm tools can all be seen, and the "slanted kitchen" – really an optical illusion – and astronaut Marc Garneau's space suit are still museum favourites. Beyond the walls visitors will find Technology Park, full of great big monuments to mostly Canadian technology, including a lighthouse, a radar antenna, and even a rocket. Also on site is the Helen Sawyer Hogg Observatory which is popular with astronomy buffs, offering films, lectures, photography sessions, and special programs throughout the year. There is a cafeteria and the Scientique gift shop on the premises.

Niagara Apothecary Museum

* c/o Ontario College of Pharmacists, 483 Huron Street, Toronto, Ontario, M5R 2R8
  LOCATION: 5 Queen Street, Niagara-on-the-Lake
* (905) 468-3845
* Open daily, May – September, 12:00 – 6:00
* Free admission

The 19th-century Niagara Apothecary Museum, an interesting piece of Niagara-on-the Lake history, can be found in the area's scenic shopping district in a mid-Victorian storefront with arched plate-glass windows and a large mortar and pestle hanging over the door. The interior gleams with polished black walnut and butternut fixtures, replicas of original crystal gasoliers, intricate plaster work, armies of bottles, flasks, and storage jars and products for anything that could possible ail a body. In former days the apothecary not only sold pharmaceutical items, but also things like paints, varnishes, veterinary supplies, and even liquor. Although the apothecary was first opened in the 1820s, it has only been at the present site since 1869 where it operated continuously until the 1960s. The pharmacist was often a key figure in the community, and three previous owners of the Niagara Apothecary served as the town's Mayor. Today it is owned by the Ontario Heritage Foundation and operated by the Ontario College of Pharmacists. Gifts and souvenirs can be purchased on the premises.

NIAGARA FALLS MUSEUM

- 5651 River Road, Niagara Falls, Ontario, L2E 6V8
- (905) 356-2151
- May – September, 9:00 a.m. – 9:00 p.m.; October – April, 10:00 a.m. – 5:00 p.m. (in winter phone ahead)
- Admission fee

The Niagara Falls Museum claims to be the oldest still-operating museum in North America, having been in existence since 1827. Privately run, it is very much an old-style commercial museum, where the exhibits aim to baffle and amaze visitors more than convey factual information – but hey, we're talking Niagara Falls! The museum has about 700,000 artifacts and some twenty-six galleries featuring early Native Americans, an Egyptian collection, an "Oriental Curios" gallery, ancient arms, and weaponry, a Hall of Dinosaurs, zoological exhibits, their "Famous Shell and Coral Collection" and an extensive mineralogical collection. Favourites with children are the mummies, the "largest Redwood tree ever felled," the Humpback Whale display, and the new "hands-on" exhibits which include fossil rubbings and paper folding. And of course it just wouldn't be the Falls without a "Freaks of Nature Gallery" and a "Daredevil Hall of Fame." Famous visitors have included Abraham Lincoln, Mickey Mantle, and King Edward VII.

NICHOLAS GAOL INTERNATIONAL HOSTEL

* 75 Nicholas Street, Ottawa, Ontario, KIN 7B9
* (613) 235-2595
* Open for visitation, daily, 11:00 – 6:00
* Free admission, tours by appointment

When the Nicholas Gaol first opened in 1862 it was known as the "Pride of Ottawa" and considered a model of modern jail architecture and practices, but by 1972 the jail was closed due to poor living conditions, lack of sanitary facilities in the cells, poor lighting, ventilation, and set-up. Today the limestone building is a testament to changing social standards and attitudes in the penal system. Canada's last public hanging was staged at the Nicholas Gaol in 1869 when Patrick Whelan was hung for assassinating one of the Fathers of Confederation, Thomas D'Arcy McGee. In 1973 the jail was taken over by the Canadian Hosteling Association and has been run as a youth hostel ever since. Hostelers sleep in the original cells, bars and all, and groups can spend the night in the warden's suites. The entire building is a fascinating artifact, retaining much of the feel and history of the original Gaol. Several of the cells have been virtually untouched, time capsules of when the jail was still functioning, and the whole floor of "Level 8," known as "Death Row," has been left as a period space, with its 1 by 2.7 metre cells. The original gallows are still on the site, and the main lobby area features cases of artifacts including punishment log books, personal items bags, disciplinary instruments like cat-o-nine-tails, and restraining devices like "come-alongs," or early handcuffs. Tours are recommended, and are held regularly throughout the year by appointment.

NORMAN ELDER MUSEUM

- 140 Bedford Road, Toronto, Ontario, M5R 2K2
- (416) 920-0120
- Admission fee, by appointment

Norman Elder, the son of a wealthy Canadian family, is one of Canada's few true eccentrics. Stepping into his museum home is like entering a 19th-century gentleman's cabinet of curiosities – only one that's gone absolutely berserk! The house itself contains over a dozen staircases, hidden tunnels, a tomb in the basement, and a wonky back extension made entirely of junk and covered with white plaster. Not an inch of wall space is left bare, displaying spears, tribal clothing, genital sheaths, Victorian hair wreaths, python skins, preserved insects from all over the word, animal pelts, a mounted lion skeleton (with human hands), and hundreds of photos of Norman himself in his travels around the world as chairman of the Canadian wing of the Explorers Club. All flat surfaces are covered with curiosities like human skulls, shrunken heads, stuffed animals (including a spaniel), hardened elephant dung, trophies, weapons, models – all of it fascinating. But not everything in Norman's house is dead – the backyard features a ferret menagerie, the hall houses hissing cockroaches, and the house pet is Robbie the Rooster. (There was a pet pig once, too, but the city put an end to that.) Norman regularly rents out artifacts to movie companies, and a scene from Cronenberg's *Naked Lunch* was filmed in his living room. The Norman Elder Museum is a must-see, but that, however, is easier said than done: there are no set hours, and visitors are only admitted when Norman isn't travelling, arranging insects in glass cases, or feeding his ferrets.

North America's Smallest Jailhouse

* Tweed Municipal Office, P.O. Bag 729,
  Tweed, Ontario, K0K 3J0
  LOCATION: Victoria Street (Highway 37)
* (613) 478-2535
* Open summer only
* Free admission

North America's Smallest Jailhouse, in Tweed, is one of at least three other North America's Smallest Jailhouses. Contenders can apparently be found in Creemore, Port Dalhousie, and Berens Rivers, and that's just in Ontario, but Tweed's little lockup is the only one open to the public. Inside is a tourist information booth, with one significant artifact, a portable wooden toilet, unfortunately not indigenous to jail, or for use by tourists. However North America's Smallest Jailhouse is worth a stopover, just to say you've been there, and that you've done time in a town called Tweed.

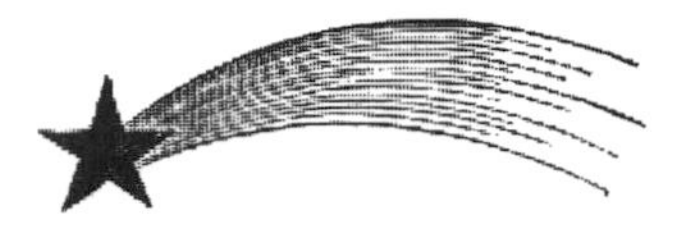

North American Black Historical Museum and Cultural Centre

- 277 King Street, Amherstburg, Ontario, N9V 2Z2
- (519) 736-5433
- Open April – November, Wednesday – Friday, 10:00 – 5:00; Saturday and Sunday, 1:00 – 5:00
- Admission fee

Amherstburg and surrounding Essex County were part of the "Underground Railroad" used in the late 18th- and early 19th-centuries by American slaves seeking freedom in Canada. This makes the town a fitting place for the North American Black Historical Museum and Cultural Centre, which chronicles and pays tribute to the black people who managed to escape to Canada, and the subsequent black culture of Essex County. The idea for a museum came about in 1964 with a man called Melvin Simpson whose vision, according to the museum, "was one of understanding and of taking great pride in knowing the history of our forefathers. Helping future generations to keep alive the dignity, strength and purpose of being that was so much a part of our past history still has an important influence on us today." The museum exhibits relevant artifacts, photographs, documents, and interpretive text and provides cultural facilities. These include the Cultural Centre on the second floor, and future plans involve the restoration of an important log house and church, the latter as "a shrine in the memory of all slaves who came to Canada seeking a better life." The Museum is also part of a self-guided tour of sites important to the Underground Railroad, information about which can be picked up at the museum.

Museum of the North American Indian Travelling College

* R.R. 3, Cornwall Island, Ontario, K6H 5R7
  LOCATION: Cornwall Island
* (613) 932-9452
* Open weekdays, 8:00 – 4:00
* Admission fee

The North American Indian Travelling College is located at the Mohawk Nation Reserve on the St. Lawrence River; it is called a "travelling college" because of the role it plays in fostering understanding and communication between different Native and non-Native groups. Outreach programs include speakers and a dance troupe who visit other First Nation reserves, schools, conferences, and various organizations. An Indian Village, also on the site, recreates traditional First Nations dwellings, and depicts the lifestyles of Cree, Ojibwa, and Iroquois peoples around the early 1700s. The Log Cabin building is home to a museum featuring Cree, Ojibwa, and Iroquois artifacts, and is also set up to teach visitors about the lifestyle of these peoples. Tours can be arranged by appointment. In the Log Cabin is the Craftshop, which gives visitors a chance to purchase Iroquois arts, crafts, and various publications.

NORTH BAY MODEL RAILROAD DISPLAY

- c/o North Bay Chamber of Commerce, P.O. Box 747, North Bay, Ontario, P1B 8J8
  LOCATION: Seymour Street at Highway 11
- (705) 472-8480
- Open summers only, call for hours
- Admission fee

The North Bay Model Railroad Club is an association of model railroad enthusiasts from all walks of life, centred in and around the North Bay area. Twenty-seven Club members, from teens to seniors, have set up a model railroad display in two refurbished green boxcars outside the North Bay Information Booth to illustrate Northern Ontario railway heritage. It encompasses area geography, transportation, trade, colonization, and industry, and features the Ontario Northland Railway, CN Rail, and CP Rail. A guide stands at the door to answer questions and help interpret the display which starts with a modern, urban rail yard, and rolls through history via rugged terrain, lakes, the era of mining, colonization, the 1800s and rock-cutting for the railways, lumber history, and ends with the romantic age of steam. Covering over ninety metres of track, it's a fun trip through time.

North Himsworth Museum

* 107 Lansdowne Street, Callander, Ontario, POH 1HO
* (705) 752-2282
* Hours are seasonal
* Admission fee

The North Himsworth Museum, a delightful seven-room building, was the home and medical office from 1914 to 1943 to a big celebrity: Dr. Allan R. Dafoe, the doctor of the famous Dionne Quints, known by the Ontario quintuplets' fans as the "Little Doc." The museum features Dafoe's medical texts, furniture, and personal effects. Best of all, it also houses a terrific selection of Quints memorabilia, including hundreds of original photos and some of the girls' clothing worn from infancy to early adulthood, all highly sought after by collectors of Quints trivia. The museum also has an Olde Tyme Barber Shop, with barbering artifacts from the last century, as well as displays on logging, sawmills, boats, and local history. Definitely worth a visit while in Callander.

Northwestern Ontario Sports Hall of Fame and Museum

- 435 Balmoral Street, Thunder Bay, Ontario, P7C 5N4
- (807) 622-2852
- Open year-round, weekdays, 10:00 – 4:30; Sundays 1:00 – 4:00
- Free admission

The Northwestern Ontario Sports Hall of Fame and Museum was established in 1978 to preserve, collect, and display the sporting heritage of Northwestern Ontario. The institution is an active one, educating the public and preserving memories, as well as inducting people yearly into the Hall of Fame. Athletes, Teams, and Builders are all recognized and the choice of Famers is made through the endorsement of citizens in Northwestern Ontario communities. An induction dinner is held annually in the fall. Display galleries feature photos, trophies, and memorabilia, along with profiles of key players, and tours and educational programs for different age and interest levels are offered. A library and archives are available for research, and gifts and souvenirs can be purchased on the premises.

Nor'Westers and Loyalist Museum

* P.O. Box 69, Williamstown, Glengarry, Ontario, KOC 2J0
  LOCATION: Off the 401, county road 19
* (613) 347-3547
* Open Victoria Day – Labour Day, weekdays, 1:30 – 5:30; Saturdays and Holidays, 10:30 – 5:30; Labour Day – Thanksgiving, weekends only
* Admission fee

Williamstown was founded in 1784 by United Empire Loyalists, many of whom joined the North West Company, at that time a competitor in the fur trade with the Hudson's Bay Company. Both companies played a tremendous part in exploring and developing Western Canada and several key historical figures came from Glengarry. These included David Thompson, who produced significant maps of North Western Canada, and Simon Fraser, whose exploration of the river that still bears his name secured British Columbia for the North West Company and for the Crown. The Nor' Westers and Loyalist Museum, founded in 1967, is housed in an old schoolhouse, *circa* 1860. The collection includes personal effects of many Glengarry area Loyalists, such as a bible, tea cups, snowshoes, trade items, guns, documents, portraits, letters and one of Thompson's precious maps. The museum also has a gallery for temporary exhibits. A brochure for a self-guided walking tour, available at the museum, will facilitate exploration of the rest of Williamstown.

Norwich and District Museum

- R.R. 3, Norwich Ontario, NOJ 1PO
  LOCATION: Stover Street North, Norwich
- (519) 863-3101
- Open late April – early December, Tuesday – Friday, 1:00 – 4:00, Sunday 1:30 – 4:30 and by appointment; July and August, Tuesday – Friday 10:00 – 4:00, Sunday 1:30 – 4:30 and by appointment
- Admission fee

Norwich Township was once home to many Quaker communities, and the Friends are still an important element of Norwich life. Reflecting this, the Norwich and District Museum is located in an 1889 Quaker Meeting House and features displays on the Quakers, as well as the pioneer heritage of the area. Period rooms and a general store recreate local history and a two-storey barn on the site focuses on local agricultural history, including farming tools and machines, and a new dairy exhibit with mural dioramas. Displays on blacksmithing, woodworking and broommaking can also be enjoyed and a "saltbox" building, currently under restoration, will become part of the museum complex in the future. Tours and educational programs are offered by appointment. The museum is also affiliated with the Norwich and District Archives which will be of interest to researchers and genealogists.

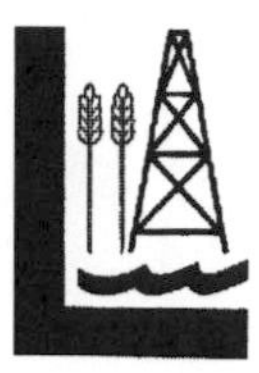

OIL MUSEUM OF CANADA

* Oil Springs, Kelly Road, R.R. 2, Ontario, NON 1PO
  LOCATION: 1.5 kilometres south of Main Street and .5 kilometres east of Highway 21
* (519) 834-2840
* Open daily, May 1 – October 31, 10:00 – 5:00 daily; open year round for booked tours
* Admission fee

The Oil Museum of Canada marks the site of the first commercial oil well in North America. Originally owned by two brothers who are remembered as the creators of asphalt, in the mid-1850s the land was sold to James Miller Williams, who began sinking his own wells and refining illuminating oil. Business went well, and a man named Hugh Nixon Shaw later drilled deep enough to produce the world's first "oil gusher." After this Oil Springs boomed, and became the first town in the world to have a totally kerosene-lighted main road. Products and technology first developed in Oil Springs are still in use today worldwide. Inside the modern Oil Museum of Canada building are truly fascinating exhibits tracing the history of oil from its geological formation to modern refining and byproducts from chewing gum to panty hose. On the grounds are a reconstruction of the first well and other early wells in working order. Tours are offered all year, as well as a self-guided driving tour of the Oil Heritage District involving a brochure and audio tapes. The tour starts with the museum and follows a receiving station, holding tanks, "jerker lines," the location of the Shaw "gusher," a machine shop and other sites of technological and historical significance.

The Old Courthouse and First Hussars Museum

- 399 Ridout Street North, London, Ontario
- (519) 434-7321 Courthouse, or (519) 471-1538 Museum
- Hours, tours are seasonal
- Free admission, donations accepted

London's Old Courthouse is the oldest surviving public building in the city of London. Built in the mid-19th century it functioned as the district court offices, courthouse and jail, and today still contains the offices for the counties of Elgin and Middlesex. Resembling a castle, the Old Courthouse is thought to have been modelled on the original English castle home of Colonel Talbot, who settled the counties. Now a National Historic Site, the facade and many other areas of the courthouse have been restored to period. The First Hussars Museum is located inside the Old Courthouse, and is intended as a tribute to the First Hussars Regiment. The Regiment was initiated in 1856 as the First London Volunteer Troop of Cavalry, and became the First Hussars in 1892. They have served in the Boer War, World Wars I and II and others, and are the sister regiment of the Prince of Wales' own Royal Hussars in the U.K. The museum includes a small collection of regimental and other military artifacts including documents, uniforms, photographs and medals. A collection of regimental film footage dating back to the 1930s is available on video and a small diorama of a tank battle *circa* 1944 can also be viewed. Tours of both the Old Courthouse and the museum are offered throughout the year by appointment.

Old Fort William

- Vickers Heights Post Office, Thunder Bay, Ontario, POT 2ZO
  LOCATION: Broadway Avenue, off Highway 61 S
- (807) 577-8461
- Hours and times are seasonal
- Admission fee

The original Fort William was built in the mid 1680s, and had three main eras. As Grand Portage under the French regime, it was a meeting place in the fur trade between 1688 and 1760; then it became an important centre for the North West Company from 1801 – 1821; and for the Hudson's Bay Company between 1821 and 1880. The fort only saw action once, in 1816, as a result of the Seven Oaks Massacre and later became a fishing centre and a Jesuit mission before falling into ruin. With industrialization, a CP Railway yard was constructed over the original site. However, in 1973 the Ontario Government built an impressive reproduction of the fort, including 42 buildings on a 50 hectare site, which now functions as one grand living history museum, recreating the lively North West Company period between 1801 and 1821. Famous for its lively recreations, realistic staff and attention to detail it offers trade shops, a farm and dairy, a naval yard, jail, hospital, First Nations encampment, an area where large cargo birchbark canoes are made and many other sights. Hobnobbing with "Pork Eaters," Native North Americans, bakers, traders and candlestick makers is encouraged, and demonstrations of breadmaking, dancing and musket firing are held regularly. Educational programs, special events and the Great Rendezvous summer bash can be enjoyed yearly. Gift shop and Canteen on the premises.

Ontario Agricultural Museum

* P.O. Box 38, Milton, Ontario, L9T 2Y3
  LOCATION: off Highway 401 at exit 320B, then north on Highway 25
* (905) 878-8151
* Open mid-May to mid-September, 10:00 – 5:00
* Admission fee

The Ontario Agricultural Museum's aim is "to stimulate awareness of Ontario's agriculture and food system and to preserve its heritage." The site holds approximately 30 buildings, grouped according to three heritage themes: Farmsteads of different periods and all they entail; Crossroads Communities, reflecting services available to Ontario residents in the past, such as a school, harness shop and church; and Display Buildings, presenting artifacts and equipment for various agricultural industries, like a pump works and drainage display. The museum and its interpretive staff convey the evolution of agriculture and rural life in Ontario. A 32-hectare expanse of old-time country living, mud, dirt, animals and all, means visitors should dress comfortably and appropriately. The site includes picnic facilities, transportation, catering facilities and a gift shop. Plenty of exciting special events are held year-round, among them a corn festival, tractor parades and Dairy Days.

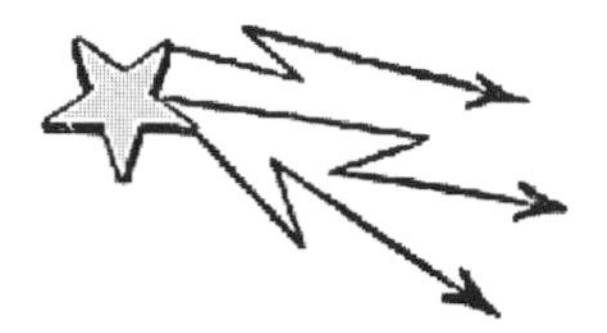

Ontario Hydro Energy Information Centres

* PICKERING: P.O. Box 160, Pickering, Ontario, L1V 2R5
  (905) 839-0465
* BRUCE: Box 1540, Tiverton, Ontario, N0G 2T0
  (519) 368-TOUR
* ROBERT H. SAUNDERS: Box 999, Cornwall, Ontario, K6H 5V1
  (613) 938-1518
* DARLINGTON: Box 1000, Bowmanville, Ontario, L1C 3W2
  (905) 623-7122
* For overall information, call Ontario Hydro at
  1-800-263-9000

To promote understanding of nuclear power and create good public relations, Ontario Hydro has set up Education Centres in four of its nuclear power stations. The Pickering Station offers a life-sized walk-in cutaway model of a CANDU reactor, hands-on exhibits, films, displays, and other models. The Bruce Development is one of the largest nuclear power centres in the world, and its Education Centre features an animated model of the station, and a special exhibit on Fission/Radiation Shielding. The huge Robert H. Saunders Station is one of North America's first and largest international stations, and the info Centre provides a spectacular view of the project. The Darlington Station has a reference area on nuclear power and the environment, fuel storage and economics, and exhibits on the history of the project and of electricity in Ontario. All the centres show films, have picnic facilities and are free of charge. Hours and schedules are seasonal and vary according to each station.

ONTARIO PARLIAMENT BUILDINGS

- Interparliamentary and Public Relations Branch, Queen's Park, Toronto, Ontario, M7A 1A2
- (416) 325-7500
- Tours by appointment, regular business hours for self-guided viewing
- Free admission

Ontario's impressive pinkish-brown sandstone Legislative Building was erected between 1886 and 1892, and is known today as simply "Queen's Park." The building, constructed in the Victorian Romanesque style, is a wonderful showpiece of intricate stonework, surrounded by grounds inhabited by statues and monuments of famous figures in Canadian history, including Queen Victoria and John Graves Simcoe. Inside the building 130 elected members of the Provincial Parliament make important decisions regarding Ontario, provincial government workers keep the province in order and there is a suite used by the Lieutenant Governor. Portraits, paintings, carvings, landscapes, mineral exhibits, statuary and other works of art throughout the building commemorate Canadian and Ontario political history. Temporary displays of artifacts from local museums and societies relevant to Ontario history are also featured. Free tours, by reservation, will explain how Parliament works, and seats in the public gallery when the Legislative Assembly is in session are offered by reservation. There is also a gift shop on the premises which features items uniquely Ontarian.

Ontario Centre for Puppetry Arts

* 116 Cornelius Parkway, North York Ontario, M6L 2K5
* (416) 246-9222
* Hours, admission fee to be determined

Puppetry is a centuries old, universal art form used as a medium to convey important information, ideas, or histories and, of course, to delight and entertain. The making of puppets, sets, costumes, storylines, sound effects, and animating the final product are only a few of the elements of this unique art form. Set up by the Ontario Puppetry Association, an organization consisting of several puppetry guilds across Ontario to promote puppetry, the Centre for Puppetry Arts functions as a training and professional development centre for puppeteers, as a display and educational facility, and a place to hold performances, educational programs, workshops and special events. The Centre for Puppetry Arts was also home to a museum collection of more than 700 wild, wicked, woolly and wonderful puppets in all sizes and shapes, mostly from the 20th century and from all over the world until recently, when the Centre donated the entire collection to the Museum of Civilization. The Centre has been moving quite frequently in the last few years, and will take a while to get back on its feet; when it does, it plans occasionally to stage small temporary exhibitions of works by Canadian puppeteers.

Ontario Science Centre

* 770 Don Mills Road, Don Mills, Ontario, M3C IT3
  LOCATION: Don Mills Road and Eglinton Avenue East
* (416) 696-3127
* Open daily, 10:00 – 6:00; Fridays, 10:00 – 9:00
* Admission fee

Since 1969 the Ontario Science Centre has been living out its mandate to "display science and technology in all its forms and to interpret the relevance and relationship of diverse or unfamiliar areas of society." Certainly, with more than two dozen live presentations, over 40 mini-theatres, knowledgeable guide-"hosts," a large auditorium, a science arcade, and more than 650 exhibits on space, earth, food, the atom, technology, transportation, matter, energy and change, the environment, fashion and the body, and Canadian resources, to name a few, how could they go wrong? Visitors can see, hear, and do a multitude of fun and educational things, like watching a laser burn a hole through a brick, finding out what a fractal looks like, viewing a 180-year-old computer, and seeing illusions, resolving confusions, and coming to all kinds of scientific conclusions. Special exhibitions, such as the memorable *Mindworks*, bring with them lecture series, special events, and interesting merchandise. There are also places to eat, a great gift shop, and first aid facilities. The Ontario Science Centre is living proof that learning can be fun!

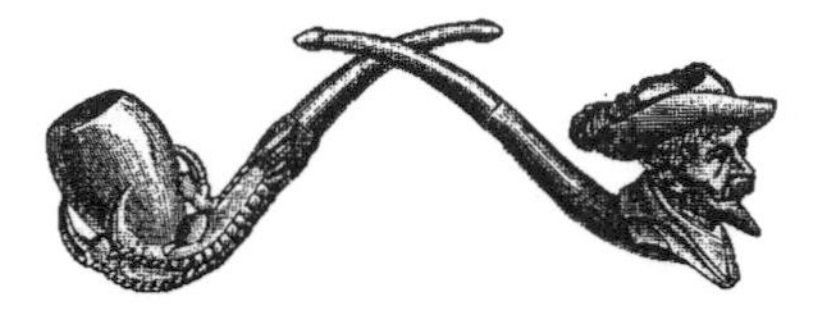

Ontario Tobacco Museum and Heritage Centre

* P.O. Box 182, Delhi, Ontario, N4B 2W9
  LOCATION: 200 Talbot Road (Highway 3), Delhi
* (519) 582-0278
* Open May – October, daily, 10:00 – 4:00; November – April, Monday – Friday, 10:00 – 4:00
* Admission fee

The tobacco industry has always been important to the culturally diverse town of Delhi, Ontario, and the Ontario Tobacco Museum and Heritage Centre was set up to preserve and interpret its provincial and national importance. At present the future of the museum is a little smoky, and it may be undergoing some physical and thematic changes in the future, but for now exhibits follow the tobacco plant's early beginnings in Native North American culture through to modern times. The cultural implications of tobacco, its uses, growing and curing, and other interesting topics are interpreted while tobacco industry equipment and tools, and a wide range of tobacco paraphernalia, like pipes, tobacco pouches, and an impressive collection of tobacco cards, make up the bulk of the artifacts displayed. When in season tobacco plants grow outside the museum so visitors can see them up close. Audio-visual presentations, tours, and educational programs and kits are offered, and there is a research library and gift shop on site.

Osborne Collection of Early Children's Books, Toronto Public Library

- Toronto Public Library, 40 St. George Street, Toronto, Ontario, M5S 2E4
  (Moving to 239 College Street, 4th floor, fall 1995)
- (416) 393-7753
- Open Monday – Friday, 10:00 – 6:00; Saturday, 9:00 – 5:00, closed Sundays
- Free admission

Ontario houses a little-known gem, the Osborne Collection of Early Children's Books, one of the world's pre-eminent collections of children's literature. According to the library, "the Osborne Collection encompasses the development of English children's literature, ranging from a fourteenth-century manuscript of Aesop's fables, through fifteenth-century traditional tales, sixteenth-century school texts and courtesy books, godly Puritan works, eighteenth-century chapbooks, moral tales and rational recreations, Victorian classics of fantasy, adventure and school stories, up to 1910 – the end of the Edwardian era." The first books were donated by English librarian Edgar Osborne in 1949, but since that time the collection has grown in size and reputation, although it is perhaps better known by international scholars than by Ontario residents. Highlights include Florence Nightingale's childhood books, and what is believed to be the original, handwritten, and illustrated version of *Goldilocks and the Three Bears*, in which Goldilocks is an old woman.

OSHAWA AERONAUTICAL, MILITARY AND INDUSTRIAL MUSEUM

- Oshawa Airport, 1000 Stevenson Road North, Oshawa, Ontario, L1P 5P5
- (905) 728-6199
- Open Easter – November 31, Tuesday – Saturday 12:00 – 5:00, Sunday 1:00 – 5:00
- Admission fee

The Oshawa Aeronautical, Military and Industrial Museum considers itself a "living, changing collection of military, industrial and aeronautical memorabilia from the war periods of our history." In other words, it serves to preserve, display, document, and interpret all aspects of Canada's military history, on air, land, and sea, with a particular focus on the Ontario Regiment, who date back to the 1850s, the role of General Motors of Canada Limited, and other local industries who contributed to the war effort. The museum is located at the Oshawa Airport, which was an important training site for Allied flyers during World War II, and was also a dropping-off point for trainees of Camp X, once a top secret spy school. Ian Fleming, the creator of James Bond, trained there. Uniforms, weapons, medals, badges, photos, memorabilia, and vehicles, many in working order, are displayed, including a fully restored Ferret scout car. The museum is completely volunteer run, and thousands of hours and elbow grease have gone into raising funds, collecting, preserving, and displaying artifacts, and getting the whole museum moving.

Owen Sound Marine & Rail Museum

- 1165 – 1st Avenue West, Owen Sound, Ontario, N4K 4K8
- (519) 371-3333
- Open June – September, Tuesday – Saturday, 10:00 – 4:30 (closed between 12:00 and 1:00); Sundays, 1:00 – 4:30, June – August
- Admission by donation

At the turn of the century, Owen Sound was a thriving port and the terminal area for two railways. The Owen Sound Marine & Rail Museum, operated by the Owen Sound Historical Society, stands as a living memory of these times. Appropriately located in a former Canadian National Railway station, the museum features scaled-down replicas of ships once seen in the area, railway artifacts and models, a lifeboat from the *Paul Evans*, various canoes and the *Tug Ancaster*, built in Owen Sound and featured on the back of the old one-dollar bill. There are also mounted photographs, marine and railway uniforms, wheels, lanterns, tools, propellers, charts, timetables, house flags, and many other objects of local historical relevance. Library facilities are available, tours can be arranged by appointment, and there is a gift shop on the premises.

Perth Museum

- c/o 80 Gore Street East, Perth, Ontario, K7H 1H9
  LOCATION: Matheson House, 11 Gore Street, Perth, Ontario
- (613) 267-1947
- Open Monday – Saturday, 10:00 – 5:00, Sunday 1:00 – 4:00
- Admission fee

Visitors to Perth may be perplexed by the large, yellow, cylindrical structure used as the town's information booth. Fact is, it's supposed to look like a giant cheese. Perth's claim to fame in the late 19th century was the production of what was then the world's largest cheddar, weighing 9,900 kg. The cheese was exhibited in Europe and the U.S. where it made an appearance at the Chicago World's Fair in 1893. (The town of Ingersoll also made a Mammoth Cheese 27 years earlier with a similar story, but it was just a chip off Perth's Behemoth block.) Today, the only glory left for the king of cheeses is a little display upstairs in the Perth Museum where a few newspaper clippings and photos are displayed, along with a vial containing a shrivelled piece of the original cheddar. The rest of the Perth Museum is delightful, featuring a fun second floor with Victorian artifacts like glove stretchers and jewellery made from a man's beard. Downstairs are restored rooms and special exhibits in the new Inderwick Wing. Guided tours are offered and there is a gift counter. The Perth Museum is located in a lovely 1840 stone house that once belonged to Senator Roderick Matheson, himself a big cheese.

Peter A. Nichol Driftwood Museum

* Rolphton, Ontario, K0J 2H0
  LOCATION: Rolphton, Moore Lake Road, off Highway 17, 15 kilometres west of Deep River
* (613) 586-2247
* Open daily, 10:00 – 8:00
* Free admission

Peter A. Nichol was born in Slavgorod, Russia, and moved to Canada when he was eleven. Here he worked making furniture, as a machinist, and in various other occupations, before he discovered his talent for transforming pieces of driftwood into works of art. He and his wife ran the Peter A. Nichol Driftwood Museum together for several years, promoting driftwood sculpting as a uniquely Canadian artform. Peter died in 1985, and Margery, his widow, continues to run what she calls the "new wave" museum. This is located in an old schoolhouse, which showcases 500 of Nichol's sculptures, as well as the work of about 40 local artisans. Nichol looked for driftwood, the eroded trunk and root system of old trees, along the Ottawa River, chose pieces according to their beauty or suggested imagery, and enhanced them through sanding, carving, and finishing. His work has been displayed in Europe and parts of Canada, and pieces are owned by anthropologist Richard Leakey and entertainer Paul Anka.

PETROLIA DISCOVERY

* Box 1480, Petrolia, Ontario, NON 1RO
  LOCATION: off the Blind Line, Petrolia, Ontario
* (519) 882-0897
* Open daily, first Saturday in May – Labour Day, 9:00 – 5:00; Labour Day – October 31, Monday – Friday, 8:30 – 4:30
* Admission fee

The Petrolia Discovery describes itself as "a field of 150 hectares . . . set aside as a living museum, a major historic, recreational and educational exhibit." The first commercial oil well and the first oil "gusher" were discovered in nearby Oil Springs, but Petrolia really enjoyed the early oil "boom." "Black gold" is still being extracted from local fields, as it was a century before, and many buildings and artifacts used in production are displayed. The Petrolia Discovery includes either guided or self-directed tours of exhibits on Imperial Oil, once located in Petrolia, the boom town, oil equipment and technology, a "gum bed" of asphalt ponds, rigs, as well as photos and films. Much of the Discovery's focus is on the many men who were pioneers in the oil industry, who both came from and travelled the world over with their oil technology and expertise. These men discovered and refined the extraction and use of oil, creating the basis for much of today's oil technology. Information and brochures are available for a driving tour of the Oil Heritage District, which covers an impressive range of oil interests, including Oil Springs and the Oil Museum of Canada.

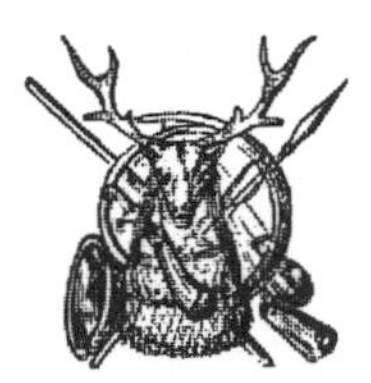

Phil Copp's Canadian Wilderness Trading Post and Wildlife Museum

- Highway 60, Dwight, Ontario, P0A 1H0
- (705) 635-2521
- Open May – Thanksgiving, 9:00 – 9:00
- Free admission

Phil Copp's Wilderness Trading Post is a rather typical tourist supply complex, conveniently located on the "gateway to Algonquin Park." It sells pine furniture, aboriginal- and pioneer-style crafts, furs, Hudson Bay items, cottage-style decorations, clothing and jewellery, t-shirts, candy, and lots of souvenir mugs and spoons. The post also does canoe outfitting, and is home to the "Hungry Bear" takeout. Phil Copp is a U.S. native who spends his spare time travelling, hunting, and gathering. He has been to Alaska, Australia, New Zealand, Hawaii, and Africa fulfilling his lifelong hunting passion and has even won the World's Championship for cat hunting. His "museum," which lines the walls of the two main shops, displays over 60 stuffed animals, including bobcats, goats, big-horned sheep, birds, wolves, and an enormous polar bear along with artifacts like spearheads and animal skulls. The slightly ramshackle exhibition is reminiscent of a gentleman's cabinet of curiosities, and descriptive cards accompany many of the items. Behind the buildings younger visitors will enjoy "Old MacDonald's Farm," a little farm-zoo with a small number of geese, ducks, sheep, and bunnies. Worth a peek while buying supplies on the way to Algonquin Park.

Pickering Museum Village

* c/o Town of Pickering, One The Esplanade, Pickering, Ontario, L1V 6K7
  LOCATION: 3 kilometres east of Brock Road on Highway 7, at the Village of Greenwood
* (905) 683-8401 or (905) 420-4620
* Open June – September, weekends and holidays, 11:00 – 5:00; July and August, Wednesday – Sunday, 11:00 – 5:00
* Admission fee

A heritage project of the Town of Pickering, the Pickering Museum Village resides on the banks of Duffin's Creek in the Village of Greenwood and recreates life of the previous century in Durham Region. A variety of buildings from the 1830s to the early 20th century, staffed by costumed guides, include a church, blacksmith shop, harness shop, the Brougham Central Hotel, a log barn, and more. Early farm equipment, mills, tractors, and other machinery and tools *circa* 1890-1930 help animate early trades and rural life. The Village also has an effective school "outreach" program, including demonstrations on early woollen textiles and "Christmas Past," and holds special events during the period between May and September. Gift shop and picnic grounds on site.

Port Burwell Marine Museum and Lighthouse

- 21 Pitt Street, Port Burwell, Ontario, N0J 1T0
- (519) 874-4343
- Open daily, July and August, 10:00 – 5:00; weekends or by appointment in June
- Admission fee

Port Burwell's Marine Museum exhibits marine artifacts from the Great Lakes, including a very fine collection of lighthouse lenses, as well as domestic and commercial items representative of the area's early history. Across the street is Canada's oldest wooden lighthouse, built in 1840. The lighthouse was restored in 1988 and, in addition to being a tourist attraction, acts as the town's symbol and information office. Brochures for self-guided historic walking tours of Port Burwell are available at both locations. This includes a scenic tour of a ship-building site, two churches, and several buildings of local importance. Port Burwell is located on Lake Erie, and offers sandy beaches, sand hills, great fishing, and "pick your own" fruit farms.

Port Colborne Historical and Marine Museum

* 280 King Street, P.O. Box 572, Port Colborne, Ontario, L3K 5X8
* (905) 834-7604
* Open daily, May – December, 12:00 – 5:00
* Free admission

The Port Colborne Historical and Marine Museum is a delightful complex of seven historical buildings that interpret and preserve local and marine history. A Georgian Revival home and carriage house sheltering a horse-drawn carriage, a wheelhouse, log schoolhouse *circa* 1835, log house *circa* 1850, blacksmith shop, and a tea room are all located on the grounds. An anchor, weighing 2.3 tonnes, from the propeller ship *Raleigh*, which sank locally in the late 19th century, is also set out for viewing, along with a 50-passenger lifeboat from the S.S. *Hochelaga, circa* 1850. Marine and local history artifacts are featured mostly in the Williams House Museum, including interactive displays and a permanent exhibition on "Who Built the Welland Canal." Arabella's Tea Room offers delicious teas between 2:00 and 4:00 every day from June to September, and is staffed by volunteers in period costume.

Prehistoric World

- Morrisburg, Ontario, K0C 1X0
  LOCATION: Upper Canada Road, Exit 758 from Highway 410
- (613) 543-2503
- Open daily, late May – Labour Day weekend, 10:00 – 4:00
- Admission fee

Stepping into Prehistoric World is like walking back in time thousands of years, and the park is full of dinosaurs. The site's one kilometre nature trail displays some 40 life-sized sculptures representing prehistoric animal evolution from the Paleozoic through the Jurassic and Cretaceous to the Cenozoic and the Quaternary periods. Visitors will see full-sized reproductions of dinosaurs and other prehistoric animals, the largest of which weighs 36.3 tonnes, staged in a natural setting. Highlights include a woolly mammoth, a Canadian duck-billed hadrosaur, a triceratops, a dinornis maximus, and a fossil-pit. New creatures are constantly being added, the construction of which is fascinating in its own right. Combining education, exercise, fresh air, and fun, Prehistoric World is a great place for school and family trips, and is the closest thing Ontario will ever get to Jurassic Park.

Pump House Steam Museum

* 23 Ontario Street, Kingston, Ontario, K7L 2Y2
* (613) 546-4696 or (613) 542-2261
* Open daily, June 1 – Labour Day, 10:00 – 5:00
* Admission fee

The Pump House Steam Museum will take visitors back to a time when steam power was considered the height of technology. Located in a waterworks station that began catering to Kingston residents in the mid 19th century, the museum still has two of its three original pumps. The building became a museum in 1973 after being restored by the Frontenac Society of Model Engineers and donated to the city. In addition to the original steam pumping engines, many smaller steam-powered engines from the Victorian and Edwardian eras are featured, including both models and originals. Engines from canning factories, knitting machines, and steamboats can be seen, along with a big "O" gauge railway. Photographs and illustrative text put the history and function of the engines in context. Tours can be arranged by appointment and a few items are available for purchase.

QUEEN'S YORK RANGERS MUSEUM

* Fort York Armoury, 660 Fleet Street West, Toronto, Ontario, M5E 1A3
* (416) 973-3265
* Open Wednesday evenings or by appointment
* Free admission

The Queen's York Rangers are one of Canada's oldest and most interesting regiments, going back to Robert Rogers' Rangers, during the Seven Years War of 1756-1763. As the Queen's Rangers they helped to distinguish themselves in the Battle of Brandywine. Later John Graves Simcoe brought his Queen's Rangers to Upper Canada in 1792, when the Rangers began cutting Toronto streets, like Yonge and Dundas, out of forest land. Many of the Rangers served in the militia, first in the War of 1812, and in 1866, the 12th York Rangers were formed, serving in World War I, and in 1936 became the Queen's York Rangers, who served in World War II. The regiment is still going strong, and has put the word "ranger" into common use. The small museum, housed in the Fort York Armoury would benefit from funding, but is jam-packed with significant artifacts, papers, and photographs. Documents signed by Simcoe, paintings owned by his wife, the original colours carried by Simcoe's Rangers in the late 1700s, and a new guidon recently presented to the Rangers by Queen Elizabeth are just a few of the gems available for viewing.

Quinte Educational Museum and Archives

- Box 220, Bloomfield, Ontario, KOK 1GO
  LOCATION: 1 Stanley Street, Bloomfield
- July and August, (613) 393-1427, off season, (613) 393-2869
- Open Tuesday – Saturday, 10:00 – 4:00, Sundays, 1:00 – 4:00
- Admission fee

The Quinte Educational Museum and Archives is an interesting facility set up to preserve the history of the one-room schoolhouse in which it is located, and education in the area at the turn of the century, representative of much rural education of the period across Ontario. About 10,000 educational artifacts and archival materials constitute the collection, including slates, desks, books, documents, and lots of old photographs. Slides and tapes can be viewed in the museum, which also mounts a special summer exhibition at the local "Educentre," letting visitors write with a quill pen, use a slate, work with dough, and participate in other fun activities reminiscent of education during the early part of this century. The local branch of the Ontario Genealogical Society also shares the museum and archival space, and will help interested researchers trace Prince Edward County genealogical history.

Redpath Sugar Museum

* 95 Queen's Quay East, Toronto, Ontario, M5E 1A3
* (416) 366-3561
* Monday – Friday, 10:00 – 3:30, closed noon – 1:00
* Free admission, tours by appointment, check with guard at the gates

Located behind the Redpath Sugar Refinery on Queen's Quay East in Toronto is a sweet little museum dedicated to the history of the Redpath family and company, and to the past and present manufacture and use of sugar. The museum is crystal-shaped inside, and painted gold, to represent a grain of raw sugar. The front area holds a theatre where groups can watch a film called "Raising Cane," and see displays on the sugar refining process. Next is a sugary variety of products from the old-fashioned cone-shaped sugar-loaf, through a delightful collection of fancy sugar cubes, to modern products like Nutra-Sweet™. Elegant implements like sugar loaf nippers, spoons, and crystal bowls, as well as industry tools, machinery, and important buildings, ships, and cane fields are shown through photographic displays. The Redpath family and the Redpath Sugar Company have played a significant part in Canadian history, and displays of family furniture, portraiture, uniforms, books, and documents clearly demonstrate this role. A delightful tribute to something we all know and love, The Redpath Sugar Museum will appeal to all age groups.

Reid and Campbell Collection

* 2013 Yonge Street, Toronto, Ontario, M4S 1Z8
* (416) 483-3553
* Open Monday – Friday, 9:00 – 6:00, Saturday 9:00 – 5:00
* Free admission

Located on the second floor of The Reid and Campbell Limited stereo shop is a wonderful private collection of audio-visual artifacts mostly sold in Canada since 1933, when the shop first opened, although there are earlier items. The owners, Peter Campbell and Keith Maitland, began holding on to interesting pieces of audio-visual equipment they sold in their shop when they realized how quickly technology changed. They continued to collect privately until they decided, for their 60th anniversary, to showcase the collection temporarily in the store. Gems include a 10" RCA blonde cabinet TV from 1947, an old Edison phonograph with wax cylinders *circa* 1915, and an enormous early cassette tape from the 1960s. Other early TVs, radios, cassette players, phonographs, and combination units are included, with descriptive labels and photographs to pan out their history and progress. Housed in a functioning shop, the collection, boasting many lovely wooden items with sculptural shapes and simple technology, is an interesting contrast to the rest of the sleek, plastic, high-tech items. The collection is not large, but it does take up a lot of shop space and is only staged occasionally, so make sure to call before making a visit.

Rideau Canal Museum

* 34 Beckwith Street, Smiths Falls, Ontario, K7A 2A8
* (613) 284-0505
* Open May 1 – October 31, Tuesday – Saturday, 10:00 – 5:00, Sunday 12:00 – 5:00; mid-June – early September, daily 10:00 – 7:00; by appointment only November – April
* Admission fee

The 202-kilometre Rideau Canal consists of a series of lakes, rivers, and canal cuts between Kingston and Ottawa, and boasts twenty-four lockstations, most of which are still hand-operated. Construction of the canal, which was intended as a wartime supply route, started after the War of 1812 and completed in 1832, an incredible engineering feat of the last century. Through its long history the canal has served more as a commercial supply and recreational boating facility than a military route, and in the winter it becomes the world's longest skating rink. Several historic sites, exhibits, restored buildings, trails, and programs can be found along its banks, with the Rideau Canal Museum being the most comprehensive of these attractions. This impressive museum is located in a mill complex dating from 1840-1899, canalside at Smiths Falls, and includes five floors. The entrance of the museum is lit up with seventy-two backlit transparencies of the canal, and upstairs the innovative "Tunnel of History" follows the canal's geological, pre-European, and settlement history through the use of dioramas. Fun, lively interactive and computerized displays and a great selection of artifacts, documents, and photographs will give visitors an overview and a new respect for the Rideau Canal and those who conceived, built, used, and still run it today.

Ripley's — Believe It or Not!™

RIPLEY'S BELIEVE IT OR NOT! MUSEUM

* 4960 Clifton Hill, Niagara Falls, Ontario, L2G 3N4
* (905) 356-2238
* Open daily, April – October, 9:00 a.m. – midnight; 10:00 – 5:00 rest of year
* Admission fee

Your mind will boggle at Ripley's Believe It or Not! Museum, a shrine to human extremes and weirdness, and a monument to morbid curiosity. The museum is chock-full of bizarre and occasionally disgusting artifacts collected by America's "modern Marco Polo," Robert Ripley. Shrunken heads, recreations of the world's funniest and weirdest epitaphs, human anomalies, enormous and tiny shoes, intricately carved grains of rice, two-headed calves, cars made out of matchsticks, a portrait of Queen Elizabeth I made out of dried beans, wreaths of human hair, medieval instruments of torture, the "Humbug-Major Sweet Machine" used in Disney's *Chitty Chitty Bang Bang*, enormous rolls of cigarette foil, miles-long chains of candy wrappers, tapestries made of the lint from clothes dryers, and the world's longest-lasting soap-on-a-rope, can all be looked at loud and clear. Perhaps most interesting are the videos and displays on Ripley's life and travels, and the history of *Ripley's Believe It or Not!* magazine, revealing a time when North America read about freakishness and extremes, instead of watching them on T.V. talk shows.

Robert Stuart Aviation Museum

- Oshawa Airport, Oshawa, Ontario, L1J 5P5
  LOCATION: Stevenson Road North, Oshawa
- (905) 728-1237
- Open weekdays, 1:00 – 9:00, Saturday and Sunday, 10:00 – 6:00
- Admission by donation

The Robert Stuart Aviation Museum is a private collection of primarily Canadian aviation memorabilia, with examples from all over the world, which has been set up in a Quonset Hut at the Oshawa Airport. Robert Stuart is a private collector and one-time airplane pilot who has always been fascinated by flying machines, and his collection is a result of over 40 years of accumulating artifacts. His museum features model planes, posters, engines, machinery, equipment, photographs, and uniforms. Also of interest is a special exhibit on Camp X, the now famous spy training school which was set up at the western limits of Oshawa during World War II. About 500 men were trained at the camp, including Ian Fleming, the creator of James Bond. As it was the drop-off point for Camp X trainees, the Oshawa Airport makes an interesting spot for the museum. Movies and tours are available by request.

Ron Morel Memorial Museum

* 88 Riverside Drive, Kapuskasing, Ontario, P5N 1B3
  LOCATION: Highway 11, along Millview Road
* (705) 335-5443 or 335-2341
* Open summer only, hours vary
* Admission fee

The Ron Morel Memorial Museum is housed inside two railway cars and a caboose, a fun place for a museum that focuses on the history of the railway and the town of Kapuskasing during the 19th and early 20th centuries. The museum includes a large HO scale model railway, railway memorabilia, a schoolroom display, special exhibits, and photographs of a prisoner-of-war camp that was located in Kapuskasing during World War II. The museum serves as a meeting house for railway and historical clubs, has a gift shop, and offers guided tours by appointment.

Royal Botanical Gardens

- P.O. Box 399, Hamilton, Ontario, L8N 3H8
  LOCATION: 680 Plains Road West, Burlington
- (905) 527-1158
- Open daily all year; outdoor garden areas, 9:30 – 6:00; Mediterranean garden, 9:00 – 5:00
- Admission fee

The breathtaking Royal Botanical Gardens is one of the world's biggest botanical gardens, consisting of 1,090 hectares of gardens and trails. It operates all year as an educational, social, and recreational institution. Grounds include the Rock Garden, Laking Garden, Arboretum, Mediterranean Garden, and Teaching Garden, where flowers, plants, trees, bulbs, annuals, medicinal plants, fruits, vegetables, herbs, and thousands and thousands of blossoms will delight every visitor. Tours, interpretive panels, and other teaching media provide information on plants and gardening. Beyond the gardens are 48 kilometres of trails, with many natural and man-made sights to enjoy. The Royal Botanical Gardens also offer over 100 courses yearly, hold delightful special events, have a reference library, and a lively membership and volunteer corps. There are restaurants and an art shop on site.

Royal Canadian Air Force Memorial Museum

* Canadian Forces Base Trenton, Astra, Ontario, KOK 1BO
* (613) 965-2140
* Open Monday – Thursday, 12:00 – 5:00 & 6:00 – 8:00, Friday, 12:00 – 5:00; June 1 – September 1, Saturday and Sunday, 10:00 – 5:00, in addition to regular hours
* Free admission

The Royal Canadian Air Force was begun in 1924 at Camp Borden, Ontario, but today CFB Trenton is considered the "Home of the RCAF," hence the RCAF Memorial Museum is located there. The purpose of the museum is to educate the public about the RCAF, and to pay tribute to those who served in the forces. Displays include selections of uniforms, equipment, photos, mementoes, flags, medals, posters, and other documents, and often focus on a particular squadron or aircraft type. Unfortunately, the museum is only floating in its present location, which appears to get smaller and smaller as new exhibits and artifacts are acquired and staged. Efforts are being made to raise one million dollars to erect a new, permanent and suitable site near the administration area at CFB Trenton. If all goes well, the new "modular concept" building will feature expandable exhibition space, external displays, and a memorial.

Royal Canadian Golf Association Museum and Golf Hall of Fame

* The Golf House, R.R. 2, Oakville, Ontario, L6J 4Z3
  LOCATION: Glenabbey Golf Course, Oakville
* (905) 849-9700
* Open Monday – Friday, 9:00 – 5:00, or by appointment
* Free admission

The Royal Canadian Golf Association Museum and Golf Hall of Fame is the home of Canada's distinguished golf heritage. The history of the game from its disputed beginnings to its present incarnation, with a focus on golf in Canada, is interpreted through artifacts, memorabilia, photographs, trophies, and equipment. The museum is located in a former Jesuit monastery and overlooks an impressive championship golf course designed by Jack Nicklaus. The Hall of Fame features outstanding men and women who have been players and builders in Canadian golf, such as George Lyon, who won the Olympic Trophy for Golf in 1904. Also on site are an archives and library, accessible by appointment only, which offer a comprehensive selection of golf-related subjects.

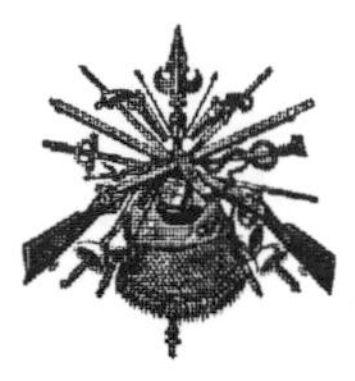

Royal Canadian Military Institute Museum & Library

- 426 University Avenue, Toronto, Ontario, M5G 1S9
- (416) 597-0286
- Museum open Monday – Friday, 9:30 – 5:30, by appointment only to non-club members; Library open 8:00 – 4:00
- Free admission

The Royal Canadian Military Institute is a long-established Toronto military club. It offers many exclusive features and rooms, one of which is the Royal Canadian Military Institute Museum. The museum has developed over the Institute's history since 1890, mostly through donations by members and their families. Artifacts from the North-West Rebellion, the South African War, World Wars I and II, the Korean War and recent peacekeeping operations include a chronologically arranged collection of small arms, ships badges, paintings, photographs, squadron badges and more from the Canadian Army, Navy, and Air Force. Most of the collection is in the museum area, although artifacts are displayed throughout the building. The Institute Library, open to researchers and club members, is one of the best small privately funded libraries in Canada, and contains an excellent collection of military books.

Royal Canadian Regiment Museum

- Wolseley Hall, Canadian Forces Detachment London, London, Ontario, N5Y 4T7
  LOCATION: corner of Oxford and Elizabeth Streets
- (519) 660-5102
- Open Tuesday – Friday, 10:00 – 4:00, Saturday and Sunday, 12:00 – 4:00
- Free admission

The Royal Canadian Regiment was established in 1883 and has participated in the North-West Rebellion, the South African and Korean Wars, and both World Wars. The two-storey, newly renovated Royal Canadian Regiment Museum is housed in Wolseley Hall, a National Historic Site, and is a memorial and display facility for events and artifacts of significance to the Regiment. The first floor has a library and the Regimental War Memorials and tributes, while the second floor features a comprehensive collection of regiment uniforms, weapons, documents, personal effects, equipment, medals, and captured enemy equipment. A mini-theatre, simulated trench-system and command post, and a diorama of the Boer War can also be examined. The museum also has a souvenir shop which offers military items like t-shirts, books, and stamps.

Royal Hamilton Light Infantry Heritage Museum

* Lieutenant-Colonel John Weir Foote, V.C., C.O. Armoury, 200 James Street North, Hamilton, Ontario, L8R 2L1
* (905) 528-2945
* Open Sundays, 1:00 – 4:00; group tours at other times by appointment
* Admission by donation

The Royal Hamilton Light Infantry was formed in 1862, originally as the XIII Battalion, Volunteer Militia of Canada, and served in whole or part in the Battle of Ridgeway in 1866, the Red River uprising of 1870, and other historically important Canadian conflicts, as well as World War II and the Boer War. The Royal Hamilton Light Infantry Museum was set up to preserve the heritage of the regiment, to distinguish its place in the development of Canada, as a tribute to those who have served the regiment through the years, and to attract new members. The museum has several rooms, all dedicated to key historical figures in the RHLI, such as the first commanding officer of the original regiment, the "unknown" soldier, a bandmaster, and the first curator of the museum. The collection includes weapons, uniforms, medals, posters and propaganda, photographs, paintings, military equipment, and other artifacts. The two Armoury buildings, one of which houses the museum, are interesting from a heritage perspective – the enormous South Drill hall is thought to be the largest building of its kind in Canada – and both have several ghost stories, including sightings of an unearthly sergeant who haunts the rifle range.

Royal Military College of Canada Museum

- Fort Frederick, Kingston, Ontario, K7K 5L0
  LOCATION: Highway 2, east of Kingston
- (613) 541-5010, ext. 6664
- Open daily, last weekend in June – Labour Day, 10:00 – 5:00
- Free admission

The Royal Military College of Canada was established in 1876 and is still in operation today. Fort Frederick, due to its long military history, was chosen as the site for the college, and Alexander Mackenzie, Prime Minister of Canada between 1873 and 1878, even worked as a stonemason on the fortifications before he went into politics. The Royal Military College Museum is located at Fort Frederick in one of Kingston's four Martello Towers, and has four floors. The lower has displays on the Royal Dockyard and the War of 1812; the main floor highlights the past and present functions and achievement of the college. The second floor features the Douglas Collection of historic weapons which was purchased from General Porfirio Diaz, former president of Mexico, and is thought to be one of the best in North America. The fourth floor contains a gun platform, which once had a removable roof. Many historical buildings can be seen beyond the museum walls, and the modern Royal Military College makes an interesting contrast and follow-up to the area's history.

ROM

ROYAL ONTARIO MUSEUM

* 100 Queen's Park, Toronto, Ontario, M5S 2C6
* 24 hour info line: (416) 586-5551, TDD (for the hearing impaired) (416) 586-5550, tour bookings, (416) 596-5572, programs, (416) 586-5797
* Open Tuesday – Saturday, 10:00 – 6:00, Sundays, 11:00 – 6:00, open to 8:00 Tuesday and Thursday, closed Monday except in summer and on school holidays
* Admission fee, free Tuesdays from 4:30 – 8:00, or all day for seniors

Since 1914, the Royal Ontario Museum has been the King of Canadian Museums, and is one of the few multi-discipline museums in the world. The addition of the McLaughlin Planetarium in 1968 and the George R. Gardiner Museum of Ceramic Art in 1987 greatly expanded the empire. The ROM's Chinese collections are, outside of China, possibly the best in the world, and the Ancient Egypt and Nubian Galleries draw international acclaim. Other features are the Dinosaur Gallery, a mounted bird collection, the genuinely terrifying walk-through Bat Cave, treasures from the Mediterranean World, a gorgeous collection of minerals, an outstanding costume and textiles collection, the European Galleries, and the exciting Discovery Gallery, which is a hands-on area. New additions include the Canadian Heritage Floor, the Roloff Beny Gallery, the Ontario Archaeology Gallery, the Gallery of Indigenous Peoples, and the Sigmund Samuel Canadiana Gallery. The ROM also has a great library, three marvelous shops, a cafeteria and full-service restaurant, and sponsors terrific educational programs, workshops, special events, and lectures.

Sainte-Marie Among the Hurons

- P.O. Box 160, Midland, Ontario, L4R 4K8
  LOCATION: Highway 12 (near Martyrs' Shrine)
- (705) 526-7838
- Open daily, Victoria Day weekend to Thanksgiving weekend, call for operating hours
- Admission fee

Sainte-Marie Among the Hurons is a recreated village and museum designed to educate the public about the first European community in Canada and the early influences between Native North American and European cultures. Sainte-Marie was founded in 1639 by French Jesuits, and was intended as a retreat for priests and as a mission to attract and convert the Huron people of the area. The clash of cultures brought many problems, like diseases to which the Native people had no natural immunity, religious and cultural interference, the disruption of the Native way of life, and conflict with the Huron's traditional enemies, the Iroquois. Understandably, by 1650 the mission was abandoned. The recreation of the Sainte-Marie mission brings to life this fascinating and truly old piece of Canadian history. It includes replica buildings, tools and equipment and is staffed by costumed interpreters. There is also an award-winning museum on the site, which features Native and European archaeological artifacts and reproductions of 16th- and 17th-century books, maps, manuscripts, and other items. There is a café and gift shop on the premises, as well as an excellent Resource Centre for research and activities associated with Sainte-Marie Among the Hurons and Discovery Harbour.

Heritage Centre of the Salvation Army and George Scott Railton Library

* 2130 Bayview Avenue, Toronto, Ontario, M4N 3K6
* (416) 481-4441
* Open Monday – Friday, 9:00 – 4:30
* Free admission

The Salvation Army was begun in 1865 in London, England, by social reformer William Booth who set out to rectify truly shocking working and social conditions in England at the time. George Scott Railton was the first official Salvation Army member to come to Canada, and his teachings, along with those of later arrivals from Britain, drew a large following in Canada. Today the Salvation Army, still a Christian enterprise, continues to thrive in all areas of social work, from running maternity hospitals to suicide prevention. The Heritage Centre for the Salvation Army, in Toronto, follows the history of the organization, highlights important events, explains its function and diversity, its role in social work and with the Armed Forces, its evolving use of music, and the Army uniform. A library and archives are housed in the same building as the centre, holding important documents, books, papers, advertising materials, periodicals, and a rare book collection including several Bibles.

Science North

* 100 Ramsey Lake Road, Sudbury, Ontario, P3E 5S9
  LOCATION: 2 kilometres off the bypass from Highway 69 at Ramsey Lake Road and Paris Street
* (705) 522-3700 or toll free in Ontario and Northern Quebec at 1-800-461-4898
* Open daily, 9:00 – 6:00, late June – Labour Day; fall and spring, 9:00 – 5:00; winter 10:00 – 4:00
* Admission fee

Housed in a building shaped like two snowflakes, Science North bills itself as Northern Ontario's largest tourist attraction. Its objective is to make visitors feel comfortable with science, with lots of hands-on, interactive, multi-media displays, accessible exhibitions, and "hosts" or stationed guides to answer questions. Many different areas of science are covered: animals and nature, rocks and minerals, air and water, astronomy and space, music, electronics, and people. Visitors can peer at the inside of their own eyes, monitor earthquakes, try prospecting, see porcupines and tarantulas, and play music by dancing on a huge keyboard. Science North also has a spectacular 3-D film with laser effects, called *Shooting Star*, that takes viewers on a trip through North America back 5 billion years in time. Special events and children's programs are offered, and there is a restaurant and gift shop on the premises. Science North sponsors outreach programs, with "science" vans that take exhibitions to remote communities, and also operates the Big Nickel Mine and the Path of Discovery.

Seagram Museum

* 57 Erb Street West, Waterloo, Ontario, N2L 6C2
* (519) 885-1857
* Open May 1 – December 31, daily, 10:00 – 6:00;
  January 2 – April 30, Tuesday – Sunday, 10:00 – 6:00
* Free admission

The Seagram Museum offers a truly comprehensive look at all aspects of the wine and spirits industry. It is housed in a spectacular two-part building, half of which is an old Seagram Company barrel warehouse, which once held up to 7,000 barrels for maturation; there is also a new main building, the incorporation of which into the old building won the Governor General's award for architectural excellence. An exciting and comprehensive collection of artifacts is on display including drinking vessels, fine artworks depicting wine and spirit history, industry vehicles and equipment, cocktail shakers, huge pieces of cork, hundreds of weird and wonderful corkscrews, stills with built-in locks, and much more. Twelve mini-theatres offer short, comprehensive videos on various themes from cork making to champagne, and recreations like the cooper, or barrel-maker's shop add life to the artifacts. The second floor holds special exhibitions such as the recent "Art of the Cocktail." The old warehouse has an upstairs display on the history of the Seagram Company, and this building also features a great restaurant, a gift shop, and a specialty liquor shop. Educational programs, courses, and special events are offered.

Seaway Serpentarium Reptile Zoo

- 800 Niagara Street North, Welland, Ontario, L3C 5Z4
- (905) 732-3685
- Open mid-May – September, Monday – Friday, 11:00 – 9:00, Saturday, 11:00 – 6:00, Sunday 12:00 – 5:00, major holidays, 12:00 – 5:00; October – mid-May, Monday – Friday, 2:00 p.m. – 9:00 p.m., Saturday 11:00 – 6:00, Sunday 12:00 – 5:00
- Admission fee

The Seaway Serpentarium holds the honour of being the first reptile zoo to be set up in a shopping mall. That means shoppers can drop in and see over 250 reptiles of about 100 different species from all over the globe. Exhibits attempt to convey the surroundings indigenous to each reptile, and educational staff are available to discuss the reptiles, answer questions and, according to the zoo, "help dispel any myths perpetrated by widespread phobias and misconceptions about reptiles." Iguanas, lizards, snakes, newts, and other scaly creatures can be seen at the Serpentarium, but the zoo, whose motto is "understand and protect," also hopes to promote captive breeding, as many of its inhabitants are rare or endangered.

SERBIAN HERITAGE MUSEUM

* 6770 Tecumseh Road East, Windsor, Ontario, N8T 1E6
* (519) 944-4884
* Open Monday – Friday, 10:00 – 4:00; Sunday, 2:00 – 4:00
* Free admission

A large population of Serbian people emigrated to Windsor between 1923 and 1929, and since that time has grown into a thriving Serbo-Canadian community. A Serbian Community Centre is a focal point of the community, and a fitting place to house the Serbian Heritage Museum. The museum collects, exhibits, and interprets artifacts and archival materials relating to Serbian heritage in the hope of creating awareness of Serbian culture, traditions, and history, and holds special exhibitions and sponsors research. Educational programs, lectures, and guided tours are also offered and the gift shop displays an interesting assortment of traditional and modern Serbian arts and crafts. Light lunches can be arranged for tour groups by request.

Sesquicentennial Museum

- Toronto Board of Education, 155 College Street, Toronto Ontario, M5T 1P6
  LOCATION: 1st floor, 263 McCaul Street, Toronto
- (416) 397-3680
- Open Monday – Friday, 12:00 – 3:00 during school year; June – August, 8:30 – 4:30
- Free admission

Sesquicentennial Museum is dedicated to education in Toronto, and "sesquicentennial" refers to Toronto's 150th anniversary, in 1984, when the museum was set up. Holdings come from the Toronto Board of Education collections and include trophies, medals, furniture, school supplies, insignia, and textbooks, as well as a collection of artwork, including portraits of key educators in Toronto and various works by Canadian artists. Many photographs are stored in the museum, where Toronto residents may find their own faces in the files, and official records, publications, press clippings, and other important documents are also archived. An audio-visual collection can also be accessed by appointment, including topics like oral histories and school reunions. The museum welcomes donations of items used in Toronto schools and a Spring Workshop invites people to help identify photographs. The museum has school programs for children, which offer an interesting contrast between old and new school methods and equipment. The strap, a symbol of outdated school disciplinary tactics, is the museum's most popular artifact.

SHARON TEMPLE

- Box 331, Sharon, Ontario, LOG 1VO
  LOCATION: 18974 Leslie Street, Sharon, Ontario
- (905) 478-2389
- Open May 1 – October 31, Wednesday – Sunday, 10:00 – 5:00 and holiday Mondays
- Admission fee

The son of Irish immigrants, David Willson moved to Upper Canada in 1801. Willson later joined the Society of Quakers but by 1812 had started his own sect called The Children of Peace. Under the direction of Ebenezer Doan, a master builder and craftsman, the Children of Peace began building a temple that was based on Willson's singular religious vision and interpretation of the Bible. Made of heavy timber, yet graceful and finely formed, the Temple's three storeys represent the Holy Trinity, while twelve pillars embody the twelve apostles. The "Davidites," as they became known, used the Temple for collecting alms, and for musical events, as music was considered an important element of worship. After Willson's death in 1866, the sect died out, and, if it hadn't been for the survival of the Temple, probably would have been completely forgotten. However, as early as 1917 the York Pioneer and Historical Society recognized the Temple's historic value and beauty, and began restoration. Today the Temple is fully operational as an historic site. The grounds include buildings such as Ebenezer Doan's relocated house *circa* 1819 and a curious outhouse with no corners, designed by Willson. The spectacular Illumination, when every window of the Temple is lit by candles, and other special events, tours, and music concerts are held annually.

Ska-Nah-Doht Iroquoian Village

- R.R. 1, Mount Brydges, Ontario, NOL 1WO
  LOCATION: Longwoods Road Conservation Area, about 6.5 kilometres west of the village of Delaware
- (519) 264-2420
- Open daily, Victoria Day – Labour Day, 9:00 – 4:30; September – mid-May, Monday – Friday, 9:00 – 4:30, weekends by appointment only; conservation area open every day from 9:00 – sunset from Victoria Day – Labour Day (and special events)
- Admission fee to conservation area

Ska-Nah-Doht is Oneida for "a village stands again," which accurately describes this recreated Iroquois village. The village represents pre-European Iroquois life about one thousand years ago and is based on data accumulated from archaeological research in the area, although a village did not stand on the actual site. The village is encircled by a palisade, and the entranceway has a maze to slow enemy infiltration. A deer run, used to trap deer, a burial area, storage lodge and pits, maple syrup works, longhouses, a sweat lodge, traps, and lookout post are some of the features. The site is located on 63 hectares of natural land, the Longwoods Road Conservation Area, which has its own resource centre, trails, skiing, snowshoeing and walking routes, camping facilities, and even a baseball diamond. Special events and a wide and important variety of school programs are offered at both sites.

Smiths Falls Railway Museum

* 90 William Street West, Smiths Falls, Ontario, K7A 5A5
* (613) 283-5696
* Open daily, April – October, 9:30 – 4:30
* Admission fee

The Smiths Falls Railway Museum, a project of the Smiths Falls Railway Museum Corporation and the Canadian Railroad Heritage Association, is located in the former CNOR/CNR railway station, *circa* 1914, which is now a National Historic Site. Near the station's two-hectare site is a unique Shurtzer Rolling Lift Bascule Railway Bridge, also with Heritage status. The museum includes 25 examples of rolling stock, of which an Alco CPR diesel 6591, CNOR/CNR steam locomotive 1112, and two operative Wickham Inspection Cars are highlights. Several passenger coaches, cabooses, box cars and gondolas are also displayed. There are displays on local railway themes, and artifacts include telegraph equipment, tools, and photographs. Visitors can roll through time on one of the Wickham cars, see other operational equipment and demonstrations, take tours and participate in special events. A railway library can be accessed by appointment and there is a gift shop on the premises.

Southwestern Ontario Heritage Village and Transportation Museum

- P.O. Box 221, Harrow, Ontario, NOR 1GO
  LOCATION: Essex County Road 23, 8 kilometres south of Essex
- (519) 776-6909
- Open April – November, Wednesday – Sunday, 11:00 – 5:00 and holiday Mondays; daily, July and August
- Admission fee

The Southwestern Ontario Heritage Village originally came about as an appropriate setting for the Historic Vehicle Society of Ontario's vehicles. It all started with a few antiquated buildings and grew into the present Heritage Village, whose delightful grounds reflect the turn of the century, and are animated with costumed guides and period artifacts. Buildings, ranging from 1826 to 1930, include a train station, church, schoolhouse, milk house, general store, various homesteads, shops, barns, and more. The Transportation Museum was built in 1982 to better display some of the vehicles and includes cars, trucks, horse-drawn wagons, bicycles, and others vehicles, like the 1893 Shamrock horseless carriage, one of only two in existence, and a 1925 LaFrance Fire Engine. School and group tours can be arranged and the site features special events such as the "Murder Mystery" and an "Art and Craft Autumnfest."

STEPHEN LEACOCK MEMORIAL HOME

- P.O. Box 625, Orillia, Ontario, L3V 6K5
  LOCATION: just off Highway 12B at the east end of Orillia
- (705) 326-9357
- Open daily, mid-June – Labour Day, 10:00 – 7:00; Monday – Friday rest of year
- Admission fee

Stephen Leacock was born in England, but as he spent most of his life in Canada, he is considered one of our greatest humorists, and was also an economist, historian, political scientist, teacher, scholar, and critic. Producing more than 64 books in his lifetime, as well as voluminous numbers of articles, correspondence, and sketches, he proved the value of his own axiom, "I am a great believer in luck and I find that the harder I work, the more I have of it." He was one of a family of eleven children whose father abandoned them when Leacock was a young adult, but Leacock's intelligence, humour, and hard work helped him through adversity. His summer home in Orillia, the "Mariposa" of his most famous work *Sunshine Sketches of a Little Town*, became his permanent home during later years, and has been restored and converted into a museum holding some 30,000 items of Leacock memorabilia. The museum holds special events yearly, has educational programs for children, and a gift shop featuring Leacock books and related items. The lovely 19-room colonial-style mansion can be rented for special events.

STRATFORD FESTIVAL ARCHIVES

* P.O. Box 520, Stratford, Ontario, N5A 6V2
  LOCATION: 363 Burritt Street, Stratford, Ontario
* By appointment only
* Fees apply for some services

As it shares the same name as Shakespeare's home town, Stratford, Ontario, has been celebrating the Bard through Shakespearean and related theatre and performing arts with the Stratford Festival since 1953. In 1967 the Festival administration set up the Stratford Festival Archives, making it the oldest formal collection of its kind on the continent and, because of its breadth, an internationally recognized theatre resource. Holdings include records of all kinds, thousands of posters, programs, prompt books, scores, scripts, press clippings, photographs, bibliographical files, technical drawings, and other documents. Costume designs and documentation accompany 1,500 actual costumes and related items. Some real gems have also been donated to the Festival Archives, such as a collection of Shakespeareana including the Fourth Folio of 1685 and one of Shakespeare's chairs. The archives have been documenting productions on videotape since 1968 and boast a thorough electronic theatre database. The Stratford Festival Archives is open to researchers only, but the staff answers thousands of inquiries every year and public exhibitions of items from the holdings are regularly staged.

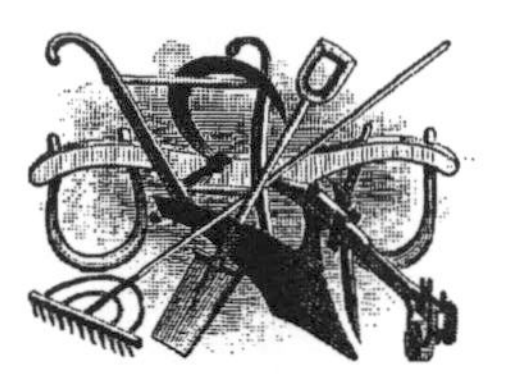

Swords and Ploughshares Museum

* Rideau Township, Ontario
* (613) 837-0149
* Hours and admission fee to be determined
* Private tours for small groups by appointment only, before 1995

The name of the Swords and Ploughshares Museum comes from the biblical quotation about "beating our swords into ploughshares and our spears into pruning hooks," reflecting the museum's dual farm and military theme. The collection combines "swords," in the form of military paraphernalia, with "ploughshares," or equipment from the country's industrial development, thus conveying the different ways Canadians have made a living and served their country. Not surprisingly, the museum was started by two private collectors of militaria, one a career, and the other a citizen soldier. The museum is not open to the public yet, as these two, along with friends and family, are busy finishing work on the building. Tours can be arranged by appointment, however, until the museum opens in 1995. So far the collection includes artillery, military vehicles, an easily dismantled "jiffy jeep," missiles, uniforms, medals, a working Bren Gun, small arms (civilian and military), and sundry antique farm implements including working horse-drawn farm machinery. The Rideau Canal Historical Arms collection will also be housed on the site, and space will be set aside for private collections.

Museum for Textiles

* 55 Centre Avenue, Toronto, Ontario, M5G 2H5
* (416) 599-5515 or (416) 599 – 5321
* Open Tuesday – Friday, 11:00 – 5:00; Saturday and Sunday, 12:00 – 5:00
* Admission fee

The Museum for Textiles began in the early 1970s as a relatively small private collection belonging to two journalists with a common love of carpets, and grew steadily to become the wonderful, comprehensive museum it is today. The building contains 12 galleries which take up 930 square metres, and houses an auditorium, lounge, offices, and storage space. The collection consists of about 16,000 textiles and related artifacts, including looms, carpets, garments, tapestries, and ceremonial cloths. The textiles on exhibit are mostly hung and draped in the open air instead of being displayed under glass. This allows really close viewing, and visitors have even been known to cop a feel or two. One of the museum's strengths is the Canadiana collection, which has close to 1,000 artifacts, including the hooked rugs and quilts so prevalent throughout Canada's history. There is also a large collection of Indonesian, South East and Central Asian textiles and strong holdings from south Central America, Peru, and Bolivia. Of interest is the Contemporary Gallery, featuring often unique wearable, usable, or purely ornamental or conceptual textiles produced by contemporary fibre artists. An on-site library can be accessed by researchers, and the Museum also holds great lectures and workshops. The gift shop features textiles, sweaters, knitted goods, jewellery, books, postcards, and other textile-related items.

Theatre Archives, University of Guelph

* c/o Archives and Special Collections, University of Guelph Library, Guelph, Ontario, N1G 2W1
* (519) 824-4120, ext. 3413
* Open Monday – Friday, 8:30 – 4:45, appointments appreciated
* Free admission

Since 1983 the University of Guelph has become the largest repository for theatre archives in Canada. Holdings include the administrative records, promotional materials, programs, set designs, scripts, reviews, and more from several large and small theatres, mostly in Ontario. The Shaw Festival Collection is an important part of the holdings, as are documents from the Tarragon, Phoenix, Open Circle, Young People's Theatre, and some pieces from the Crest, Factory Theatre, Royal Alexandra, and Stratford Festival. Important related collections include an excellent variety of Shaviana belonging to world-renowned George Bernard Shaw scholar Dan H. Laurence, which includes clippings from Shaw's beard, and the only known collection of materials relating to the Canadian Workers' Theatre Movement, which was strong in the 1930s. Much of the archive's holdings has been catalogued by computer, which makes it an excellent resource for theatre researchers.

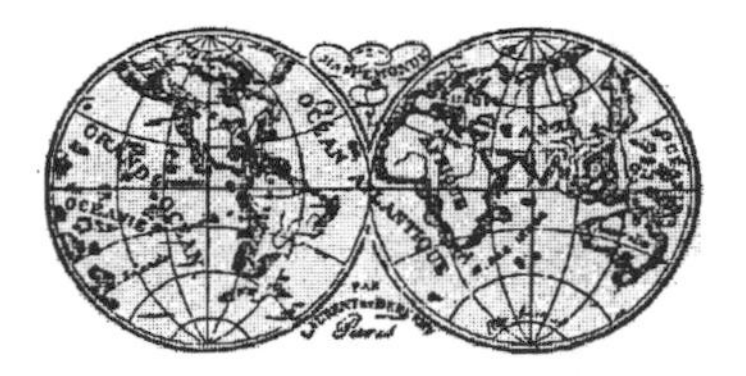

Thomas Fisher Rare Book Library

- 120 St. George Street, Robarts Library, University of Toronto, Toronto, Ontario, M5S 1A5
- Library (416) 978-5285
  University of Toronto Archives (416) 978-5344
- Open Monday – Friday, 9:00 – 4:45, closed statutory and university holidays
- Free admission

The Thomas Fisher Rare Book Library is an outstanding collection of rare books and manuscripts from Europe and Canada, dating from the 3rd century B.C. The library is named after an early resident of the area, Thomas Fisher (1792-1874), an English immigrant who settled in 1821 and became an active citizen and merchant. Holdings include the private collection of Fisher's ancestors, the Fisher Collections, which feature Shakespeare and Shakespeariana, English antiquities and topography, and etchings by Wenceslaus Hollar. Other collection areas encompass theology, philosophy, science and medicine, classical, European, and English literature, theatre history, maps and atlases and Canadiana from the University of Toronto Archives. The oldest printed book is *circa* 1470, and the oldest manuscripts are Greek papyri starting from the third century B.C. The library's entrance has an area designated for a series of temporary exhibitions such as a recent feature called "The Atlas as a Book: 1490 to 1900." An excellent and fascinating resource and educational facility and, besides, it's the only rare book library in the world housed in a building shaped like a turkey.

Thornhill Antique Clock Museum

* 447 Mullen Drive, Thornhill, Ontario, L4J 2N9
* (905) 731-1695, or (416) 409-7736 for 24 hour directions
* Open Monday – Friday, 1:00 – 4:00; weekends and group tours by appointment
* Admission fee

The newly expanded Thornhill Antique Clock Museum is a truly impressive private collection of clocks from Canada, the U.S., Britain, France, Australia, Switzerland, Holland, and China, spanning 1650 to 1940. All the timepieces are fascinating, but highlights include a great collection of British grandfather clocks, Dutch hooded and stool clocks, an original tower clock *circa* 1850, gaggles of cuckoo clocks, neon bar-style clocks from the thirties and forties, and a really ticking collection of Canadian clocks including Pequegnat clocks. Don't expect a standard setting, as the museum is rather oddly located in a functioning suburban home in Thornhill, which, of course, has been taken over by an army of time machines. Even the garage is inhabited by an enormous, one-tonne neon Lipton Real Estate Clock which presided over Toronto's Pantages Theatre between 1925 and 1940. Possibly Canada's only, and certainly the best, if not the most unusual, clock museum. Unless booked in advance, tours are self-guided with the aid of a binder.

Timber Village Museum

* P.O. Box 640, Blind River, Ontario, POR 1BO
  LOCATION: east end of Blind River on Highway 17, beside the Travel Info Centre.
* (705) 356-7544
* Open April – Labour Day weekend, daily, 10:00 – 6:00
* Admission fee

The Blind River area has seen many important phases of Ontario's history. Originally inhabited by the Mississagi people, it was travelled by the voyageurs, and later set up as a Hudson's Bay trading post. By the mid-1800s it became an important area for logging and wood processing. The Timber Village Museum is dedicated to the area's logging industry, and will give the visitor a sense of what a lumberjack's life was like at the turn of the century through displays of saws, logging tools, logging stamp hammers, camp utensils, and a portable forge, as well as larger items stored outside, like the Crazy Wheel, used to brake logs while going downhill. An exhibit prepared by the local Mississagi people can also be enjoyed as well as photographs, carvings, a rock display, and the Timber Village Art Gallery. Special events are offered year-round and lectures are staged during the summer.

TIMMINS MUSEUM
NATIONAL•EXHIBITION•CENTRE

Timmins Museum: National Exhibition Centre

- 220 Algonquin Boulevard East, Timmins, Ontario, P4N 1B3
  LOCATION: 70 Legion Drive, South Porcupine
- (705) 235-5066 or (705) 235-5063
- Open all year, Monday – Friday, 9:00 – 12:00 and 1:00 – 5:00; Saturday and Sunday, 1:00 – 5:00
- Free admission

One of 23 National Exhibition Centres in Canada, the Timmins Museum: National Exhibition Centre is a multi-purpose facility that "interprets the culture and traditions of our land" through travelling and permanent displays on many local and national themes. Temporary exhibitions are staged in the Jury and Lake Galleries of the Centre, including works of traditional or contemporary art, historical themes, and science and technology. The Centre's Museum area discusses Timmins history, from Precambrian times through today's developments. As Timmins is famous for its mining, examples of high grade gold ore, fluorescent minerals, ore suites, and samples from the Costain Mineral Collection can all be viewed, as can a display on the local Porcupine Camp, and films on mining in the amphitheatre. Visitors can also enjoy the Porcupine Pete Gold Mine and operate mining equipment. Lots of special events, workshops, openings, and educational programs are offered throughout the year and there is a gift shop on the premises.

Tivoli Miniature World

- 5930 Victoria Avenue, Niagara Falls, Ontario, L2G 3L7
  LOCATION: one block from Clifton Hill
- (905) 357-4100
- Open Easter weekend – late October, 9:00 a.m. – 6:00 p.m., July – August, 9:00 a.m. – 10:00 p.m., or later
- Admission fee

"The world is at your feet," or so they say, when you visit Tivoli Miniature World. It's a theme park full of more than 90 meticulous miniature recreations of famous landmarks from all over the world, including the Acropolis, the Vatican, the Statue of Liberty, the Eiffel Tower, the Towers of the Kremlin, the Great Pyramids of Egypt, and the CN Tower. Great for a quick trip around the world and, of course, big photo opportunities. The workshop where each feature is made is part of the Tivoli experience, so visitors can watch the craftspeople producing the little wonders. Free train rides around the site are offered, and the viewing deck puts you on top of the world. A gift shop, live entertainment, patio cafeteria, and landscaped grounds make it a fun place to spend a few wee hours.

Todmorden Mills Heritage Museum and Arts Centre

* c/o East York Parks and Recreation Department, 850 Coxwell Avenue, East York, Ontario, M4C 5R1
  LOCATION: 67 Pottery Road, East York; take the Don Valley Parkway to Bayview North
* (416) 425-2250
* Open May 1 – September 30, Tuesday – Friday, 10:00 – 4:30, weekends and holidays, 11:00 – 4:30; October 1 – December 30, Tuesday – Friday, 10:00 – 4:00; January – May by appointment
* Admission fee

Todmorden Mills, in the Don Valley, is the site of an industrial complex that began in 1795. In 1821 the Mills were sold to two men who came from Todmorden, England, and since that time the area has been called Todmorden. Today Todmorden Mills' six-hectare site includes the restored Parshall Terry House, begun in 1797, the William Helliwelll House from 1838, a brewery, the relocated Don Train Station, and the Eastwood and Skinner Paper Mill, built in 1795 for flour and later converted to paper, which sports a chimney now considered a Toronto landmark. Displays on traditional brewing, distilling, flour milling, paper and brick making can all be enjoyed on the site; the Helliwell brewery is used for special exhibits and the paper mill functions as an art centre. A nature preserve of parkland, woodland, and wildflowers is in the development stage. The Mills also offers a range of exhibitions, educational programs, special events, lectures, and workshops. There is a gift shop.

Toronto Museum of Childhood

* 121 Brunswick Avenue, Toronto, Ontario, M5S 2M3
* No permanent location as yet
* (416) 964-8255

The Toronto Museum of Childhood is an active organization with a lively assortment of artifacts, but it is still in its infancy. A search for suitable facilities has been ongoing for several years. Meanwhile, the collection of toys, clothing, furniture, musical recordings, books, and ephemera related to toys and childhood from Canada and all over the world, is growing. The museum has an active membership, volunteer corps, and board, and stages small displays across Toronto for various events. It also holds its own happenings, like a recent Hallowe'en Heritage Hoe-Down dance for ghosts and goblins, and stages lectures, educational programs, and demonstrations of things like bubble blowing, and the making of simple wind-up toys. Should be a lot of fun when it gets big.

Toronto Fire Department Museum

- Toronto Fire Academy, 895 Eastern Avenue, Toronto, Ontario, M4L 1A2
- (416) 392-1599
- Open weekdays, 8:00 – 4:00
- Free admission

The Toronto Fire Department was officially set up in the 1870s to deal with city fires, although volunteer departments had existed for several decades before that time. The current building for the Toronto Fire Academy was built in 1969, as a training facility, and a museum room was set aside to preserve Toronto and other Ontario fire history. Since 1969 the museum has been filling up with artifacts dating as far back as 1840. Most noticeable are two life-sized fibreglass mannequins of Harry and Dan, the last two horses used by the Toronto Fire Department, retired in 1930, pulling an original, fully-restored horse wagon from the 1880s. There is also a "Merryweather" horse-drawn steam pumper from 1865 and a pumper from 1932 that was used on Toronto's Centre Island. Smaller artifacts like helmets, trophies, some uniforms and photographs can be seen in display cases. The museum is currently undergoing renovations, and plans for the future include examples of more modern equipment and photographs, and a greater focus on the Toronto Fire Department. Although the museum is open year round, it is most popular during the academy's Open Houses, which are held two or three times a year, and during Fire Prevention Week and "Kids' Summer," when fire safety displays, awards ceremonies and the occasional new truck parked outside the academy can be enjoyed.

TORONTO'S FIRST POST OFFICE

- 260 Adelaide Street East, Toronto, Ontario, M5A 1N1
- (416) 865-1833
- Open Monday – Friday, 9:00 – 4:00, Saturday and Sunday, 10:00 – 4:00
- Free admission, tours by appointment

Toronto's First Post Office, now a National Historic Site, was built in 1833, part of a complex of historic buildings including the Bank of Upper Canada. During the years 1833 to 1839, the post office served about 9,000 inhabitants of what became the City of Toronto in 1834. After 1839 the building was used as a Catholic boys' school, part of a biscuit factory, and a warehouse for eggs, among other things. Since 1983, 150 years after it first opened, the site has been run as a museum by the Town of York Historical Society, winning an Award of Merit from the Toronto Historical Board and an Award of Excellence from the Ontario Historical Society. Toronto's First Post Office offers school programs, including tours by costumed interpreters where children can write letters with a quill pen and learn about Toronto's early years. The sending of Christmas letters and Valentines on special stationery, which can be perfumed with rose petals and sealed with wax and ribbon, is encouraged at the office. Lectures, tours, and fun special events like an annual Valentine-making bee are held year round, and a functioning post office, shop, and philatelic centre are also featured.

Treasure Chest Museum at Paisley

* Queen Street North, Paisley, Ontario, NOG 2NO
* (519) 353-7176 or (519) 353-5642
* Open daily, July and August, 11:00 – 5:00; late May – late June, weekends from 11:00 – 5:00; other times by chance or appointment
* Admission fee

The Treasure Chest Museum at Paisley contains scores of interesting items from across Canada, all collected by local resident Norman E. Hagedorn, with the aid of his wife. In 1988 Hagedorn generously donated his lifelong collection to the Town of Paisley, which now owns and operates the unique Treasure Chest Museum. The modern, concrete museum was built by Norman and has two display floors. The first floor features items of mainly agricultural interest, including farm tools and equipment, tractor seats, oil lanterns, a blacksmith's forge with smithing tools used by Norman himself, and a 60-apple-per-minute peeler. Upstairs showcases homier items, including about 330 oil lamps, 150 different toilet sets, glassware, china, furniture, laundry machines, sewing machines, copper kettles, butter-makers, clocks, and a bottle collection. A delightful result of what Norman calls "the Urge to Collect" and a fine gift to Paisley.

UKRAINIAN MUSEUM OF CANADA, ONTARIO BRANCH

* 620 Spadina Avenue, Toronto, Ontario, M5S 2H4
* (416) 923-3318
* Open Tuesday – Friday, 1:00 – 4:00
* Free admission

The Ukrainian Museum of Canada was founded in 1944 and has several branches across Canada. Its purpose is to demonstrate the Ukrainian contribution to Canada since immigration began in the 1890s, and to "bring to life the cultural, social and historic heritage of Ukrainian pioneers in Canada." The museum has about 40,000 artifacts in its holdings, which include a textile collection of kilims, textiles, weaving and embroidery, regional costumes, folk art, religious artifacts, dolls, ceramics, books, photographs, maps and decorative objects, such as *pysanky*, or elaborately painted Easter eggs. The Ontario branch holds lectures, courses, and workshops throughout the year and conducts tours by appointment. The museum will also provide travelling exhibitions of reproductions of Ukrainian court dress from the 8th to 18th centuries, regional headdresses, and folk dolls.

Uncle Tom's Cabin Historic Site

* R.R. 5, Dresden, Ontario, NOP 1MO
  LOCATION: Kent County Road 40, 1 kilometre southwest of Dresden off Park Street
* (519) 683-2978
* Open May – early September, Monday – Saturday, 11:00 – 5:00, Sunday, 1:00 – 5:00; late September, Monday – Saturday, 12:00 – 5:00, Sunday, 1:00 – 5:00
* Admission fee

Josiah Henson was born a slave in Maryland in 1789 and escaped to Upper Canada in 1830 through the Underground Railroad, the clandestine travelling route for U.S. slaves escaping to Canada. In 1841 he and a group of abolitionists bought 80 hectares of land in the Dresden area and established a vocational school. Henson also became a preacher, met with Queen Victoria in Windsor Castle, and narrated his fascinating life story to the Anti-Slavery Society in Boston. This narrative attracted the attention of writer Harriet Beecher Stowe, who met with Henson and modeled the main character in her novel *Uncle Tom's Cabin* after him. The complex in Dresden features six buildings, including Henson's house, a 19th-century church, fugitive slave house, sawmill, agricultural building, and two interpretive buildings. Artifacts include 19th-century agricultural and domestic items, furniture, ceramics and glass, buggies and sleighs, items of slavery, and rare books and documents relating to Henson and Beecher Stowe. Uncle Tom's Cabin Historic Site is part of the Canadian Black Heritage Tour.

Upper Canada Migratory Bird Sanctuary

- St. Lawrence Parks Commission, R.R. 1, Morrisburg, Ontario, K0C 1X0
  LOCATION: Highway 2, 14 kilometres east of Morrisburg
- (613) 537-2024
- Open daily, dawn – dusk, April – November; feeding daily at 2:30 p.m., mid-September to end of October
- Free admission

Located in Ontario's Parks of the St. Lawrence, the Upper Canada Migratory Bird Sanctuary is a haven for bird watchers. The area is a refuge for a wide variety of migratory birds, and features Canada Geese, who seasonally flock to and from the site. Feeding and banding of ducks and geese is performed during the migration period in the fall and the best viewing times are March or late October to early November. Guided Nature Tours will bring visitors close to the birds in their natural habitat and provide relevant tips and information, and a Visitor Centre features displays on the institution's history and has an observation tower from which the entire sanctuary can be viewed. Educational programs are also offered.

Upper Canada Village

- R.R. 1, Morrisburg, Ontario, KOC 1XO
  LOCATION: Highway 2, 11 kilometres east of Morrisburg
- (613) 543-3704
- Open daily, Victoria Day Weekend – Thanksgiving weekend, 9:30 – 5:00; off-season walking tours and other times by appointment
- Admission fee

Upper Canada Village is a big, bustling recreated rural community *circa* 1860, located on the St. Lawrence River. It represents a village of about 500 people, working and living much as they would have done when the area was still called Canada West. The site features costumed interpreters, some of whom are completely "in role" and will talk to visitors as the 1860s village dwellers they portray. The village has more than 30 buildings including mills, factories, farms, houses, a hotel, church, a school, a cheese factory, engine house, printing office, doctor's home, and more, all furnished and staffed to period. Horse-drawn "carry-alls" will take visitors around the village if they prefer not to walk, and horse-drawn bateaux can be enjoyed during the summer. Special events, educational programs, and research facilities are offered. Don't miss the gift shop, cafe, cafeteria, hotel restaurant, or Children's Activity Centre. There is also a golf course nearby.

Museum of Visual Science and Optometry

* School of Optometry, Columbia Street, University of Waterloo, Waterloo, Ontario, N2L 3G1
* (519) 885-1211, ext. 3405
* Open Monday – Friday, 8:30 – 4:30, and evenings by appointment
* Free admission

The Museum of Visual Science and Optometry offers a close-up look at the history of visual science and optometry from its very beginnings, with a focus on Canadian and Ontario history. Located in the University of Waterloo School of Optometry, the modern, high-tech environment makes a perfect foil for the historical collection, demonstrating how far the visual sciences' technology, practice, and equipment have come. The museum first opened in the early '70s, and since then the collection has grown to include over 800 spectacles, eyeglasses, lorgnettes, and pince-nez going back to 1650. That means visitors can eyeball everything from early Chinese spectacles to army-issue American combat glasses from the Vietnam war, and see artifacts made of everything from tortoise shell to sterling silver. There are also some lovely and interesting examples of glasses cases, including one carved to resemble a small book. Historical instruments of all descriptions will be of particular interest to those in the visual science field, as will furniture designed for the profession. Postage stamps with vision-related themes are displayed, and the museum has an important archives and a collection of many rare and unusual books. Group tours available by request.

Voyageur Heritage Centre

* P.O. Box 147, Mattawa, Ontario, P0H 1V0
  LOCATION: Samuel de Champlain Provincial Park, Highway 17, 13 kilometres west of Mattawa
* (705) 744-2276
* Open summers only; off-season by appointment
* Admission fee for park, museum free

The Voyageur Heritage Centre opened in 1988 as part of the celebration of the declaration of the Mattawa River as a Canadian Heritage River. An educational centre focused on the fur trade was fitting to the area as apparently about 80% of the trade, mainly operated by the Hudson's Bay Company and the North West Company, passed through the Mattawa River route over the course of about two centuries, starting in the early 1600s. The Native North Americans and the voyageurs, mostly of French origin, were the front-line men of the trade, hence the main focus of the museum is an enormous replica of a *canot de maitre*, the type of vessel used by the voyageurs. These held up to a dozen men, and would begin a trip full of trade goods and return loaded with beaver pelts. Other artifacts and items of interest in the centre include various canoes, oars, travelling trunks, models of voyageurs in traditional toque and sash, Native items, maps, banners, and more. Canoe excursions, self-directed hikes, and children's programs are offered, and a self-guided tour booklet for the centre is also available.

Welland's Giant Outdoor Murals

* c/o 800 Niagara Street, Seaway Mall, Welland, Ontario, L3C 5Z4
  LOCATION: Welland, Ontario
* (905) 788-3000
* Open all year, no charge

Welland may be a small town, but its history looms large in the form of 28 giant murals painted on various buildings and surfaces throughout the area. The murals were painted in a binge during the late 1980s and early '90s, and executed by various artists from all over Canada, except for the last mural, which is the world's largest paint-by-numbers painting, to which about 1,000 people contributed. Important events in Welland's history, such as the story of the Welland Canal, industrial, political, social, and military history, various forms of transportation, important local figures, clubs, and Welland's multicultural population are all depicted in the styles and interpretations of various artists.

WHITE OTTER CASTLE

* Friends of the White Otter Castle, P.O. Box 2096, Atikokan, Ontario, POT 1TO
  LOCATION: White Otter Lake, 48 kilometres from Ignace
* Hours, admission fee to be determined

White Otter Castle is an incredible rustic log cabin-castle in the bush, completely designed and constructed by one man. James Alexander McOuat came to Canada from Scotland at the turn of the century and settled in 1903 on White Otter Lake, an isolated spot forty-eight kilometres from Ignace in Northern Ontario. Here McOuat single-handedly built a three-storey log castle, tower and all, hoisting and hewing logs weighing up to nine hundred kilograms and portaging window-glass and supplies through the bush completely on his own. During his lifetime Jimmy became known as the "Hermit of White Otter Castle" – he never saw a motor car or streetcar – and loved the bush and its wildlife. Popular legends abound about McOuat: one story claims he built the castle because he was determined to disprove an insult given him as a child that he would "die in a shack"; another claims the castle was intended to house his childhood sweetheart, who was of noble birth. McOuat drowned in 1918 and mystery has also surrounded the nature of his drowning, the finding of his body, and the location of his grave. By the late '80s the castle was doomed to decay in the wilderness, but thanks to the efforts of a group called the Friends of the White Otter Castle and various government grants, a massive restoration project is currently underway that will make the castle an important landmark and tourist attraction. Visitors can contact the Friends of the White Otter Castle for more information.

William Ready Division of Archives and Research Collections

- McMaster University Library, 1280 Main Street West, Hamilton, Ontario, L8S 4L6
- (905) 525-9140, ext. 24737, 22079, or 24738
- Open October to April, Monday – Friday, 9:00 – 5:00; the first Saturday in every month, 9:00 – 1:00; other times by appointment
- Free admission

The William Ready Division of Archives and Research Collections houses many important documents and papers of significance to Canadians. National literary figures including Pierre Berton and Farley Mowat are represented in the holdings as are records of publishing companies like Macmillan of Canada and McClelland and Stewart. A collection of items from small presses, and the work of "radical" and "underground" groups and peace and labour organizations is continually growing. The pre-1800 collection contains over 30,000 volumes focusing on English and European works including Swift, Defoe, and Pope, while post-1800 holdings feature works by Samuel Beckett, D.H. Lawrence, and Ezra Pound. The Bertrand Russell Archives is also part of the collection, and includes about 250,000 documents. The William Ready Division of Archives and Research Collections is open to students, scholars, and interested parties and standard archival practices are in effect.

Woodland Cultural Centre

- P.O. Box 1506, 184 Mohawk Street, Brantford, Ontario, N3T 5V6
  LOCATION: via Highway 2 and 53 (Colborne Street) and on to Locks Road, which becomes Mohawk Street
- (519) 759-2650
- Open Monday – Friday, 9:00 – 4:00; Saturday & Sunday, 10:00 – 5:00; closed school Christmas holidays
- Admission fee

The Woodland Cultural Centre is an educational facility that includes a museum, research library, publishing house, First Nations language program, educational research centre, and gift shop. The centre also hosts special events and programs throughout the year, most notably the annual winter Snowsnake Tournament and a handicraft bazaar in November. The museum displays and art gallery follow the history of the Iroquoian and Algonkian people through prehistory, and from European contact up to the present. A recreated Neutral village, from the Woodland Period, interprets what life was like for the First Nations peoples hundreds of years ago. Exhibits include a replica of the interior of a 19th-century longhouse, a collection of Neutral Iroquoian pipes, Cree and Ojibway bandolier bags, and the Indian Hall of Fame. The gallery area displays many exciting works of contemporary art by Native artists and the Special Exhibit Gallery holds temporary features in a variety of media on varied subjects. The Museum Shop offers many Native-made crafts and works of art and a good selection of books.

Wye Marsh Wildlife Centre

- P.O. Box 100, Midland, Ontario, L4R 4K6
  LOCATION: Highway 12, opposite Martyrs' Shrine
- (705) 526-7809
- Hours and programs are seasonal
- Admission fee

The Wye Marsh Wildlife Centre is "committed to promoting environmental awareness and enhancing public understanding of the crucial role the wetlands play within the environment." It accomplishes this through an exciting variety of educational and recreational programs for all ages. Wildlife and nature trails can be explored on foot, canoe, cross-country ski, or snowshoe, depending on the season. Educational programs include canoe excursions, and fun things like the "Birds of Prey" bird demonstrations, "Nature's Engineers" which teaches all about beavers, and "Wet and Scaly," which interprets the life and times of frogs, toads, salamanders, turtles, and snakes. Combined visits with the nearby Huron Indian Village teach school groups the nature and survival skills that were necessary to the aboriginal way of life, like starting a fire without matches. Wye Marsh also has a Visitor Centre, gift shop, Seniors' Garden, a floating boardwalk in the marsh, and an observation tower.

LOCATION INDEX

Christian Island

Historic Fort Sainte-Marie II
Clarksburg
Beaver Valley Military Museum

Cloyne

Circular Saw Museum

Cobalt

Bunker Military Museum
Cobalt-Coleman Firefighters' Museum
Cobalt's Northern Ontario Mining Museum/The Heritage Silver Trail

Cobourg

Dressler House

Cochrane

Cochrane Railway and Pioneer Museum

Colborne

The Big Apple and Brian McFarlane's Hockey Museum

Commanda

Commanda General Store Museum

Cornwall

Ontario Hydro Energy Information Centre

Cornwall Island

Museum of the North American Indian Travelling College

Delaware

Ska-Nah-Doht Iroquoian Village

Delhi

Ontario Tobacco Museum and Heritage Centre

Don Mills

Museum of Contraception
Ontario Science Centre

Dorset

Leslie M. Frost Natural Resources Centre

Downsview

Kortright Centre for Conservation

Dresden

Uncle Tom's Cabin Historic Site

East York

Todmorden Mills Heritage Museum and Arts Centre

Elliot Lake

Elliot Lake Nuclear and Mining Museum

Essex

Southwestern Ontario Heritage Village and Transportation Museum

Fort Erie

Fort Erie LaFrance Firefighting Museum
Fort Erie Railroad Museum
Historic Fort Erie
Mildred M. Mahoney Silver Jubilee Doll's House Gallery

Goderich

Huron Historic Gaol

Gravenhurst

Bethune Memorial House

Guelph

The Arboretum, University of Guelph
Kortright Waterfowl Park
McCrae House
Theatre Archives, University of Guelph
Haliburton
Canadian Canoe Museum

Hamilton

Canadian Football Hall of Fame and Museum
Canadian Warplane Heritage Museum
Dundurn Castle
Hamilton Children's Museum
Hamilton Military Museum
Hamilton-Scourge Project
Hamilton Museum of Steam and Technology
Royal Hamilton Light Infantry Heritage Museum
William Ready Division of Archives and Research Collections

Holland Centre
Comber Pioneer Village

Huntsville
Muskoka Pioneer Village

Ignace
White Otter Castle

Ingersoll
Ingersoll Cheese Factory Museums and Sports Hall of Fame

Kapuskasing
Ron Morel Memorial Museum

Kars
Swords and Ploughshares Museum

Keene
Lang Pioneer Village

Kingston
Museum Ship Alexander Henry
Canadian Forces Communication and Electronics Museum
Correctional Services of Canada Museum
Fort Henry
International Ice Hockey Federation Museum
MacLachlan Woodworking Museum
Marine Museum of the Great Lakes
Miller Museum of Geology and Mineralogy
Pump House Steam Museum
Royal Military College of Canada Museum

Kingsville
Jack Miner's Migratory Bird Sanctuary

Kinmount
Highland Cinema Collection

Kitchener
Doon Heritage Crossroads
Joseph Schneider Haus

Kleinburg
Kleinburg Doll Museum
McMichael Canadian Art Collection

Komoka
Komoka Railway Museum

London
Archival Teaching and Research Museum
Banting Museum and Education Centre
Fanshawe Pioneer Village
Guy Lombardo Music Centre
London Museum of Archaeology and Lawson Prehistoric Indian Village
London Regional Children's Museum
Old Courthouse and First Hussars Museum
Royal Canadian Regiment Museum

Manitoulin Island
Mounted Animal Nature Trail

Marten River
Marten River Provincial Park Logging Camp

Mattawa
Voyageur Heritage Centre

Midland
Dracula's Museum of Horrors
Huron Indian Village and Huronia Museum
Martyrs' Shrine
Sainte-Marie Among the Hurons
Wye Marsh Wildlife Centre

Milton
Ontario Agricultural Museum

Morrisburg
Crysler Farm Battlefields Park and Queen Elizabeth Gardens
Prehistoric World
Upper Canada Migratory Bird Sanctuary
Upper Canada Village

Niagara Falls
Criminals Hall of Fame and Wax Museum
The Daredevil Adventure
Elvis Museum
Guinness World of Records

Houdini Hall of Fame
House of Frankenstein Wax Museum
J.F.K. Assassination Exhibit
Laura Secord Homestead
Louis Tussaud's Waxworks
Lundy's Lane Historical Museum
Movieland Wax Museum
Niagara Falls Museum
Ripley's Believe It or Not! Museum
Tivoli Miniature World

Niagara-on-the-Lake
Fort George National Historic Site
French Perfume Factory Outlet and Museum
Niagara Apothecary Museum

North Bay
Dionne Quints Museum
North Bay Model Railroad Display

North York
Black Creek Pioneer Village
Canadiana Collection, North York Public Library
Irving E. and Ray Kanner Heritage Museum
Ontario Centre for Puppetry Arts

Norwich
Norwich and District Museum

Oakville
Royal Canadian Golf Association Museum and Golf Hall of Fame

Ohsweken
Her Majesty's Royal Chapel of the Mohawks

Oil Springs
Oil Museum of Canada

Orillia
Stephen Leacock Memorial Home

Oshawa
Canadian Automotive Museum
Oshawa Aeronautical, Military and Industrial Museum
Robert Stuart Aviation Museum

Ottawa/Hull
Agricultural Museum
Bytown Museum
Canadian Museum of Caricature
Canadian Museum of Civilization
Canadian Museum of Contemporary Photography
Canadian National Collection of Insects and Related Anthropods
Canadian Museum of Nature
Canadian Parliament Buildings
Museum of Canadian Scouting
Canadian Ski Museum
Canadian War Museum
Canadian Women's Movement Archives
Central Experimental Farm
Currency Museum, Bank of Canada
Centre for Research on French Canadian Culture
Laurier House
National Archives of Canada
National Aviation Museum
National Library of Canada
National Postal Museum Hull, Quebec
National Museum of Science and Technology
Nicholas Gaol International Hostel

Owen Sound
Billy Bishop Heritage Museum
Owen Sound Marine-Rail Museum

Paisley
Treasure Chest Museum at Paisley

Penetanguishene
Discovery Harbour

Perth
Garden for the Blind
Perth Museum

Petrolia
Petrolia Discovery

Pickering
Ontario Hydro Energy Information Centre
Pickering Museum Village

Port Burwell
Port Burwell Marine Museum and Lighthouse

Port Colborne
Port Colborne Historical and Marine Museum
Port Hope
Canadian Firefighters' Museum

Port Rowan
Backus Heritage Conservation Area

Prescott
Fort Wellington National Historic Site
Forwarders' Museum

Rockwood
Halton Country Radial Railway Museum

Rolphton
Peter A. Nichol Driftwood Museum

St. Jacobs
Maple Syrup Museum of Ontario
The Meetingplace

St. Joseph
Fort St. Joseph National Historic Park

St. Thomas
Elgin Military Museum
Jumbo

Sault Ste. Marie
Forest Pest Management Institute

Scarborough
German Canadian Heritage Museum
The Guild

Sharon
Sharon Temple

Smiths Falls
Rideau Canal Museum
Smiths Falls Railway Museum

South Marysburgh
Mariners' Museum Lighthouse Park

Stoney Creek
Erland Lee Museum Home

Stratford
Stratford Festival Archives

Sudbury
Big Nickel Mine/Path of Discovery
Centre franco-ontarien de folklore
Science North

Thornhill
Thornhill Antique Clock Museum

Thunder Bay
Centennial Conservatory
Centennial Park 1910 Logging Camp
Chippewa Park Wildlife Exhibit
Northwestern Ontario Sports Hall of Fame and Museum
Old Fort William

Timmins
Timmins Museum: National Exhibition Centre

Tiverton
Ontario Hydro Energy Information Centre

Toronto
Addiction Research Foundation Museum
Allan Gardens
Ashley's Crystal Museum
The Baldwin Room, Metro Reference Library
Bata Shoe Museum
Beth Tzedec Reuben and Helene Dennis Museum
Campbell House
Canada's Sports Hall of Fame
Canadian Broadcasting Corporation Museum
Canadian Museum of Health and Medicine
Canadian Heritage Project Heritage Centre
Canadian Lesbian and Gay Archives
Canadian National Exhibition Archives
Casa Loma
Dance Collection Danse
Dentistry Museum

Ed's Theatre Museum
Enoch Turner Schoolhouse
Fashion Resource Centre
George R. Gardiner Museum of Ceramic Art
Girl Guides of Canada Archives
The Grange
Historic Fort York
Archives on the History of Canadian Psychiatry and Mental Health Services
H.M.C.S. HAIDA Naval Museum
Hockey Hall of Fame
Holocaust Education and Memorial Centre of Toronto
Joan Baillie Archives of the Canadian Opera Company
Mackenzie House
Marine Museum of Upper Canada
McLaughlin Planetarium
Museum of Mental Health Services
Merril Collection
Metropolitan Toronto Police Museum and Discovery Centre
Metropolitan Toronto Reference Library Arts Department
Metropolitan Toronto Zoo
National Ballet of Canada Archives
Norman Elder Museum
Ontario Parliament Buildings
Osborne Collection of Early Children's Books
Queen's York Rangers Museum
Redpath Sugar Museum
Reid and Campbell Collection
Royal Canadian Military Institute Museum and Library
Royal Ontario Museum
Heritage Centre of the Salvation Army and George Scott Railton Library
Sesquicentennial Museum
Museum for Textiles
Thomas Fisher Rare Book Library
Toronto Museum of Childhood
Toronto Fire Department Museum
Toronto's First Post Office
Ukrainian Museum of Canada, Ontario Branch

Tweed

North America's Smallest Jailhouse
Wasaga Beach
Nancy Island Historic Site

Waterloo

Biology-Earth Sciences Museum
Canadian Clay and Glass Gallery
Doris Lewis Rare Book Room, University of Waterloo
Museum and Archive of Games
Seagram Museum
Museum of Visual Science and Optometry

Welland

Seaway Serpentarium Reptile Zoo
Welland's Giant Outdoor Murals

Whitby

Cullen Gardens and Miniature Village

Williamstown

Nor'Westers and Loyalist Museum

Windsor

Serbian Heritage Museum

Wroxeter

Gingerbread Doll Museum

SUBJECT INDEX

Forest Pest Management Institute
Jack Miner's Migratory Bird Sanctuary
Kortright Waterfowl Park
Metropolitan Toronto Zoo
Mounted Animal Nature Trail
Phil Copp's Canadian Wilderness Trading Post and Wildlife Museum
Seaway Serpentarium Reptile Zoo
Upper Canada Migratory Bird Sanctuary
Wye Marsh Wildlife Centre

Communication

Bell Homestead
Canadian Broadcasting Corporation Museum
Canadian Forces Communication and Electronics Museum
Reid and Campbell Collection

Conservation

Agawa Bay Exhibit Centre
Algonquin Park Visitor Centre
Backus Heritage Conservation Area
Kortright Centre for Conservation
Leslie M. Frost Natural Resources Centre
Wye Marsh Wildlife Centre

Curiosity and Amazement

The Big Apple and Brian McFarlane's Hockey Museum
Cullen Gardens and Miniature Village
Daredevil Adventure
Dionne Quints Museum
Dracula's Museum of Horrors
Guinness World of Records
Houdini Hall of Fame
House of Frankenstein Wax Museum
J.F.K. Assassination Exhibit
Jumbo
Louis Tussaud's Waxworks
Niagara Falls Museum
Norman Elder Museum
Prehistoric World
Ripley's Believe It or Not! Museum
Tivoli Miniature World

Education

Archival Teaching and Research Museum
Canadian Heritage Project Heritage Centre
Enoch Turner Schoolhouse
Museum of the North American Indian Travelling College
Quinte Educational Museum and Archives
Sesquicentennial Museum
Woodland Cultural Centre
Entertainment
Canadian National Exhibition Archives
Conklin Collection of Vintage Carnival Equipment
Dressler House
Ed's Theatre Museum
Elvis Museum
Museum and Archive of Games
Guy Lombardo Music Centre
Highland Cinema Collection
Jumbo
Movieland Wax Museum
Reid and Campbell Collection

Gardens and Arboreta

Allan Gardens
The Arboretum, University of Guelph
Centennial Conservatory
Central Experimental Farm
Crysler Farm Battlefields Park and Queen Elizabeth Gardens
Garden for the Blind
Royal Botanical Gardens

Government

Campbell House
Canadian Parliament Buildings
Laurier House
Mackenzie House
Ontario Parliament Buildings

Historic Houses and Sites

AECL Research, Chalk River Laboratories
Banting Museum and Education Centre
Bell Homestead

Bethune Memorial House
Billy Bishop Heritage Museum
Bytown Museum
Campbell House
Canadian Parliament Buildings
Casa Loma
Commanda General Store Museum
Crysler Farm Battlefield Park and Queen Elizabeth Gardens
Dionne Quints Museum
Dressler House
Dundurn Castle
Erland Lee Museum Home
Fort George National Historic Site
Fort Henry
Fort Malden
Fort St. Joseph National Historic Park
Fort Wellington National Historic Site
The Grange
Her Majesty's Royal Chapel of the Mohawks
Historic Fort Erie
Historic Fort Sainte-Marie II
Historic Fort York
Joseph Brant Museum
Joseph Schneider Haus Museum and Gallery
Jumbo
Laura Secord Homestead
Laurier House
Loyalist Cultural Centre
Lundy's Lane
Mackenzie House
Martyrs' Shrine
McCrae House
Mildred M. Mahoney Silver Jubilee Doll's House Gallery
Mill of Kintail Museum and Conservation Area
Nancy Island Historic Site
Niagara Falls Museum
North America's Smallest Jailhouse
North Himsworth Museum
Oil Museum of Canada
Old Fort William
Ontario Parliament Buildings
Perth Museum
Sharon Temple
Stephen Leacock Memorial Home
Todmorden Mills Heritage Museum and Arts Centre
Toronto's First Post Office
Uncle Tom's Cabin Historic Site
White Otter Castle

Industry and Commerce

AECL Research, Chalk River Laboratories
Algonquin Park Logging Museum
Big Nickel Mine/Path of Discovery
Centennial Park 1910 Logging Camp
Cobalt's Northern Ontario Mining Museum/The Heritage Silver Trail
Commanda General Store Museum
Elliot Lake Nuclear and Mining Museum
Forwarder's Museum
French Perfume Factory Outlet and Museum
Ingersoll Cheese Factory Museums and Sports Hall of Fame
MacLachlan Woodworking Museum
Maple Syrup Museum of Ontario
Marten River Provincial Park Logging Camp
Mississippi Valley Textile Museum
Niagara Apothecary Museum
Nor'Westers and Loyalist Museum
Oil Museum of Canada
Ontario Hydro Energy Information Centres
Ontario Tobacco Museum and Heritage Centre
Oshawa Aeronautical, Military and Industrial Museum
Petrolia Discovery
Pump House Steam Museum
Redpath Sugar Museum
Rideau Canal Museum
Seagram Museum
Swords and Ploughshares Museum
Timber Village Museum

Todmorden Mills Heritage Museum and Arts Centre
Voyageur Heritage Centre

Law and Order

Campbell House
Correctional Service of Canada Museum
Criminals Hall of Fame and Wax Museum
Huron Historic Gaol
Metropolitan Toronto Police Museum and Discovery Centre
Nicholas Gaol International Hostel
North America's Smallest Jailhouse
Old Courthouse and First Hussars Museum

Literature

Baldwin Room
Canadian Lesbian and Gay Archives
Canadian Women's Movement Archives
Canadiana Collection, North York Public Library
Doris Lewis Rare Book Room, University of Waterloo
Centre for Research on French Canadian Culture
McCrae House
Merril Collection
Metropolitan Toronto Reference Library Arts Department
National Archives of Canada
National Library of Canada
Osborne Collection of Early Children's Books
Stephen Leacock Memorial Home
Stratford Festival Archives
Theatre Archives, University of Guelph
Thomas Fisher Rare Book Library
Uncle Tom's Cabin Historic Site
William Ready Division of Archives and Research Collections

Local Interest

Arkona Lion's Museum and Information Centre
Athens Historical Murals
Bowmanville Museum
Brantford and Area Sports Hall of Recognition
Bytown Museum
Canadiana Collection, North York Public Library
Cobalt-Coleman Firefighters Museum
Cochrane Railway and Pioneer Museum
Elgin Military Museum
Irving E. and Ray Kanner Heritage Museum
Joseph Schneider Haus Museum and Gallery
Lundy's Lane Historical Museum
Mississippi Valley Textile Museum
Northwestern Ontario Sports Hall of Fame and Museum
Norwich and District Museum
Owen Sound Marine and Rail Museum
Perth Museum
Port Burwell Marine Museum and Lighthouse
Port Colborne Historical and Marine Museum
Quinte Educational Museum and Archives
Ron Morel Memorial Museum
Sesquicentennial Museum
Timmins Museum: National Exhibition Centre
Todmorden Mills Heritage Museum and Arts Centre
Toronto Fire Department Museum
Toronto's First Post Office
Welland's Giant Outdoor Murals

Marine and Naval

Museum Ship Alexander Henry
Canadian Canoe Museum
Discovery Harbour
Forwarders' Museum
Hamilton-Scourge Project
H.M.C.S. HAIDA Naval Museum
Marine Museum of the Great Lakes
Marine Museum of Upper Canada
Mariner's Park Museum

Nancy Island Historic Site
Owen Sound Marine and Rail Museum
Port Burwell Marine Museum and Lighthouse
Port Colborne Historical and Marine Museum
Rideau Canal Museum
Voyageur Heritage Centre

Medicine

Archival Teaching and Research Museum
Banting Museum and Education Centre
Bethune Memorial House
Canadian Museum of Health and Medicine
Dentistry Museum
Archives on the History of Canadian Psychiatry and Mental Health Services
Museum of Mental Health Services, Toronto, Inc.
Niagara Apothecary Museum
North Himsworth Museum
Museum of Visual Science and Optometry

Military

Beaver Valley Military Museum
Billy Bishop Heritage Museum
Bunker Military Museum
Canadian Forces Base Borden Military Museum
Canadian Forces Communication and Electronics Museum
Canadian War Museum
Canadian Warplane Heritage Museum
Crysler Farm Battlefield Park and Queen Elizabeth Gardens
Discovery Harbour
Dundurn Castle
Elgin Military Museum
Fort George National Historic Site
Fort Henry
Fort Malden
Fort St. Joseph National Historic Park
Fort Wellington National Historic Site
Hamilton Military Museum
Hamilton-Scourge Project
Historic Fort Erie
Historic Fort Sainte-Marie II
Historic Fort York
H.M.C.S. HAIDA Naval Museum
Joseph Brant Museum
Laura Secord Homestead
Lorne Scots Regimental Museum
Lundy's Lane Historical Museum
McCrae House
Nancy Island Historic Site
National Aviation Museum
Old Courthouse and First Hussars Museum
Old Fort William
Oshawa Aeronautical, Military and Industrial Museum
Queen's York Rangers Museum
Robert Stuart Aviation Museum
Royal Canadian Air Force Memorial Museum
Royal Canadian Military Institute Museum and Library
Royal Canadian Regiment Museum
Royal Hamilton Light Infantry Heritage Museum
Royal Military College of Canada Museum
Swords and Ploughshares Museum

Multiple Focus

Canadian Museum of Civilization
Canadian Museum of Nature
C.H.P. Heritage Centre
National Archives of Canada
National Library of Canada
Royal Ontario Museum
Timmins Museum: National Exhibition Centre

Public Service

Canadian Firefighters' Museum
Cobalt-Coleman Firefighters' Museum
Currency Museum, Bank of Canada
Fort Erie LaFrance Firefighting Museum
National Postal Museum

Ontario Hydro Energy Information Centres
Heritage Centre of the Salvation Army and George Scott Railton Library
Toronto Fire Department Museum
Toronto's First Post Office

Religion and Cultural Identity

Beth Tzedec Reuben and Helene Dennis Museum
Canadian Lesbian and Gay Archives
Canadian Women's Movement Archives
Centre franco-ontarien de folklore
Centre for Research on French Canadian Culture
Erland Lee Museum Home
German Canadian Heritage Museum
Her Majesty's Chapel of the Mohawks
Holocaust Education and Memorial Centre of Toronto
Huron Indian Village and Huronia Museum
Irving E. and Ray Kanner Heritage Museum
Joseph Schneider Haus Museum and Gallery
London Museum of Archaeology and Lawson Prehistoric Indian Village
Loyalist Cultural Centre
Martyrs' Shrine
The Meetingplace
National Archives of Canada
National Library of Canada
North American Black Historical Museum and Cultural Centre
Museum of the North American Indian Travelling College
Nor'Westers and Loyalist Museum
Norwich and District Museum
Serbian Heritage Museum
Sharon Temple
Ska-Nah-Doht Iroquoian Village
Ukrainian Museum of Canada, Ontario Branch
Woodland Cultural Centre

Rocks, Minerals, and Mining

Bancroft Mineral Museum
Big Nickel Mine/Path of Discovery
Biology-Earth Sciences Museum
Canadian Museum of Nature
Cobalt's Northern Ontario Mining Museum/The Heritage Silver Trail
Elliot Lake Nuclear and Mining Museum
Miller Museum of Geology and Mineralogy
Niagara Falls Museum
Ontario Science Centre
Royal Ontario Museum
Science North
Timmins Museum: National Exhibition Centre

Science and Technology

AECL Research, Chalk River Laboratories
Biology-Earth Sciences Museum
Hamilton Museum of Steam and Technology
McLaughlin Planetarium
National Museum of Science and Technology
Ontario Hydro Energy Information Centres
Ontario Science Centre
Science North
Timmins Museum: National Exhibition Centre

Social History

Addiction Research Foundation Museum
Bata Shoe Museum
Canadian Automotive Museum
Canadian Canoe Museum
Canadian Museum of Caricature
Canadian Museum of Civilization
Canadian Clay and Glass Gallery
Canadian Museum of Contemporary Photography
Canadian Museum of Health and Medicine
Canadian Lesbian and Gay Archives
Canadian National Exhibition Archives
Museum of Canadian Scouting

Canadian Women's Movement Archives
C.H.P. Heritage Centre
Circular Saw Museum
Commanda General Store Museum
Conklin Collection of Vintage Carnival Equipment
Museum of Contraception
Correctional Service of Canada Museum
Currency Museum, Bank of Canada
Dentistry Museum
Dionne Quints Museum
Fashion Resource Centre
French Perfume Factory Outlet and Museum
Museum and Archive of Games
George R. Gardiner Museum of Ceramic Art
Gingerbread Doll Museum
Girl Guides of Canada Archives
Guinness World of Records
Hamilton Children's Museum
Highland Cinema Collection
Archives on the History of Canadian Psychiatry and Mental Health Services
Kleinburg Doll Museum
London Regional Children's Museum
MacLachlan Woodworking Museum
Maple Syrup Museum of Ontario
Museum of Mental Health Services, Toronto, Inc.
Mildred M. Mahoney Silver Jubilee Doll's House Gallery
Mississippi Valley Textile Museum
National Archives of Canada
National Library of Canada
National Postal Museum
Niagara Apothecary Museum
Niagara Falls Museum
Ontario Centre for Puppetry Arts
Ontario Tobacco Museum and Heritage Centre
Osborne Collection of Early Children's Books, Toronto Public Library
Quinte Educational Museum and Archives
Redpath Sugar Museum
Reid and Campbell Collection
Ripley's Believe It or Not! Museum
Royal Ontario Museum
Salvation Army and George Scott Railton Library
Seagram Museum
Sesquicentennial Museum
Southwestern Ontario Heritage Village and Transportation Museum
Swords and Ploughshares Museum
Museum for Textiles
Thornhill Antique Clock Museum
Toronto Museum of Childhood
Toronto's First Post Office
Treasure Chest Museum at Paisley
Museum of Visual Science and Optometry

Sports and Recreation

The Big Apple and Brian McFarlane's Hockey Museum
Brantford and Area Sports Hall of Recognition
Canada's Sports Hall of Fame
Canadian Canoe Museum
Canadian Football Hall of Fame and Museum
Canadian Ski Museum
Conklin Collection of Vintage Carnival Equipment
Museum and Archive of Games
Guinness World of Records
Hockey Hall of Fame
Ingersoll Cheese Factory Museums and Sports Hall of Fame
International Ice Hockey Federation Museum
Northwestern Ontario Sports Hall of Fame and Museum
Royal Canadian Golf Association Museum and Golf Hall of Fame

Transportation

Canadian Automotive Museum
Canadian Canoe Museum

Cochrane Railway and Pioneer Museum
Fort Erie Railroad Museum
Halton Country Radial Railway Museum
Komoka Railway Museum
North Bay Model Railroad Display
Oshawa Aeronautical, Military and Industrial Museum
Owen Sound Marine-Rail Museum
Rideau Canal Museum
Ron Morel Memorial Museum
Smiths Falls Railway Museum
Southwestern Ontario Heritage Village and Transportation Museum

Villages

Backus Heritage Conservation Area and Backus Heritage Village
Black Creek Pioneer Village
Comber Pioneer Village
Doon Heritage Crossroads
Fanshawe Pioneer Village
Huron Indian Village and Huronia Museum
Lang Pioneer Village
London Museum of Archaeology and Lawson Prehistoric Indian Village
Museum of the North American Indian Travelling College
Muskoka Pioneer Village
Pickering Museum Village
Sainte-Marie Among the Hurons
Ska-Nah-Doht Iroquoian Village
Southwestern Ontario Heritage Village and Transportation Museum
Todmorden Mills Heritage Museum and Arts Centre
Upper Canada Village

Youth and Childhood

Museum of Canadian Scouting
Museum and Archive of Games
Gingerbread Doll Museum
Girl Guides of Canada Archives
Hamilton Children's Museum
Kleinburg Doll Museum
London Regional Children's Museum
Mildred M. Mahoney Silver Jubilee Doll's House Gallery
Osborne Collection of Early Children's Books
Toronto Museum of Childhood